MW01277709

Created and Directed by Hans Höfer

INSIGHT GUIDES

UMBRIA

Edited by Paul Otto Schulz
Principal Photography: Bill Wassman

Managing Editor: Dorothy Stannard

APA PUBLICATIONS

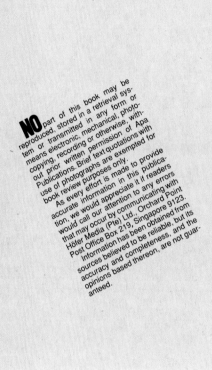

NO part of this book may be reproduced, stored in a retrieval system or transmitted in any form or means electronic, mechanical, photocopying, recording or otherwise, without prior written permission of Apa Publications. Brief text quotations with use of photographs are exempted for book review purposes only.

As every effort is made to provide accurate information in this publication, we would appreciate it if readers would call our attention to any errors that may occur by communicating with Höfer Media (Pte) Ltd., Orchard Point Post Office Box 219, Singapore 9123. Information has been obtained from sources believed to be reliable, but its accuracy and completeness, and the opinions based thereon, are not guaranteed.

UMBRIA

First Edition
© **1992 APA PUBLICATIONS (HK) LTD**
All Rights Reserved
Printed in Singapore by Höfer Press Pte. Ltd

ABOUT THIS BOOK

even in the days when Italy was the ultimate destination of any "Grand Tour", Umbria never lay directly on the main thoroughfare. For the hordes of poets, artists and philosophers wishing to broaden their horizons, the primary attraction was Rome, and the stretch between Florence and Rome generally involved the speediest route, from the Uffizi Palace straight to the Vatican.

Umbria was of interest only to travellers prepared to wander off the beaten track – and so it has remained to this day. But for all those in search of the true Italy, the region, often referred to as the "green heart of Italy", is hard to beat. It is a heart with variable temperament, inclinations and valleys, all well worth exploring.

Revealing the hidden heart of regions and cities comes naturally to Apa Publications, which has published almost 150 Insight and City Guides to destinations all over the world. Although based in Singapore, Apa maintains editorial offices in England and Germany, both of which got together to produce *Insight Guide: Umbria*. The Munich office put its close links with Italy to good use by assembling the German edition; the London office re-worked the text for an English-language readership, adding a considerable amount of new material. The result: a genuine European Community collaboration.

The original material was assembled by project editor **Paul Otto Schultz**. In his days working on Germany's *Merian* travel magazine, he found that the best way of discovering a region was always to leave enough time to observe. His love for Italy intensified when he worked as editor of the German edition of Franco Maria Ricci's Milanese art

and culture magazine *FMR*. Schultz now lives as a freelance journalist and author in Munich. He is editor of the series *Klassische Reiseziele* (Classic Travel Destinations).

The new material for the English edition was provided by **Christopher Catling**, a veteran Apa contributor whose love of Italy showed through when he edited *CityGuide: Florence*. "Umbria has been unjustly neglected," he says. "It contains some of Italy's most interesting and attractive cities, such as Assisi and Perugia, and some of its frescoes are regarded as the greatest work of the medieval period in Italy."

The Writers

Schultz brought together a broad range of interests to provide the text for this book. **Wolftraud de Concini**, a writer and translator in Pergine near Trent in northern Italy, readily accepted the challenge of providing the introductory chapter.

One of **Leo Linder**'s main preoccupations has, for years, been to follow the courses of Europe's major rivers, all the way from source to estuary, and convert his experiences into documentary films and books. In 1989 he made a film about the River Tiber, a tour that he repeated for this book.

Karsten Welte is an actor and director. Among his TV films, Apa's editors were particularly impressed by his portrait of the Umbrian town of Gubbio. Welte lives in Eberspoint on the River Vils in Bavaria.

Munich-born **Ute Diehl** studied art history in Giessen and Rome. She has now lived in Italy for over 20 years, with homes in Rome and Trevi. Her journalism has appeared in the *Frankfurter Allgemeine Zeitung*.

Schultz   *Catling*   *de Concini*   *Linder*   *Welte*

Vincenzo delle Donne qualified as a radio and TV journalist with the RAI. He not only works for a variety of Italian newspapers, but also for the German newspaper *Süddeutsche Zeitung* and the *Westdeutsche Rundfunk* broadcasting corporation. He lives in Arezzo. It is also from Arezzo that **Susanne Bloss** reports on topics that correspondents in Italy usually only just touch on – themes such as the history of art, arts and crafts and cuisine.

Virgilio Jafrate was born and continues to live in Munich, where he works as a publisher and translator. Together with engineer **Wilfred Taschner**, he follows the exciting hobby of researching some of the less well-known parts of Italy, including Umbria.

Heinrich Decker has made a name for himself as writer, photographer and publisher of art-historical publications on Italy. He was responsible for providing the text and photographs for the chapter on the Umbrian Romanesque.

Wolfgang Boller worked as an editor for *Merian* and the German *Zeit* magazine in Hamburg. Hailing originally from Mainz, the freelance journalist and travel writer now lives in a village in Rhine Hesse.

Ute York was responsible for compiling the Travel Tips. Her work as a journalist takes her halfway round the world, though in private she acknowledges that Italy is her favourite country. To be more precise: a Tuscan village only a few valleys away from Umbria. "Everything I know about Italy, I have from first-hand experience," she says.

Herbert Lechner works as a leading editor on a number of magazines such as *Grafik* and *Kunst* in Munich. **Peter Treutler** is more difficult to pin down: his work as a cameraman takes him all over Europe. It was during a weekend free from filming that he came

across Umbria's "Truffle King". For his works on Roman history, **Theodor Mommsen** was awarded the Nobel prize for literature in 1902. His account of the fateful Battle of Lake Trasimene is reprinted here.

The Photographers

Insight Guides are renowned for their consistently high standard of photography. Top-quality images enable people, landscapes and events to speak to the reader more directly than any form of written description. This fact is clearly demonstrated by *Insight Guide: Umbria*. For portraits of the people, we have to thank primarily the keen eye of American photographer **Bill Wassman**, whose work in this book is the result of just one of many Apa assignments.

The Munich photographer **Gisela Nicolaus** is first and foremost a specialist in landscapes. **Gerd Weiss**, also from Munich, has spent years exploring and capturing on film the less well-known regions of Italy. The young photographer and author **Hans Jörg Künzel** travelled through the region while based in Rome. The result is an impressive array of Umbrian impressions.

Our thanks also go to the photographers of the **Bilderberg** agency, which contributed a number of shots to this volume. Last but not least, **Thomas Höpker**, one of the most successful photographers in Germany, provided some wonderful impressions from his stay in Orvieto.

The original German text was translated by **Ginger Künzel** and **Susan Sting**, under the supervision of **Tony Halliday**. The managing editor of the English edition was **Dorothy Stannard**.

Diehl

delle Donne

Jafrate

Wassman

Nicolaus

History and Culture

<u>Preceding pages</u>: Classic 15th-century buildings of Urbino, set in the hills of Umbria.

Places

Maps

TRAVEL TIPS

**For detailed information
see page 279**

WELCOME

"Tell me about Umbria."

"Well, it's the province next door to Tuscany."

"I see."

It is as if you had asked about Cinderella and been told instead about her glamorous sister. As we all know, however, the prince fell in love with the more modest beauty and was rewarded with Cinderella's love because he recognised her true worth. Cinderella's fairy story could also be the story of Umbria. Umbria asks to be discovered for itself, not compared with Tuscany. Once you have discovered it, you will probably agree with Saint Francis, who, speaking of his home after travelling far and wide, said: "I have never seen anything more pleasing."

Saint Francis himself continues to have a contemporary relevance. He viewed all of Creation and all the creatures of the earth with brotherly love. Growing up in such a beautiful region, it would be hard not to fall in love with the sun, the moon, the stars, and all the birds, flowers and fruits of God's Creation. Even so, it was a distinctly odd thing to do in the 13th century when the beasts of the earth were seen as low and inferior creaures, created, according to Genesis, for man's use and exploitation.

Saint Francis now is seen as the first of the "greens"; indeed, he was officially declared patron saint of ecology in 1979 and it was entirely approriate that the Worldwide Fund for Nature should have held its major conference in 1988 in Saint Francis's birthplace, Assisi. Happily, the landscapes which so charmed Saint Francis, the hilltop towns and wooded valleys, the wildlife and the gentle scenery, have survived unspoiled. Happily, too, this is not a region that appeals to tourists en masse and Umbria, dubbed the "Green Heart of Italy" remains a quiet place for those who enjoy simple, natural pleasures.

A story will illustrate that. A colleague who bought a small property in the green hills near Orvieto made friends with a neighbour who always liked to stop for a chat, a kind of problem-solving session, on his way to the town. Occasionally he would pull a small white object out of his pocket and hand it over without a word. It was a white truffle, tastier and rarer than the black, a present to be savoured; a few shavings grated over a dish of spaghetti transforms a humble meal into a dish fit for an emperor. Nothing could be more typically Umbrian than this quiet generosity; and nothing more typical of Umbria than the truffle – an elusive rare nugget of pure pleasure for those with the sensitivity to find it.

Preceding pages: seasonal contrasts – Easter near Gubbio; Trevi rises above the plains; the Basilica di San Francesco in Assisi, one of the symbols of Umbria; a rainy day. **Left,** young participants at the *Ciostra della Quintana* in Foligno.

"The clouds lie like dark smoke above the Apennines: Umbria, expansive, intense and green, looks down from its sloping mountains. Salve, green Umbria…!"

– Giosuè Carducci, At the Springs of Clitunno, 1876

When, several years ago, Italian tourist agencies proclaimed Umbria "the green heart of Italy", they were plagiarising the words of the Italian poet Giosuè Carducci, a rhetorical and prolific writer of the 19th century. For once, however, they were not dealing in half-truths.

With its huge woods and meadows, its fields and gardens meticulously planted with cereals, vines and olive trees, Umbria is as green and rural as environmental protectionists might wish the entire surface of the earth to be. And it is certainly at the heart of Italy: from here to the alpine border in the north is the same distance as to the sole of the "boot" in the south; and from here the Tyrrhenian coast to the west and the Adriatic coast to the east are equidistant.

Strangely enough, this tiny land, which is just about as large as Corsica and makes up not even 3 percent of the entire area of Italy, could be considered a microcosm of the country – in an economic, cultural and social sense. The statistics for Umbria are almost always on a par with the mean for the rest of Italy, whether they relate to the numbers of people employed in agriculture and industry, the level of education or ownership of cars, per capita income, population growth or the temperature and amount of rainfall. The wealthy and enterprising northern region of Italy, with its flourishing industry, and the poverty-stricken sluggish south, with its often backward agricultural society, meet in Umbria. Here, in the middle of the Italian peninsula, is the so-called "third Italy", where the extreme differences between north and south are balanced out.

Harmonious is the word which best describes the Umbrian landscape, about half of

which is comprised of mountains and the other half of hills. The Apennine mountains, which form the long, 900-mile/1,400-km backbone of Italy, are nowhere so uniform as in Umbria. Here the peaks are almost all under 5,000 ft (1,500 metres) in height, the one exception being Monti Sibillini in the southeast (though this is actually more a part of Abruzzi than Umbria). The hills, made up of sandstone and layers of marl, are less rugged and harsh than those of the neighbouring region of Tuscany to the west, less

rounded than those in the Marches to the east; and the few plains found here are not nearly as far-reaching and expansive. Everything is gentle, balanced and easy on the eye, even in the towns.

Sparsely populated: Only Perugia and Terni, the two provincial capitals of this region of 815,000 people, boast more than 100,000 residents. Aside from these two cities, Foligno is the only municipality with more than 50,000 inhabitants. The rest are small towns, villages and hamlets. The wealth, much of which is generated in the factories and industrial plants of Perugia and Terni, is displayed in an unaffected manner; the poverty, present

Preceding pages: the green heart of Italy. Left, tilling the soil. Above, the Palazzo del Capitano del Popolo in Assisi.

throughout the mountain regions, despite the far-reaching social reforms of recent years, is borne with dignity.

Umbria is seldom a topic of conversation among Italians, either in a positive or negative sense. With its self-imposed modesty and reservation, it is no wonder that the fifth-smallest Italian region, which is cut off from the sea and merely skimmed by the major traffic routes, is often overlooked by the government in Rome as well as by the streams of tourists that pass through Italy annually. This is a great pity: Umbria is well worth discovering.

For many years, the bulk of its visitors have been pilgrims on their way to Assisi, the

Ubaldus of Gubbio – there is a wealth of castles, fortresses and watchtowers. These date from the Middle Ages when Umbria was drawn into the conflict between emperor and pope, whereby Umbria eventually came under papal authority. Although the citizens of Umbria repeatedly revolted against papal power, the Church retained the upper hand and employed every means within its power to maintain its sovereignty over the region.

Perugia's Rocca Paolina is the most forceful embodiment of Church repression; this huge fortress, built by Pope Paul III in 1540 to keep the citizens of Perugia in check was torn down and left in ruins by those same citizens in 1848 at the beginning of the first

birthplace of St Francis, or Norcia, where St Benedict was born. The hordes of pilgrims who come annually to pay tribute to these two saints, the most important in the history of Western religion, have earned Umbria a reputation for religiosity.

History of conflict: In fact, Umbria has a turbulent history, which began 3,000 years ago with the ancient Umbrians and the Etruscans and reached its zenith during the time of the Roman Empire. Aside from the churches of pilgrimage – and these include not only those dedicated to St Francis and St Benedict, but also to St Clare of Assisi and St Clare of Montefalco, St Rita of Cascia and St

Italian War of Independence; in a last brutal act of retaliation, Pius IX sent an army of the Swiss Guard to quell the city in 1859, which it did with such brutality that the event is still remembered as the "massacre of Perugia". Only the following year, 1860, after nearly a thousand years of rule by the Papal States, did Umbria finally gain its freedom, when Garibaldi's troops liberated Perugia.

Religious authority, sustained for several centuries, has had a lasting effect on the conduct of the Umbrian people. Visitors to Umbria who enjoy its timeless qualities perhaps owe a special thanks to the strict restraints practised by the Church. Time has been marked by few changes in the region, and much of its medieval character is still intact. Not only in Assisi, but also in Città di Castello, in Foligno, Gubbio, Montefalco, Narni, Norcia, Orvieto, Perugia, Spello, Spoleto, Todi and Trevi – to name just the larger towns of the region – visitors can immerse themselves in medieval history.

After the 12th and 13th centuries, when the commercial and pilgrim routes which had brought worldly wealth and influence to Umbria were rerouted through Tuscany and along the coast, these towns became backwaters. The whole region found itself on the sidelines. None of the native families was powerful enough to rule Umbria for any

Erasmo da Narni "Gattamelata", Braccio "Fortebraccio" da Montone, the Baglionis and the Vitellis were all Umbrian soldiers of fortune whose loyalty could be bought for a price. The Umbrian saints also possessed a fighting spirit: St Francis overcame the most intense opposition to follow his vocation. A wealthy merchant's son, he placed himself at the side of the poorest of the poor. He guided Christianity back to the path of Christ and preached the unity of man and nature.

St Benedict of Norcia was also a pioneering force in the church. He founded western monasticism. His pragmatic philosophy of *Ora et labora*, "prayer and work", was completely different from the one inspiring the

length of time, and so the people of the region were forced to bow to the influence of the Church.

Saints and soldiers: Many adapted to this (at least they felt secure under the Church's rule), but for others it was too restrictive and they chose to break out: they plunged either into the adventure of war or into religion. This explains why a land as small as Umbria produced so many famous military heroes – and so many saints. Niccolò Piccinino,

contemplative religious societies of the Byzantine Orient. Made patron saint of Europe in 1964, he has been described as one of the architects of the modern world.

The spirit of Umbria is perhaps best personified by the artist Pietro Vannucci from Città della Pieve, who has gone down in art history as "Perugino". His pictures, painted around 1500, reflect all the tensions of the times but use harmonious colours and calm, gentle forms, a style which Perugino passed on to his pupil Raphael. This tendency towards balance is Umbria's contribution to Italian art and culture, a contribution still evident today.

<u>Left</u>, a storm gathers. <u>Above</u>, a fertile land. <u>Following pages</u>: a region steeped in history: the city of Orvieto.

DECISIVE DATES

Up to the 10th/9th millennia BC: Paleolithic age (evidence of stone tools found along the Tiber, Chiascio, near Norcia, Orvieto and along the shores of Lake Trasimeno).

3rd Millennium BC: Middle and late Copper age (Rinaldone culture; graves in cliff-side caves). Middle Bronze Age; so-called Apenninian culture (ceramics with meandering and spiral patterns; archaeological finds near Perrano, Titignano, Gualdo Tadino).

10th–8th century BC: Early Iron age; later period of the so-called Protovillanova culture (finds near Orvieto, Terni, Spoleto, Norcia).

8th century: BC Founding of the Etruscan city-states.

7th–3rd century BC: The Etruscans, Picenti and Gauls of the Etruscan city-states of Perugia and Orvieto succeed in forcing the Umbrian *gentes* out of the Tyrrhenian and Adriatic coastal areas into the Apennine region.

310 BC: Victory of the Romans over the Etruscans near Perugia.

4th century BC: Composition of the Eugubine Tablets, codifying local religious practices, the only surviving example of the ancient Umbrian language.

299 BC: Attempts by Rome to consolidate its position in central Italy lead to wars with the Etruscans, Umbrians, Sabines and Gallic Senones.

295 BC: Defeat of the Senones and Etruscans near *Sentinum* (today's Sassoferrato); Rome controls eastern Umbria.

220 BC: The Via Flaminia is built.

217 BC: Hannibal defeats the Romans at the battle of Lake Trasimeno.

177 BC: Road built from Nocera Umbra across the Scheggia Pass to Fossombrone and Fano.

47–2 BC: Sextus Propertius, from Bevagna near Assisi, writes his lyrical love poems.

40 BC: Following the murder of Caesar (44BC) Octavius lays siege to Perugia where his main rival for power, Lucius, sought refuge. Perugia is sacked and burned to the ground. Octavius declares himself the Emperor Augustus, and out of the ashes of Perugia comes the dawn of the new Imperial Age.

AD 13–14: Italy is divided into so-called *regiones* for purposes of collecting taxes; the 6th Augustal region is Umbria.

493–554 Italy ruled by Ostrogoths.

529 Benedict of Norcia founds the Benedictine order.

552 Totila the Goth is killed by the Roman general, Narses, near Gualdo Taldino.

571: Teutonic Lombards invade Umbria and found the Dukedom of Spoleto; the western portion of Umbria remains Byzantine.

756: Pepin the Short, king of the Franks and father of Charlemagne, helps Pope Stephen III drive the Lombards out of Umbria, which becomes part of the Papal States.

774: Charlemagne sanctions the Papal States in return for being crowned Holy Roman Emperor by

Pope Leo III and grants the Pope sovereignty over Tuscia (present-day Tuscany) and Orvieto; confirmed by Emperor Otto I (962) and Henry II (1020).

885: The Saracens plunder Italy until being defeated at Garigliano (915).

11th century: Foundation of independent municipal *comuni*.

1075–1250: The constant conflict between the papacy and the German emperors leads to the consolidation of urban power; rise of Perugia.

1181–1226: Life of Saint Francis of Assisi.

1228: Construction begins on the Basilica di San Francesco in Assisi..

1230/36–1306: The life of Franciscan poet Jacopone de'Benedetti da Todi, composer of the *Stabat Mater* as well as of pamphlets condemning Pope Boniface VIII.

1296–98: Giotto paints his frescoes in the upper church of the Basilica di Francesco in Assisi

1308: Founding of the university and school of law in Perugia.

1309–77: The Popes retreat to Avignon; temporary fall of the Papal States.

1328: Earthquake (Norcia and Preci were especially hard hit).

1348: The plague strikes.

Pre-1350: Beginnings of faïence production in Deruta.

1357–68: The papal legate, Cardinal Gil D'Albornoz, re-establishes papal authority in Umbria; his *Constitutiones Aegidiane* form the constitution of the Papal States up until 1816.

15th century: Restoration of the papacy; despite schisms and consular opposition, the popes, with the aid of diplomacy and successful *condottieri* (mercenaries), consolidate their political position.

1416–24: The *condottiere* Braccio Fortebraccio from Montone rules (after 1420 with Papal consent) over vast areas of the Papal States; but his dream of creating his own kingdom is carried with him to his grave.

About 1420: The artist Ottaviano Nelli, regarded as the founder of the Umbrian school of painting, works in Gubbio.

1430–1502: Life of Niccolò da Foligno (known as Niccolo Alunno), pupil of Nelli.

1432: The artist Masolino da Panicale working in Todi.

1445–1523: Life of the artist Pietro Vannucci, known as Perugino.

1454–1513: Life of the artist Pinturicchio from Perugia.

1456: The artist Giovanni di Piamonte working in Città di Castello.

1492–1503: Pope Alexander VI Borgia.

1507: Establishment of the *Prefettura di Montagna* in Norcia to administer the mountain villages of the Valnerina.

1521–44: War between Emperor Charles V of Germany and Francis I of France over power in Europe; the popes (Clement VII, Paul III) shift between the two adversaries.

1527: After the sack of Rome, the troops of Charles V ravage the Papal States.

1540: Defeat of Perugia in the Salt War against Paul III, so called because Perugians revolted against the raising of a salt tax;construction of the Rocca Paolina as a symbol of papal authority.

1559: The Treaty of Carteau-Cambrésis, between Spain and France, leads to the stabilisation of the multi-republic status of Italy, which comes under Spanish influence.

1567–69: The artist Federico Barocci working in San Lorenzo, Perugia.

1599: Earthquake in the area around Cascia.

1611: The Flemish artist Denis Calvaert painting in Santa Maria, Montone.

1703: The most severe earthquake to date in the Valnerina results in 2,000 casualties (800 in Norcia alone; other earthquakes in Umbria: 1730, 1751, 1832, 1859 and 1979).

1796: Italian campaign of Napoleon Bonaparte.

1797: Treaty of Tolentino; the Papal States relinquish sovereignty over Emilia-Romagna.

1798: French campaign in the remainder of the Papal States: arrest of Pope Pius VI; creation of the provinces of Trasimeno (capital: Perugia) and Clitunno (Spoleto).

1807–08: The former Papal States are absorbed into the French Empire. Italy is now nominally a republic under French control – the first time Italy has been united since the Roman era.

1809: Arrest of Pope Pius VII.

1814–15: Re-establishment of the Papal States, following the downfall of Napoleon, by the Congress of Vienna.

1831: Influenced by the July revolution in France, revolts occur throughout the Papal States where Pope Leo XII and his successor, Gregory XVI, rule despotically; Austrian troops crush nationalistic and liberal democratic uprisings.

1846: Political and administrative reforms under Pope Pius IX.

1848: Radicalism in the Papal States; Pius IX flees to Gaeta; Giuseppe Mazzini proclaims the republic.

1849: Austrian troops occupy the Papal States. The French march into Rome.

1859: Bloody uprising in Perugia crushed by Swiss Guard.

1860: Giuseppe Garibaldi's "March of the Thousand"; troops from Piedmont march into the Papal States; plebiscite over annexation by Piedmont.

1861: Umbria joins the Kingdom of Italy.

1870: After the departure of the French, Italian troops occupy Rome; end of papal sovereignty.

Late 19th century: Terni becomes the industrial centre of Umbria.

1896–1926: Construction of the railway connection Spoleto and Norcia (discontinued in 1968).

1920-23: Fascism takes control; destruction of socialist and communist organisations, especially in Terni (numerous court cases).

1926: Mussolini founds the University for Foreigners in Perugia.

Post-war: Heavily bombed industrial centres in Perugia and Terni benefit most from Marshall Plan aid, while the agricultural regions develop an economy based on tourism and food production.

VIDE·EBSTV·AFE·RVDHYSVPV·EPVS·TET
VIKVMAKERESNIMV·AOTV·IVCIF·VCEF
REMBETV·ADCIV·VSFENEVFVNI·BETV·ROFV
AIKNE·BETV·ADCI☐STETV·BABIV·RDVSEBETE
PDE·BETV·RVNIBETV·TDA·FRCINE·BETV
ETVS·REDAIKNE·BETV
       OVNTIA·KATLE·TIBELSTAKAE·EST·SVM
FED·NENFADV·bEDSIADV·OEDIIEI·BABIV·APE
FEDIAFES·MENINE·KVDbLASIV·BAbIA·TIbIT
RLV·ADCIA·STDVOLLA·BIKLA·TVNE·CINV·MAIV
NIDAOKLV·CESKLA·SNAFA·ASNAFA·VNNEN·B
ENEV·ESVNV·RVNIBETV·OVNTE·IVCIE·ANN
DE·SECAKNE·PETDVNIAFED·NAFINE·BDATDVF
AE·BVTV·KATLES·SVFA·OAOTV·SVBABIAB·SV
YS·AFLENIES·RDVSEbIA·KADFV·KDEMAFDA·AF
EPV·MEDIFV·ADCIA·FVNI·FVDFVCIFV·CESTIKA
FVSTIN·ANbIB·CINV·NVCIS·AOFDEFVPAFV·TIV
V·BEDCA·BDEOFEB·BEDTV·FVPE·NVCINE·BED
JEL·BEDTV·CESTIbIA·FEPVWE·FEDSNIOMV·KATLE
·I·EDVS·FDVSEKAFV·ISVNF·KDEMAFDV·FDVSEKF
A·APCEIFV·KATLV·FVDFVCIFV·ANNFEPIA·FEDSNIOMV
JEFEDSNIOMV·EENFEDSVN·FDAFEDSNIOMV·SV
ENFV·CESKLES·CVBEFES·FEDSNIOMV·CESTIKAFV·AC
LFV·STAFIFAFV·SVFA·FVSFDA·FEDSFV·IEFDV·EDV
AMAP·EFV·FVCE·DEKAFIPVS·FVNE·BEDFV·BEDCA·F
SOFFIB·CESKLV·SNAFVASNAFV·VNNEN·BEDFV·F
ECESTIKAFV·FEFDVNIAFEDNAFINE·BDATDVAF
IKNIS·FEDSNIOMV·FEDFSFINIA·ISVNF·KIACLES·F
LLESSNAFE·ASNAFES·SECAKNIS·SFINIAMNA·FEDSNIO

Despite numerous allusions to the Umbrians in the writings of the scribes of antiquity, despite the famous Eugubine Tablets of Gubbio, despite archaeological finds, we still know almost nothing about their history. On the contrary, the pieces of evidence that are to be found only raise more questions.

Herodotus, called by Cicero "the father of history," reports that two rivers flowed out of the region "above" the land of the Umbrians in a northerly direction. These were the Carpis and the Alpis, and they merged with the Istros which we know today as the Danube. Some historians believe that Carpis and Alpis were names for the Drina and the Sava, the Inn and the Salzach or the Inn and the Drava. This may or may not be the case, but what is clear is that the "Umbrians" had obviously already settled in Upper Italy at the time of Herodotus.

The Umbrian tribes: Pliny the Elder also reported widespread settlement by the "Umbrians". According to him, they were one of the oldest *gens* of Italy, and the Etruscans are said to have conquered 300 of their cities. The region they occupied reached from the mouth of the Umbro (today's Ombrone) to the Adriatic Sea. Mantua, Ravenna and *Ariminum* (today's Rimini), as well as the vanquished cities of *Butrium* (near Ravenna) and *Spina* (south of the Po Delta) were founded by the Umbrians. According to Pliny, they wrested from the Sikuli and the Liburni the area extending from the coastal region to the *Aternus* River (today's Pescara). In the interior of the country, the Umbrians occupied a region which extended well beyond Umbria's later boundaries. In 1134 BC, they founded *Ameria*, today's Amelia.

On the other hand, the Umbrians lost their founding settlement of Cortona to the indigenous tribes; and the Pelasgi chased them out of the region around *Reate* (today's Rieti), where they settled and assumed the name Sabines. Eighty years before the Trojan War (c.1260 BC), the Pelasgi and the Umbrians had formed an alliance to force the Ligurians to emigrate to Sicily.

Left, detail of one of the Eugubine Tablets. **Above**, on the Via Flaminia.

In short, the scribes of antiquity generally classified the Umbrians as a sort of aboriginal tribe whose lands, at the turn of the first millennium BC, stretched from the alpine region to Rome, from Rucellae and Grosseto to Ravenna and Pescara. These scribes, however, in using the term Umbrians, engaged in a gross generalisation – there was never one unified tribe of this name controlling the entire region during that period.

Philological research provides a little more information. The Magrè inscriptions, found

near Shio, lend more support to the theory of Herodotus. The inscriptions suggest a linguistic affinity between tribes of the Indo-Germanic language group of northern Europe and those of the Umbrian-Sabellian group. The Umbrian-Sabellian group was divided into various *gentes* with different names and different cultures. In the south were the Samnites, Lucani and Brutti; in central Italy were the Equi, Marsi, Vestines and others; in the west, the Volski settled, and in the northwest, the Sabines. The Umbrians lived in the north. But when this tribe appeared, its name, where it came from and what it meant – the scribes make no mention. Herodotus called this folk the *Ombrikoi*, meaning "people along the water". In Latin, this simply was changed into *Umbri*. But the question remains, to which "water" was Herodotus referring? Was it the land bordering the Carpis and Alpis or the area around the mouth of the Ombrone?

Indo-Germanic immigrants: We can only conclude from all this that the Umbrians were originally Indo-Germanic migrants from the north. When they arrived they found, in the heart of Italy, a fertile land watered by lakes (most of which have since disappeared). The rivers and streams were teeming with fish and it was a region of rich vegetation as well as being home to a wide variety of

not far from Perugia, is a prime example of this civilisation. Other archaeological finds near Terni, Parrano, Titignano and Gualdo Tadino provide evidence that the region which later came to be known as Umbria was traversed by numerous tribes as they migrated from the north across the Apennines to the flat plains around Terni and Rieti in the south. One of the most impressive finds testifying to this fact is the necropolis of Monteleone di Spoleto, where, among other things, a war chariot was found. This chariot can be seen today in the Metropolitan Museum in New York City.

The era of the Etruscans: The widespread "nation" of the various *gentes*, referred to by

animals. The immigrants were confronted with a native population whose roots can be traced back to the late Paleolithic age, a fact supported by archaeological finds from that epoch in the valleys of the Tiber and the Chiascio and along the plateau of Norcia. Although finds from the early and middle Neolithic age are scarce, a few have been unearthed near Norcia.

Evidence of an imported civilisation with Indo-Germanic origins dates from the late Neolithic age. The region of this civilisation, stretching from the Arno to the Tiber, from Fiora to Lake Bolsena, is today known as Rinaldone. The tomb of Poggio Aquilone,

Pliny as the Umbrians, experienced its first defeat when the Etruscans advanced to the Tyrrhenian coast. It should be pointed out, however, that most of the population remained in their settlements; only the ruling class was ousted. At the end of the 7th century BC, the Tiber formed Etruria's eastern boundary. One of the border towns was Todi, whose name comes from the Etruscan word *tular*, meaning border. Mantua and *Spina* were important centres of Etruscan power.

It was also in the 7th century BC that the Trojans began to threaten the Adriatic coast. In the south, the Sabines spread out around the region of Rieti. In the 4th century, the Adriatic coast from Ancona to Pescara was lost to the Picenti, and in the north the Gauls were threatening. They had been streaming into Upper Italy since the end of the 5th century BC – the Lingoni occupied the territory west of Ravenna, while the Senoni conquered the coastal region from Rimini to Ancona, the so-called *ager Gallicus*.

Even though various segments of the population were driven into the Apennine valleys, where they also settled, it would be incorrect to refer to them collectively as the Umbrians. They comprised tribes, such as the Camertes and the Tadinati, who were anything but friendly with one another. Thus, the Eugubine

before they were conquered and absorbed. Through the establishment of colonies such as *Sena Gallica* (Senigallia) and *Castrum Novum* (Giulianova), the Adriatic coast was secured. In the year 247, a road was built along this coast, and in 220 that road was joined to Rome by the Via Flaminia (today the N3 road, still forming the major north-south route through Umbria). The eastern Apennine region was thus totally under Roman control. The Romans had already begun the conquest of the northern Apennine region with the founding of *Arminium* in the year 268. A mere two years later, they ruled this entire region. In order to secure the hinterlands, as well as to protect the southern

Tablets (bronze tablets codifying ancient Umbrian religious practices, today displayed in Gubbio's Palazzo dei Consoli) contain curses, some of which are directed against the hostile "brothers" in the region around today's Gualdo Tadino.

The rise of Rome: Rome's victory over the Gauls at *Sentinum* (near Sassoferato) in the year 295 BC, as well as a successful campaign against the Senoni in 283, sealed the fate of the Umbrian tribes. Although they were allies of Rome, it was only a question of time

exit of the mountain pass across *Camerinum* (Camerino), the colony of *Spoletium* (Spoleto) was established in the year 241. Thus, Rome's conquest of the Umbrians was complete. The tribes had to supply large numbers of troops to assist Rome in its war against the Gauls in the year 225. One of these warriors, a cohort of the Camertes, gained fame under the Roman banner.

We know little about the domestic politics of Umbria during these centuries. However, changes in the language give rise to the theory that large numbers of immigrants moved from the east into the region west of the Apennines after the 5th century BC. The

Left, Etruscan necropolis near Orvieto. **Above**, an Etruscan vase.

Nucerini Camellani, from whom Nocera Umbra got its name, originally came from *Camerinum*, and the *fratres Atiedii* of the Eugubine Tablets originated in *Attidium*, a settlement north of today's Matelica. This brotherhood – perhaps a caste of priests – presents us with one of the rare written works from the second or first century, evidence which provides information about certain inhabited areas around Gubbio. The legendary seven bronze tablets contain not only various curses directed against enemy tribes, but also sacrificial instructions, native names for gods and the structure of the ruling authority. In general, it is thought that the Umbrians lived under an aristocratic struc-

tem of artificial irrigation. On the other hand, two characteristics of agriculture which are still evident today are typically Umbrian. These are the famous white cattle of the region, originally bred as sacrificial animals, blessed at the Clitunno spring and then taken to Rome to be offered to the gods; and the population's ability, through clever management, to make optimal use of the land in the mountainous regions.

Hannibal's campaign: The residents of Umbrian towns first gained Roman citizenship through the Lex Iulia in 217BC, but by then the region had long since ceased to harbour thoughts of independence from Rome. Had it been otherwise, the course of

ture. According to the Eugubine Tablets of Gubbio, this structure was of a hierarchical nature and was divided into the following levels: territorial units, called *tribus*; *plaga*, which were weapon-carrying troops; and *gentes*, meaning families.

While the advance of Rome in the 3rd century BC consisted solely of military and logistical measures in the bordering regions, the subsequent introduction of Roman coins, the Roman legal system and Roman titles, such as *quaestor*, proved the extent of the new rulers' influence. However, the civilisation of the Etruscans also left its mark. It was the Etruscans who introduced the sys-

history might have been very different. After his spectacular victory over the Romans at the Battle of Lake Trasimeno, Hannibal marched to Spoleto, fully expecting the Umbrians to join his army and march with him to attack Rome itself. The citizens of Spoleto turned him away; if their hearts had been set against Rome, who knows what would have been the future for this ambitious young soldier intent on "world" power. Ten years later, when Hannibal returned, Umbrians showed equal lack of interest in a Punic "liberation" of their land.

The name Umbria first appears during the rule of Caesar Augustus. It was the designation for the 6th Augustal region, an administrative unit governing extremely heterogeneous territory. The northernmost portion, between the Bidente River and the upper reaches of the Savio, reached almost to the sea. From there, the border stretched to the mouth of the Rubicon, running along the Adriatic coast to Esino, then following the river's path into the interior of the country before changing to a southerly direction where the river joined the Esinate. It continued on to Monti Sibillini and then followed the Nera river to Velino where it ran to the south of Terni and Narni, reaching the Tiber below Otricoli. The Tiber formed the western boundary. It was not until reaching region, such as Rimini, Senigallia and Camerino. The Augustal administrative boundaries were based on natural borders and ethnicity – factors which played no role in later times.

Still in use at the time of the territorial reforms under Emperor Diocletian, the term Umbria disappeared during the time of the Ostrogoths and the Lombards. It became the "Dukedom of Spoleto" in official records as well as in colloquial speech. Not until the United Kingdom of Italy was founded did the name "Umbria" re-emerge.

Travelling around Umbria, you will see evidence of the ancient Umbrians and Etruscans everywhere in the form of the

Umbertide that the border turned northward, continuing to the main ridge of the Apennines where it once again reached the area between the Bidente and Savio rivers.

Numerous important centres were excluded by this Augustal boundary, without which it would be hard to imagine Umbria today. Città di Castello, Perugia, Chiusi and Orvieto are just a few of them. On the other hand, the former boundary embraced villages which today are not included in the

<u>Left</u>, portraits of Caesar Augustus; Etruscan warrior. <u>Above</u>, mosaic from a Roman villa in Umbria.

massive walls that still surround many cities, including Perugia and Spoleto; though these were later heightened, the lower courses, of massive monoliths, date to the first millennium BC. The best museum for pre-Roman material is the Museo Archeologico Nazionale dell'Umbria in Perugia. Almost every Umbrian town has its surviving Roman temples, arches and amphitheatres but the best remains are at Carsulae, north of Terni, where you can see the impressive ruins of a complete Roman town, founded around 220 BC on the Via Flaminia and praised for the beauty of its buildings by Tacitus and Pliny.

Malice and breach of confidence were, in principle, foreign to Theodoric, King of the Ostrogoths. He was a hero, a Teutonic military commander and prince of war. His soldiers were his family. They were willing to sacrifice their lives for him. But he was also full of fear and hatred and he nursed a pathological mistrust.

Byzantine ambitions for power: When Odoacer had removed the youthful Romulus Augustulus from the throne, the western Roman Empire had ceased to exist. But the emperor in Byzantium still had ambitions to consolidate his power. Ravenna, Perugia, Narni and Todi, all in upper Italy, still belonged to him. And he had allies.

The Byzantine emperor, Zeno, viewed the former empire as a gameboard for his clever moves. His perception of the character of the Germanic tribes, their dissension and their greediness, formed the basis of his politics. He pitted Germans against Germans: the Ostrogoth Theodoric against Odoacer, the upstart from the tribe of the Skiri. They were victims of this same emperor; both were generals of the Byzantine court, both were kings and military commanders. If they did not destroy each other, then at least one of them would perish.

Zeno had been watching with mistrust the bloody rivalries for the leadership of the palace guard in Ravenna as well as Odoacer's military successes leading to a coup d'état. The first king of Italy had paid homage to him, but he had held too long to his claim to the throne within a united empire and had become too powerful. On the other hand, the Germanic settlers in the eastern provinces were becoming a nuisance with their constant attacks and plundering. Their alarming migrations had come to a halt in Pannonia and Moesia (today's Hungary, Slovenia and Bulgaria). The Ostrogoth tribal chieftain, Theodoric, had grown up as a hostage in the court of Byzantium and, as a youth, was

already considered a favourite of the emperor. Thus it was possible to reach an understanding with him, and Zeno was able to win him as an ally against Odoacer. Theodoric was given the difficult task of reconquering that portion of the empire.

The empire of Theodoric: The hero rose to the occasion. With four giant steps, he attained his historical position as Theodoric the Great. His triumphal march, with an army of 20,000 warriors, left a trail of blood. Three times he was victorious over Odoacer, at Isonzo, near

Verona and along the Adda. He drove him out of the territory. And, finally he laid siege to Odoacer in the fortress of Ravenna.

Ravenna, a lagoon city, impossible to conquer by land, was Rome's largest naval base on the Adriatic. Additionally, it controlled the most strategically important land routes in northern Italy: the Via Flaminia which led to Rome and the Via Emilia which led to Piacenza, with branches leading to Genoa, Aquileia and across the Brenner Pass (Via Claudia Augusta).

The fate of these first two kings of Italy was sealed in Ravenna. During a joint meal on 15 March, in the year 493, Odoacer and

Preceding pages: the Roman springs at Clitunno, north of Spoleto; Queen of the Lombards Theolinde at her wedding to Duke Agilulf. Left, Agilulf with two warriors. Above, a warrior's helmet.

his followers were massacred. Odoacer was killed by Theodoric himself. According to the chronicles of history, "Theodoric plunged his sword straight through him in the Lauretum Palace." It is said that Odoacer's last words were: "Where is God?"

The kingdom of the Ostrogoths assumed the Roman Constitution as the basis for official order. Roman law and tax privileges, as well as the old Roman offices, remained virtually unchanged. The Goths claimed one third of the conquered territory. They bore weapons and served as soldiers. Theodoric ordered the establishment of grain reserves and the construction of churches, palaces and aqueducts.

lishment of the old Roman Empire. He commissioned two commanders-in-chief to eliminate the Goths. They were Belisarius, commander of the imperial guard, and Narses, a palace official and a eunuch.

Theirs was to be a long battle and their adversary, Totila the Goth, was no mean tactician. For a long time the Goths held the upper hand and an interesting insight into Totila's character is provided by a meeting that took place between him and Saint Benedict in AD 542, towards the end of the lives of both men. Benedict had now all but retired to the monastery that he founded at Monte Cassino. Totila, who was making a triumphal progress through central Italy,

Theodoric the Great died at the age of 70 hated as a heretic king who rode straight into hell on a horse which was not even his own, loved as a ruler and hero, and glorified in legend as Dietrich from Berne. The kingdom of the Ostrogoths continued to exist for exactly 26 years after his death.

Theodoric bore no sons. Thus his daughter, Amalasuntha, ruled as regent for his grandson Athalaric, who was a minor and in ill-health. When she ordered the drowning of a cousin and co-regent in a bath on the island of Martana in Lake Bolsena, the Byzantine emperor, Justinian, used this murder as an excuse to begin the battle for the re-estab-

which had been laid waste by his armies, had heard of Benedict and decided to test his prophetic powers. According to the account given by Pope Gregory in his *Dialogues*, Totila sent Riggo, the captain of his guard, dressed in purple robes, to impersonate him. Benedict greeted Riggo with the words "Put off those robes, my son, for they do not belong to you".

Totila himself then came to see Benedict and prostrated himself before the great saint. They later spent some time in conversation, during which Benedict tried to persuade Totila to abandon his onslaught. The meeting ended with Benedict's prophesy that

Totila would succeed in sacking Rome but would die within 10 years and not enjoy his conquest – a prediction that came true.

The end of the Gothic wars: The final confrontation came in AD 552, literally 10 years after Benedict's prediction. Narses commanded an army of 30,000 men. With the aid of his superior troops and his outstanding capabilities as a military commander he defeated the Goths near Tagina (today Gualdo Tadino in the province of Perugia). Totila was killed by a spear in the back as he fled.

It took another 10 years, however, before Narses finally defeated the rump of the Ostrogothic cavalry. The last of the army was wiped out at the foot of Monti Lattari

with all of their goods and possessions, should immediately leave Italy and under no conditions ever bear arms against the Romans again."

That was the end of the Gothic wars. The Gothic kings had ruled over Sicily, Dalmatia and a portion of Pannonia, as well as inner Noricum and Raetia. Nine kings had ruled this empire. Five of them were murdered, one was deposed and one fell in battle.

The winner's joy in victory, however, was shortlived. Although Narses, as a favourite of Justinian and the notorious Theodora, achieved royal respect after his conquest of the Goths, Emperor Justin II, successor to Justinian, saw him as a threat. It seemed that

near Pompeii. The last king of the Goths fell in a one-on-one battle. Roman soldiers mounted his head on a lance and, according to the chronicler Procopius, "paraded him before both armies; before the Romans in order to motivate them, and before the Goths to force them to surrender. The Goths, however, had no intention of admitting defeat, but continued fighting until nightfall." It was not until the next day that the 1,000 survivors announced their willingness to retreat; "and it was agreed that the remaining Barbarians,

Left, the boss of a battle shield. **Above**, shield plaquette depicting a rider on horseback.

the ruler of Ravenna was once again one who had amassed too much power. At the suggestion of Empress Sophia, Narses was relieved of his authority. In her words, "The time has come to send him back into the Serail where he can weave plots with the women." Also recorded in history, though not authenticated, is his answer: "I will weave a plot so thick that the empress will never be able to undo it." This story is probably mere speculation; even so Narses had already calculated his revenge – he called the Lombards into the country.

The Lombards in Italy (568–774): Chroniclers have never really accepted that the

Lombardic conquerors were formally invited into Italy behind the emperor's back. The source of the story was Paulus Diaconus, a monk and himself a Lombard, writing about 200 years after the event occurred. It is possible that Diaconus based his story on supposition or perhaps even a pack of lies. But it is known that he was well acquainted with the royal court in Pavia and had seen through the motives behind the migration of nations. He must also have known that the Armenian Narses, only a few years after supposedly being branded a traitor, was given a hero's funeral in Byzantium with all the accompanying honours.

In the writings of Paulus Diaconus con-

cerning the ailing commander, the following reference is found: "Whereupon, out of hate and fear, he retreated to Naples in Campania. And soon thereafter, he dispatched his courier to the Lombards with the message that they should immediately abandon the unfertile fields of Pannonia and hasten to Italy with the aim of conquering that country which has an extraordinary abundance of all resources. At the same time, he sent various types of fruits and other crops of the land to these Lombards so that, upon seeing these, they would be convinced to come."

The story of the Lombards in Italy has certain elements of a blockbuster novel. It is

no exaggeration to say the Lombards held the future of western civilisation in their hands, the well-being of a Europe which did not yet even exist. They could have prevented the fall of the Roman Empire, or certainly delayed it. If they had supported the Byzantine Empire, they could have nipped in the bud the power of the Popes over the Holy Roman Empire of German Nations. But, instead of all this, they joined forces with their arch enemy. They gambled away the empire like a handful of nuts.

The rule of Alboin: Affected by a severe case of political myopia, the Lombards marched on to the stage of European history. Continuing in this same tempo, they massacred the Gepids, their Germanic brothers in the Hungarian lowlands, before being forced out by the Avars. King Alboin led a trek of 200,000 Lombards, plus 20,000 Saxon warriors, across the Alps. Included in this procession were prisoners taken during the battles of destruction, including many women and children. One of these was Princess Rosamond, daughter of Kunimond, the king of the Gepids whom Alboin had killed in battle.

They came as victors and rulers, wild and bearded men with the backs of their heads shaved. Their hair was parted in the middle and matted strands hung down over both sides of their foreheads. They wore clothes of linen with colourful stripes, and footgear which was laced crosswise up to their knees. They stormed into the country with a force that could be likened to a natural disaster. They paid no attention to Roman law. They acted according to their own laws and exhibited an aggressiveness which the imperial ruler in Ravenna and the Roman bishop came to fear. Murdering and plundering, they laid waste to the region to which they later returned and settled, still known today as Lombardy.

Alboin captured the city of Pavia and raised it to the status of a royal residence. In Milan, he crowned himself king of Italy. During the course of his incursions into upper Italy, he founded, among others, the duchies of Florence, Spoleto, the Marches and Abruzzi. Each duke (from *duces*, or leader) ruled a sizeable territory and owed allegiance to the king. The duke of Spoleto was to become, along with those from Fiaul and Benevento, the most powerful and the most dangerous of Lombardic rulers.

Alboin was not a stereotypical conqueror. He was strong-willed, ambitious, vindictive, but he was full of contradictions. In Pavia, for example, he acted with foresight and was conciliatory. The resistance offered by the people of this town made his blood boil and yet, when he finally entered the city as conqueror, he ordered that his opponents be treated with leniency. But he was not always so merciful and wise. He was also primitive and brutal – a tasteless and superstitious barbarian. He forced Rosamond, the daughter of the king, to marry him.

In a drinking spree in the royal palace, Alboin toasted his bride with a gruesome tankard he had had fashioned from the skull who had conquered so many enemies, met his death, defenceless and deceived by the cunning of a woman."

The Lombards found themselves trapped in a triangular web of worldly and religious authority. And the more they thrashed about in this web, the more tightly they were caught. On the one side, was the Pope. Despite the Lombards' conversion to Christianity (6th–mid-7th century), they were unable to win the Pope's support. And then there were the warlike pillaging Franks – a new and sinister power within the old empire. Finally, there was the threat from the imperial puppet player operating from far-away Byzantium. The Dukedom of Spoleto, with its obstinate ruler,

of the defeated Kunimond. He passed this to Rosamond and, according to Paulus Diaconus, "ordered her to drink merrily with her father". The chronicler leaves no room for doubt that this macabre tankard actually existed. He says he saw it with his own eyes.

In a conspiracy with her lover, Rosamond arranged for the murder of King Alboin in his sleeping chambers. In the words of Diaconus, "in the end, this audacious man, lay caught between the imperial governor of Ravenna, the exarch, and the duchate of Rome (the metropolitan area belonging to the Pope). To make matters worse, it was (or at least it considered itself) independent.

The empire of the Lombards was built on precarious foundations and survived the periods from one war to the next only by means of forming constantly changing alliances: with the Avars against the rebellious dukes or with loyal princes against the Avars, with the consent of the Franks against Ravenna, with the exarches against the Pope and with the Pope against the dukes of Spoleto and Benevento.

Left, Gospel illustrations served to spread the message of Christianity among the Germanic peoples. **Above**, the siege of Rome by the Ostrogoths in the 6th century.

Lombardic kings were often involved in civil wars and exhausted their strength in many a fraternal strife. They threatened Rome repeatedly, called into question the power of the Church as an important authority and brought an end to the power of the Byzantine emperor over Italy.

The influence of the Frankish kings: Even so, the men with the matted hair were able to defend their authority for more than 200 years, especially in the northern and central regions of the peninsula. They settled in Lombardy and Tuscany, in Umbria and Campania. They never succeeded in conquering Rome. They marched forward as far as Bari, but their bold vision of a united Italy

never came to be. They had a total of 22 kings of which three or four played an important role. Six kings were murdered, three chased out of the country and one was defeated in battle. After being besieged by Charlemagne at Pavia for seven months, King Desiderius capitulated and the Lombards disappeared from the pages of history.

Ironically, Charlemagne was the son-in-law of Desiderius, the father of Charlemagne's second wife, Desiderata. Desiderius viewed the arranged marriages of both of his daughters as clever political manoeuvring on his part. He also fancied himself in a more advantageous position relative to the Roman

duchate than he was. Thus, Desiderius saw himself as a powerful ally to both the Frankish and Bavarian thrones, and could not understand how it came to pass that the reins of power slipped so quickly through his hands. First, the Roman bishop intervened the moment he gained the apostolic throne. Stephen III notified Charlemagne: "If this marriage plan is true, then it could only have been arranged by the devil. This is certainly not a holy marriage, but rather a filthy relationship…"

Amazingly, it was not Charlemagne, but Desiderius who tried to put an end to the marriage by purposefully and wantonly annoying his son-in-law. He took in Charlemagne's widowed sister-in-law and requested that Pope Hadrian declare her two sons as the Frankish kings. Charlemagne decided to rid himself of Desiderata. He loaded her on to an ox cart and sent her home to her father.

Desiderius once again engaged in concentrated attacks against Rome and Hadrian, backed into a tight corner, called on Charlemagne to assist him. Charlemagne arrived in Lombardy soon thereafter with his armoured cavalry. After conquering Pavia, he vanquished the last Lombard king to a monastery on the other side of the Alps and accepted, as new ruler over both empires (*Rex Francorum et Langobardum*), the homage of the dignitaries.

The Lombard empire had crumbled, but it retained a small degree of independence into the 9th century. Benevento remained free. The princes of Spoleto, now vassals of the Frankish crown, still ruled until 1247, when the duchy was absorbed by the Papal States.

That period of independence was critical to the development of Umbria. The Lombards, who had begun as barbarian warriors, became able administrators after their defeat by Charlemagne. It was the Lombardic Duke Faroaldo II who, inspired by Saint Benedict, founded the great monastery at San Pietro in Valle, in the Velnerina, and the chain of Lombardic fortifications in that same valley brought a measure of peace to what had been a lawless region. Above all, the Lombardic style of building laid the foundations for the characteristic and intriguing Umbrian Romanesque style.

<u>Above</u>, Charlemagne on horseback. <u>Right</u>, Lombardic enamelled reliquary.

OR·FALE
TRVS·

D̄I GR̄A
VENECI
Ę DVX

The Roman Papa was already the wealthiest property owner in Italy by the time Pope Gregory (590–604) came to power. The *Patrimonium Petri* (Peter's Patrimony) consisted of lands which had been inherited, donated or wrested from others. Most of these properties were located in the central and southern part of the Italian peninsula.

The curia's pride in its possession of its new territories, however, was short-lived. The Lombardic King Aistulf annulled the donations made by both of his predecessors with a stroke of his quill. He based this decision on the "imported" law of the Lombards: the possessions of the king are in all cases inviolable. Pope Stephen II was extremely angry with Aistulf. The spiritual leader had, by the 8th century, already adopted the title *Il Papa* (the diminutive form of "father"), but he certainly did not treat King Aistulf in a very fatherly way, even though this king respected him as the head of the Church. Instead he described him as a roaring lion: "Godless, accursed, a bitter enemy who is in the hands of the devil, a wicked king, tyrant and a child of the devil".

Earlier Lombardic rulers kept more in line with the wishes of Rome's religious leaders. Luitprand, for example, presented the conquered city of *Sutrium* (today's Sutri in the province of Viterbo) to the "holy Apostles Peter and Paul" out of his own free will. Under international law, this act was not entirely above board since *Sutrium* belonged to the emperor of Byzantium who would have liked to have it back. Luitprand's successor, Ratchis, was a bit more cautious. He made presents only of the properties belonging to his own crown and donated the land for the founding of monasteries. It was these donations, and others, that Aistulf annulled.

Pepin the Short: Aistulf had already proved troublesome. He conquered Ravenna, chased out the exarch and laid claim to Rome. He dared to try to collect taxes in the duchate. Pope Stephen saw his position of authority

Preceding pages: a lion, symbol of St Mark, on the facade of Orvieto cathedral. **Left**, Peter with the key to Heaven. **Above**, Titian's portrait of Pope Leo X.

threatened. He went to Gaul to seek an alliance with the Frankish steward named Pepin, requesting him to save the Church from this diabolical Lombard. Pepin the Short (father of Charlemagne) had risen through the ranks as a courtier of the Merovingians. He had an insatiable appetite for power but lacked dynastic legitimacy. He offered the Pope a deal which would be beneficial to both of them. The Church must put itself at the mercy of the protective power of Pepin, while at the same time raising itself, as a religious insti-

tution, above all temporal thrones. It seems that he knew what the Pope's decision would be: Pepin had ensured that his visitor was well taken care of.

Stephen knew how to interpret the symbols of the time. Using the authority invested in him by the apostle Peter, he made Pepin king of the Franks and granted him the title once reserved for the Byzantine emperor: *Patricius Romanorum*. The rules of the game were laid down in such a way that the Roman "Papa" could not lose. As the newly named protector of the Romans and their house saints, Pepin stormed with the fury of war over the Lombards. He defeated Aistulf twice and, in a fit of joyous philanthropy, presented St Peter with property which did not even belong to him: the exarchate of Ravenna including Istria and Venice, the duchies of Spoleto and Benevento and the southern portion of Lombardy and Corsica. In other words, a substantial portion of Italy.

The Pepinian Gift, however, was nowhere as important as the so-called Donation of Constantine. Successive popes, from Stephen on, claimed that Constantine the Great, who was the first Roman emperor to convert to Christianity, had bequeathed everything – nothing less than the whole Roman Empire – to the Church. The Donation gave the Church sole ownership of the city of Rome, the

the judicial foundation of the entire Papal States for the next 1,000 years. Dante was later to state, with justice, that all the troubles of Italy could be laid at the door of Constantine's bequest.

The expansion of the Papal States: In the course of the next 1,000 years, the geographical boundaries of the Papal States were continually changing. Sometimes an ambitious insolent nephew of the Pope would break a piece off for himself; or sometimes the territory would be increased through gifts or inheritance. At its largest, the Papal States represented an area about as large as Switzerland (41,000 sq. km/16,000 sq. miles) and stretched from the Tyrrhenian Sea all the

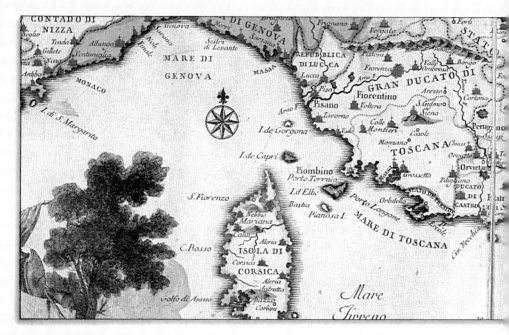

Lateran, all the provinces of Italy and the entire Western World, not to mention inconceivable privileges. But could it be proved?

Miraculously, documents containing the deeds of donation were produced and ceremoniously ratified at the tomb of Saint Peter; this sacral setting was meant to reinforce the authenticity of what were patently forged documents setting out the right of the Church to exercise territorial power in Italy. At a stroke, the apostle Peter was posthumously transformed from a poor humble fisherman into the biggest landed property owner in Italy and all his successors into princes of the Church. The documents formed

way to the Adriatic. Around the year 1200, the Holy Father reclaimed unconditional sovereignty over the former *Patrimonium*, the exarchate, the Pentapolis (the Adriatic league of cities including Rimini, Pesaro, Fano, Senagallia and Ancona), the March Ancona, the Dukedom of Spoleto, the county of Bertinora and the Mathildian inheritance (an extremely large area between the Arno and Po rivers). This was about half of Italy, taking in the regions of Latium, Abruzzi, Umbria, the Marches and many parts of Tuscany and Emilia Romana.

The art historian Gregorovius, an authority on Italy, visited Spoleto during his travels

(1860). The art historian wrote, "Upon journeying through this small empire of the Popes, as I have been doing for the past several weeks, from the depths of central Latium all the way to the border of Tuscany, it must be admitted that this was a magnificent monarchy. Surely any king would have been pleased to have worn the crown of this kingdom."

The popes' insatiable appetite for more land and more power led to a great amount of bloodshed. They threatened those who defended their own land with the loss of eternal salvation. They persecuted their opponents long after their deaths. When the once-powerful but defeated Lombard king, Aistulf, broke his neck, Pope Stephen II raged in

Given that the documents gave the whole Roman Empire to the Church, the fact that Saint Peter's successors only laid territorial claim to half of Italy appears modest. Yet what little the Church owned, it clung on to tenaciously and doubts as to the authenticity of the document were dismissed by the curia over a period of almost 1,000 years with the peculiar rationale that "what should not be could not be".

Even so, the Papal States were politically, militarily and economically untenable right from the start. The Pope based the administration of the territories on that of the bureaucracy within the imperial exarchates. The papal legates ruled with an arbitrariness

anger: "the tyrant Aistulf, child of the devil, who thirsted after the blood of the Christians and destroyed the Church, this man has been slain by God's hand and relegated to the depths of Hell."

The Popes shied at nothing to defend their rights of ownership and were willing to use any means, no matter how questionable, to achieve their ends. It is now known that documents containing Constantine's bequest were forged at the monastery of St Denis.

Left, this 18th-century map shows the extent of the Papal States. **Above**, *Virgin and Child* in the church of Santa Maria Nuova in Gubbio.

which could be likened to that of orthodox land overseers. The papal army of 15,000 soldiers existed to sustain papal authority. The threatened power was fearsome, but established power was even more fearsome.

At the beginning of the 19th century, the government of the Papal States resembled that of a despotic principality ruled by a dictator at the mercy only of God. The laws of the Church were enforced through judicial inquisition and police authority. There were Jewish ghettos and state censorship. Those caught in possession of banned books were thrown into the dungeons. Religious commandments were also civil laws. Children were forced to denounce their own parents.

St Peter, however, could never really reap the harvests of his pantry. Although the direct taxes within the Papal States were higher than elsewhere in Italy, and the feudal Pope, Martin IV, was known to have enjoyed such huge quantities of fat eels from Lake Trasimeno that he died from them, these wonderful properties were actually more of a burden than a pleasure. There were constant disputes with the insolent feudal barons, with dynasties demanding their independence and with autocratic magistrates. Despite substantial income, the debts were, in general, even more considerable. Not even the increase from 600 to 2,100 of the number

of positions which were for sale eased the financial troubles of the papacy. The increase was ordered by Pope Leo X, a businessman of limited abilities, who remarked, "Let us enjoy the papacy as long as God has given it to us".

The fall of the Papal States: It was a long time before the end finally came. The first blow was struck when Napoleon annexed the Papal States and placed them under the Republic of Italy. While in prison Pope Pius VII renounced the temporal feudal authority of the Church (1813). Pius subsequently retracted the renunciation as having made under duress: "We demand the return of our lands because they are not our personal inheritance but rather the inheritance of St Peter who received them personally from Christ." After the fall of Napoleon the apostolic pilgrim returned triumphantly to Rome. The Pope once again allowed the use of the inquisition but forbade torture. The restoration of the Papal States was secured at the 1815 Vienna Congress by the curia cardinal and Secretary of State, Ercole Consalvi.

During the Italian Wars of Independence that followed, it was actually proposed by church supporters that the popes should be made president of a federal Italy. That was not to be.

Victor Emanuel II, king of Sardinia, was crowned king of a united Italy in February 1861. This led to an official breach with the Vatican. In a referendum, the union of the Papal States with Italy was rejected by a vote of 133,681 to 1,507.

The temporal authority of the Pope was finally annulled in the Capitol in 1870. A law passed in 1871 limited the sovereignty of the Pope to the Vatican, the Lateran Church and the Castel Gandolfo and guaranteed him a yearly pension of 3,225,000 lire. The problem, however, remained unsolved; the papacy could not accept a renunciation of its authority over the Papal States. Pius IX, with the conviction of his newly won infallibility, reacted obstinately to the suggestions of a compromise: *Non Possumus* ("We cannot"). He could well afford to decline the pension.

The conflict was finally ended by the Lateran Treaty of 1929, an agreement between the Italian fascist state and the papacy. The state recognised papal sovereignty over the Vatican City and Catholicism as the country's only religion. The papacy recognised the Italian state and accepted the loss of all other papal territories as irreversible. The treaty was enshrined in the Italian constitution of 1948. From the *Patrimonium Petri*, only 44 hectares (109 acres) now remained in the northwest of Rome. The Vatican City, under the sovereignty of the Pope, had a population of 520, a palace guard, a bank, post office, coat-of-arms and its own flag (yellow and white) as well as four extraterritorial churches and almost a dozen palaces.

Left, Angelo Brunetti announces the new constitution promulgated by Pope Pius IX on 14 March 1848.

LUCREZIA BORGIA

The priors of Spoleto accepted with pleasure and curiosity the invitation of their new regent to a reception in the castle La Rocca. The impossible had happened. According to the will of the Pope, a woman was to govern a city within the Papal States. This was a real first; the cities had always been governed by a papal legate, usually a cardinal. And to top matters off, the designated woman was the most admired, and yet the most detested female in all of Rome: Lucrezia Borgia.

Lucrezia was an illegitimate daughter of the unscrupulous Pope Alexander VI and his mistress, Vannozza, and sister of the terrible Cesare. Reportedly, she had engaged in the sin of incest with both father and brother. She was known as a mistress of intrigue and a poisoner as well as an irresolute pawn in the political manoeuvring of her father. At 19 years of age she had been engaged twice and had married twice.

The dignitaries, in their splendid embroidered garb, were blinded by her beauty at the reception and banquet. Contemporary poets praised her graceful appearance, her congeniality, cleverness and education. Lucrezia was a slender and extremely elegant young lady, with a mane of blonde hair and lively blue eyes.

On 15 August 1499, Lucrezia presented her accreditations, a letter from the impious Pope: "My dear sons, I send you greetings and apostolic blessings. We have entrusted the office of protectorate of the castle as well as governor of Spoleto and Foligno, with all their districts, to the well-loved daughter, the duchess of Bisceglia, the noble lady, Lucrezia Borgia…"

The daughter of the Pope was a pawn in the games of the Vatican. She had ended her pre-arranged marriage to her first husband, Giovanni Sforza, after five years. In the interest of diplomacy, she then married Duke Alfonso from Bisceglia, a nephew of the king of Naples. This young man of 17 was handsome, passionate and innocent, and it seemed that Lucrezia really loved him. The happiness lasted exactly one year after which time Alfonso disappeared from Rome, influenced by fear. It was noted that: "The duke of Bisceglia…has secretly fled…He has abandoned his bride, who is in the sixth month of her pregnancy, and she is constantly in tears."

Lucrezia governed from the castle for almost five weeks and no doubt felt very much at home in this most splendid building, the most striking symbol of papal power in Umbria (it was later turned into a maximum security prison, whose recent inmates included members of the Red Bridgades; now it is under restoration and will reopen as an arts centre). She settled a disagreement between the neighbouring communes of Spoleto and Trevi. One document with her stamp of approval and signature has lasted throughout the centuries: *Placet ut supra Lucrezia Borgia*.

Finally, the young husband and father-to-be responded to the demands of his father-in-law and returned to Rome. Perhaps he loved Lucrezia more than life itself. Alexander ordered the young couple to hasten to the castle at Nepi, half way to Rome, where he enthroned his daughter. Soon thereafter, the couple joined him in Rome where their first son was born in November.

In July of the following year, Alfonso was severely injured in an attack by hired killers on the steps of St Peter's. Disappointed by the failed assassination attempt, Cesare had the young husband strangled in his bed while he was supposed to be convalesing.

Lucrezia saw Spoleto one more time. In January of 1502, in a travelling costume of red silk and ermine, she rode through the streets of the city with her entourage. The 22-year-old widow was on a journey to her wedding with Alfonso d'Este, the duke of Ferrara.

A chronicler acclaimed her beauty, cleverness, vivaciousness, grace and humanitarianism. Ariosto and Titian were guests at her court. The people respected and loved her. It is said that the immorality attributed to her during the first half of her life is very questionable. Nothing has been documented and it may all be fabrication.

Lucrezia bore five children in Ferrara. Then, at the age of only 39, she died of a miscarriage. No portrait was left which can with certainty be said to be hers, and no sculpture. Her grave is nowhere to be found.

THE RISE AND FALL OF ANDREA BRACCIO

On 2 June 1424. at the foot of the Abruzzian city of L'Aquila, Andrea Fortebraccio (the name means Stongarm), "Braccio" for short, "Prince of Capua, Count of Foggia, Montone and Perugia, representative of the kingdom of Sicily, governor of both Abruzzis" armed himself for his last battle. The military commander, born on 1 July 1368 in Perugia to the family of the "Brachi", was at the peak of his career and said to be unbeatable. Eulogists trace his family tree back to the victorious Hannibal. A biographer wrote that he was "of average stature, with a rosy face, giving him a pleasing appearance. He combined military strictness with a common modesty and a courtly nature."

As the third son of Count Oddo, Andrea grew up in the mountain village of Montone near Perugia. After 1393, he shared the lot of so many aristocratic families of Perugia: exile. Eventually, lacking income, he sought employment as a *condottiere*, or mercenary.

Alberigo da Barbiano, of the Kingdom of Naples, another notorious *condottiere*, was his first "employer", and he served in Barbiano's so-called company of St George. But the opportunities to gain fame were few and far between and Braccio decided to change allegiance. He turned to Pope Innocent VIII. But in Rome, too, his time of service was short. The papal *condottiere*, Mostardo da Forli, was the victim of an uprising, and the army was disbanded. Once again, Braccio found himself in the service of Barbiano, but this time he was given a *condotta*, a contract, and 12 horses. His rise to power began.

Barbiano battled in Emilia Romana against the Pope and Venice. Facing his opponent on the Reno, he realised that he was greatly outnumbered. His only chance was a retreat across the river. However, the banks of the Reno were steep and high, and the ford was difficult to cross. While Barbiano and his commanders searched for a way out of this dilemma, Braccio breezed into the tent of the *condottiere* and presented the following strategic plan: they should dig an expansive semi-

circular trench with a wall, starting at the Reno and circling back to the river. A handful of chosen soldiers would be responsible for the defence, giving the remaining troops the opportunity to cross over the river.

The plan succeeded. Barbiano raised Braccio's wages and placed 150 cavalry troops under his command. However, success bred envy, and Braccio only narrowly escaped an attempt on his life by jealous commanders. In fear, he fled to the Pope's army once again.

Braccio's career as *condottiere* really took off in 1407. He was chosen as *Signore* of Roccacontrada, thus gaining a base from which to assemble troops and plan military operations. With his troops, at first quite modest in number, he brought cities such as Fano, Ancona and Fermo under tribute. And, to increase the wealth of his troops, he demanded large sums of money from powerful communes such as Bologna and Cesena in return for a guarantee of their "independence".

In his military exploits, Braccio developed a new strategy, one which would be recorded in military history as *Scuola Braccesca*. He divided his troops into separate battle units led by commanders. Rather than engaging them all at once, he used one unit at a time, so ensuring a constant supply of fresh reserves.

His military strength made Braccio a popular ally. King Ladislaus of Naples tried to lure Braccio over to his side to assist him in consolidating his power. On the one hand, Braccio was a nuisance, but on the other hand, the king needed him if he was to succeed in his plan to annex the Papal States and Tuscany. Ladislaus promised him Perugia, and Braccio agreed. In 1406, he launched his first attack against his hometown.

The city, realising its impending defeat, informed Ladislaus that it would succumb to his rule if he promised to remove the dreaded *condottiere*. The king of Naples believed he could kill two birds with one stone and agreed to Perugia's request. Trying to overpower Braccio through trickery, Ladislaus ordered him to come to Rome which he had conquered shortly before. But Braccio got wind of the king's plan and claimed he was indisposed. In league with the Florentines, he chased the Neapolitans out of Rome on 2 January, 1410.

At the time of Ladislaus' death, in 1414, Braccio was well on the way to becoming the most powerful man in central Italy. In the summer of 1416, with papal approval, he ordered his troops to march against Perugia for the third time. Between the Tiber and the village of San Egído, in a battle fought in sweltering heat on 15 July, he defeated the troops of Carlo Malatesta, who had been called in to supply an auxiliary army. The fighting lasted seven hours. Braccio had anticipated the thirst of his troops and ordered containers filled with water to be placed behind the lines. Thus, each time a division pulled back, fresh water awaited them and their horses. It was this foresight that allowed Braccio to win the battle. Malatesta and his soldiers were taken prisoner. The battle itself was immortalised by Paolo Uccello, who painted three versions of it, one of which (*Battle of San Romano*) is in the National Gallery's Sainsbury Wing in London, while the others are in the Uffizi, Florence, and the Louvre, Paris.

The former exile marched triumphantly into the city of his birth, forced the government to swear its allegiance and installed a puppet regime. His political opponents were thrown out and any uprisings were brutally crushed. Braccio compensated for his dictatorship by becoming a patron of the arts. He also improved the facilities of the town. The Loggia di Fortebraccio, to the left of the cathedral steps, is all that remains of an elegant house he had built for himself in 1423 in Renaissance style; under his orders the city's fortifications were strengthened. A canal to Lake Trasimeno was built for strategic purposes.

Braccio encouraged festivals, and reintroduced the *Battaglia dei Sassi*, the Battle of the Stones, at the beginning of the 15th century in honour of the Perugian martyr San Ercolano. The game's origins can be traced back to Roman gladiatorial contests. Every 2 March the *compagnia del sasso* organised a battle between two groups for the occupation of a certain piazza, usually the cathedral square.

The conflict was opened by youths with slingshots, the so-called *lanciatori*. These were followed by up to 2,000 men armed with clubs, who battled with one another until one of the groups retreated. Despite the fact that the combatants wore leather jackets padded with hair and dressed in helmets, this "game" often resulted in injuries and even fatalities.

In 1417, during the Council of Constance, Braccio once again occupied Rome – as he said, "for the future pope" – and proudly proclaimed himself *Almae Urbis Defensor*, "protector of the life-giving city". The new pope, Martin V, had no choice but to enter into a coalition with this absolutist in the Papal States. He elevated him to "vicar" of the Church. When these two men signed the treaty in Florence in 1420, the population took to the streets, chanting: "*Braccio valente vince ogni gente; Papa Martino/non vale un quattrino*" – "Braccio, the true hero, masters the entire world; but for Pope Martino nobody cares a quattrino."

Soon, however, Martin was rid of this nuisance. Braccio became embroiled in the chaos surrounding the succession to the Neapolitan crown and set himself up as an opponent of papal politics. Near L'Aquila, he forced a fatal decision. His army was heavily outnumbered by that of the enemy, under the command of one of his former "pupils", Jacopo Caldora. To Caldora's astonishment, Braccio allowed him and his forces to march uninhibited into the valley.

It was a fatal mistake for Braccio. After eight hours his army were obliterated. Trying to escape unrecognised, the defeated hero tossed aside his shining helmet. However, he was recognised, injured in the neck and brought to Caldora's tent. Braccio refused medical assistance, went on hunger strike and died 3 days later on 5 June.

Pope Martin V decreed three days of celebration in honour of the event. He ordered Braccio's body to be brought to Rome and buried in unconsecrated ground. The body was thrown into a grave on the outskirts of the city. Many years later, a grandson had his remains brought to Perugia for a proper burial in the church of San Francesco al Prato. During renovation of the church in the 19th century, Braccio's remains were exhumed and placed in the university museum. An inscription reads: "*Mars* raised me to power, *Mors* (death) caused my defeat."

An invisible line divides the northern and southern portions of the Italian peninsula, a line which some refer to as a wall. The division remains in the minds of Italians, over 130 years after General Giuseppe Garibaldi and his legendary 1,000 youthful soldiers landed in the west Sicilian harbour city of Marsala. His intention was to drive the Spanish viceroy out of the south, thus liberating that part of Italy that was still under papal control, paving the way for unification with the north.

In a way, Umbria straddles that dividing line because it was under the control of the powerful Papal States for centuries and formed a sort of buffer zone. However, the Umbrians of that time were also extremely eager to be a part of the new Italian nation that politicians and theorists were striving to create in the north, following the temporary unity forced by Napoleon but which collapsed after the 1815 Vienna Congress. Economic factors combined with political fervour were the reasons. It could not exactly be said that Umbrians were well off under their worldly-religious Roman rulers. Umbria was dismissed by these rulers as the "countryside", a backward region; inevitably social problems increased as the population continued to grow.

The Italian nation: When the troops of Piedmont conquered Umbria on 11 September, 1860, forcing the Papal States to retreat, the people of the region therefore had great expectations of the new rulers from the royal court of Savoy. Like those in the other southern Italian regions, the Umbrians hoped for improved conditions within a united Italy. They particularly believed that there would be an economic upswing when the "foreign powers", the Spanish troops brought in to bolster the power of the Papal States, were expelled from the country and regional unity was established. In reality, however, things turned out very differently, and the enthusiasm for the Risorgimento, the national "resurrection", soon ebbed.

Economic and social decline, which had began during the centuries when Umbria was under various governmental and administrative systems, could not be reversed overnight. Thus, when asked about the change from the Papal States to a national state, many Umbrians are still of the opinion that they jumped out of the frying pan and into the fire. They reply in a tone of voice which is a mixture between Roman and Florentine. Instead of leading to the hoped-for economic boom, the measures taken – currency re-

form, tax reforms and the elimination of the existing internal customs barriers – proved to be the last blow for the already weak economy of the region.

Hardest hit was the extensive handicrafts sector of the economy, involved in textiles and ceramic production. This sector was not able to compete with ever-increasing industrialisation and was thus thrown into a deep crisis. Additionally, the dissolution of the landed estates, which belonged mainly to the church, favoured the rise of large estate ownership. And an old system of economic exploitation from feudal times, the *mezzadria*, the semi-lease, experienced a rebirth. It was

<u>Preceding pages</u>: a band plays at a street festival in Gubbio. <u>Left</u>, street encounters. <u>Right</u>, Franciscan friars are part of the scenery in Assisi.

the only method by which large property owners could manage their estates. The *mezzadria*, which can still be found in some regions throughout the south, functions in such a way that the peasants without any property farm the land of the large estate owners. When the crops are harvested, the peasants and the estate owner divide the goods equally. Thus, the Umbrians had replaced their old subservience with a new kind. What's more, living conditions were thereby worsened rather than improved.

The start of the age of industrialisation: Although, geographically speaking, Umbria does not belong to the Mezzogiorno, the economically underdeveloped south of Italy,

There was never any shortage of governmental reconstruction programmes. The first of these was passed by the Roman parliament at the beginning of the 20th century. It contained measures to assist the economically underdeveloped Mezzogiorno which, at the time, included Umbria. Contemporary historians claim that the law was only passed because the peasants had taken to the streets. These measures, designed to fuel industrial development and to reduce the existing economic differences between north and south, also brought about the establishment of medium and small-size plants for the mass production of goods that had previously been the staple of cottage industries. Some com-

there were many economic and social parallels in the development of the two regions during the time following the establishment of the Italian nation. Economic decline, which was inevitably accompanied by the loss of many traditional forms of making a living, migration from the rural areas to the cities and the ever-increasing poverty of the rural population (even though it was nowhere near as dramatic as in the south); this was the price that had to be paid for the national state. The fact that these structural problems still exist today is proved by the level of government subsidy, which is just as high here as it is in the southern regions.

panies founded during this period have since achieved national and international markets. A good example of this is the Perugini factory, located in the suburbs below Perugia, which produces chocolate and which, along with the Buitoni pasta factory, is one of the region's biggest employers.

Statistics show, however, that the numbers of people employed in the new industrial branches is relatively small. Despite these excessive imbalances between industrial, agricultural and service industry sectors, only a small percentage of the population of Umbria chose the path of migration to the more prosperous regions of northern

Italy, or to the Americas, as an escape from their poverty. This was due mainly to the fact that Umbria has a relatively small and stable population; the pressures of a rapidly rising birth rate were never as acute here as in southern Italy, and poverty, theough real enough, was never so acute as to force Umbrians to leave the land of their birth.

Umbria today: According to the last census, Umbria has a population of 818,226. The clear trend toward zero population growth is continuing. Sociologists interpret this as a result of couples choosing to limit their family size so as to achieve a higher standard of living, much like that in the industrial centres of the north. However, there is a small but

Agriculture: According to the latest statistics, about 33,000 people, 11.2 percent of the population, make their living in the agricultural sector. About 50 years ago, the figure represented almost two-thirds of the population. This demonstrates how quickly the changes, even in this secluded region, landlocked and confined, have come about. The number of people involved in agriculture, however, is still enough to cultivate 93 percent of the territory. This figure is rapidly diminishing, however, because rising agricultural wages mean that it is no longer profitable to hire workers for traditional, labour-intensive operation, such as oil and

important difference. If the population were to be spread out equally over the entire region, it would mean, using today's figures, a population density of 97 people per sq. km (248 people per sq. mile). That means that Umbria's population is far less dense than that of other northern regions such as Lombardy, Liguria or Piedmont. The population density in those regions is two to three times that of Umbria. This means that problems, especially those associated with big city life,

Left, mechanisation reached rural areas around the turn of the century. **Above**, haymaking in the Piano Grande.

wine production or the cultivation of tobacco and turnips. These types of cultivation also need artificial irrigation during the summer. Not every Umbrian farmer can afford to install such costly technology.

Developments within the cattle and pig-farming sector are slightly different. Although the production statistics are also declining, this sector represents the backbone of present-day Umbrian agriculture. The reputation of Umbrian pig breeders reaches far beyond the boundaries of the region. The tender meat, praised by connoisseurs as a true delicacy, is without equal. The pigs raised around Norcia, the *norcini*, are renowned and the region's farmers produce a substantial proportion of the salami and *prosciutto* consumed in northern Italy. Aside from the breeding of cattle and pigs, sheep farming is also widespread in the mountainous regions of Umbria.

Small-scale industry: Since 1950, Umbria has developed so rapidly that it now counts as one of the most industrialised regions of central Italy, second only to Tuscany. This is astonishing because almost all the raw materials must be imported. There are very few exceptions – one of them is the abundant clay, which is used in the production of bricks; the raw materials for cement are also found here.

Almost all of Umbria's industry is concen-

produce enough electricity to meet its own needs and must import an ever-increasing amount, at a high price, from France, Switzerland and Austria, this natural source of power is extremely important. Umbria's inexpensive power is mainly used within the region and has led to the establishment of many new factories. However, the electrical power plants do also supply other regions and cities too – for example Rome. The "light" of the eternal city is powered mainly by electricity coming from Umbria.

The developments of the last decades have enabled new methods of industrial production to be put into use. Thus, a branch of industry came into being which was for-

trated in the south, along the river Nera, which drives the turbines of power stations supplying electricity to factories around Terni and Narni. Here, a large number of metal-working and chemical factories have been introduced. But growth-oriented industrial plants have also been established in the areas surrounding Città di Castello, Perugia, Bastia, Foligno and Spoleto. They are all located either on the banks of the Tiber or in the Valle Umbra. Only a few of these factories employs more than 1,000 workers, however.

Umbria is richly blessed with water resources. These are increasingly used in the production of electricity. Since Italy cannot

merly almost non-existent here, but which is now indispensable to the agricultural sector: the food-processing industry. For the past several years, agricultural products that were once transported to northern Italy are now processed in Umbria and distributed and sold from there. In former times, Umbria's raw products were sold to the north, with enormous transportation costs, and then reimported as finished products at further great expense. Today one of the region's most lucrative food products is the truffle: the village of Scheggio, in the Valnerina, is home to the Urbani truffle industry, which collects and processes 80 percent of the truffle products consumed in Italy, and commands 40 percent of the world market.

Tourism: Tourism has become an increasingly important economic factor within the region. For the regional planners, however, the figures could be increased even more. With its wealth of cultural attractions and beautiful landscpe, Umbria enjoys culturally oriented tourism rather than mass tourism. But it is no longer an insider's tip. Umbria registers well over 1 million overnight stays a year. Until now, however, these tourists have tended to stay for only a few days, visiting Assisi and Perugia before going on to Rome or Florence. The economic benefits of this type of tourism are, it has become all

too clear, relatively modest.

Among Umbria's cities, Perugia is the most popular destination for visitors. This is probably because of its central location: from here, one can easily make day trips to other cultural attractions. A major problem is that tourist infrastructure and accommodation lags behind that found in other areas in Italy. Movements are, however, underway to correct this problem; in particular, fast roads are under construction linking the region to the rest of Italy and Norcia is rapidly developing

Left, sleeping it off in Citta di Castello. **Above**, irrigation near Lake Trasimeno.

as a winter sports centre, with new ski resorts, hotels and holiday apartments.

Ever since the Romans, plagued by traffic, car emissions and stress, discovered nearby Umbria as a natural refuge for rest and relaxation, the region has functioned as a weekend retreat for those living in the capital. Anyone who wants to preserve his peace of mind, and who has enough money in the bank, buys a townhouse in Orvieto or a piece of property in an undeveloped part of Umbria. The times when it was possible to get a bargain on a villa there are long gone, although prices are still cheaper than in Tuscany. Shrewd real estate agents got wind of the money to be made in the area and earned themselves a pretty profit. Nowadays it is only the relatively wealthy few who can afford the idyllic country life – an idyll which perhaps never really existed.

Culture: After a series of golden ages, lasting for many generations, Umbria's culture declined, little by little, into mediocre provincialism. The culture reached its nadir in the 19th century, a low point which continued into the 20th century. It only began to flower again when the university was established in Perugia. The university did not gain renown until 1926 when the *Università Italiana per Stranieri* (the University for Foreigners) came into being. Since that time, thousands of foreign students from all over the world have travelled to Perugia to learn the Italian language. Here, where some of Italy's most famous language professors teach, the surroundings are ideal. Students can also acquaint themselves with the region's rich cultural tradition.

Present-day Umbria would like to build on this tradition, and its modern image-makers are keen to emphasise the region's culture. Two cultural festivals have attained international recognition. Spoleto celebrates the *Festival dei Due Mondi*, the Festival of Two Worlds, featuring international performers – from Europe and the Americas. Jazz concerts of equally high quality are staged throughout the summer months. Collectively known as Umbria Jazz, these concerts have become a high point in the Italian social calendar. Numerous smaller events take place throughout the year. Whether through musical concerts, theatrical performances or the fine arts, the Umbrians want to carve a special place for themselves in modern Italy.

Throughout history, the Umbrians have been forced into subordination. First by the Etruscans, then the Romans, later by Goths, Lombards and Franks and, finally, by the Papal States. Whenever their cities reached a certain level of independence, their freedom was immediately threatened – and not only externally. There was constant infighting among the citizens. Even Goethe observed in Terni a "peculiar provincial and municipal zeal; they all cannot stand each other."

Local patriotism: But even today the Umbrians place great weight on their heritage and roots. This is manifested in, among other things, a marked local patriotism. Ancient rivalries which, from a historical point of view, have long been laid to rest, continue to have an influence.

The people of Spoleto, proud of their ancient Roman origins, look down on the residents of Perugia, Orvieto and Todi as inferior because of their Etruscan past, an attitude of superiority that dates back, ultimately, to a battle in which the Etruscans were defeated by the Romans in 283 BC. Equally, many Umbrian towns feel a deep hostility towards Assisi for "monopolising" the St Francis industry – we are not talking here about modern tourism; revenue from pilgrims has been enriching Assisi almost since the day of the saint's death, and many nearby towns claim that the itinerant preacher was as much their saint as Assisi's.

Campanalismo is an Italian phenomenon, but one which is especially strong in Umbria. It is that bond of loyalty, some would say parochialism, that cements a community of people all of whom were born within the sound of the city's ancient bells. It must be understood that in Umbria nearly every community regards itself as a "city" and that *campanalismo* is just as strong in a tiny community like Paricale or Bevagna, with a population of only a few hundred souls as it is in Assisi or Perugia.

Another aspect of pride in *campanalismo*

is that it excludes friendships even with people from the next hilltown. Towns which are only a few miles distant are considered "foreign" and the population is seen as possessing certain undesirable peculiarities. Invisible but deep trenches divide the various provinces, as do the different accents. Perugia and Assisi are only 16 miles/25km apart, facing each other across the Tiber. Yet that river also marks a linguistic boundary between the land of the ancient Etruscans (Perugia was a major Etruscan frontier town) and the land of the ancient Umbrians, still detectable today in the different dialects spoken in these two cities.

The gruff tones of the Terni residents are very different from the singsong tones of people in Foligno (which make every statement of fact sound like a question). These people view Todi as lying *de lae*, over there, behind the mountains, a town which they have merely heard about.

Agriculture: The Umbrians look back proudly on a long tradition of agriculture, although nowadays only about a quarter of the population is tied to the land. The villages in the higher lying regions of Umbria are

Preceding pages: Assisi is most impressive when viewed from below; critical observers; Mona Lisa's smile also comes from Umbria. **Left,** *Una bella*. **Right,** *Un bello*.

experiencing a steady decline in population. The soil of Umbria isn't ideal, and the farmers must work hard to make their land productive. Fields in the mountainous regions are small and steep, and until very recently were still cultivated by oxen-drawn plough. Mechanisation is a very recent innovation.

An additional hardship is that, up until two decades ago, the tenant farmers had to deliver half of their annual crops to the landowners. Umbria, like Tuscany, is a land of the *mezzadria*, the semi-lease, and although Umbrian farmers are renowned for their extreme stoicism it was discontent with this system which led to the spread of communism in the rural areas.

might as well give the opposition a try.

Under Communism, Umbria has developed agricultural co-operatives for the more efficient marketing of local products and seen a big improvement in infrastructure: new roads linking the more remote areas of Umbria to major cities have enabled farmers to get their produce to city consumers for the first time. For this the Umbrians are grateful; they have begun to attain a modest prosperity and are able to earn a living that does not depend upon turning Umbria into some sort of tourist theme park or living museum, an idea that horrifies local people.

Love of the land: Almost all the 800,000 Umbrians have relatives in the countryside.

Political answers: Communism in Umbria may seem something of a paradox – why should Umbria Verde (the gentle green country of Saint Francis) become Umbria Rosso (red Umbria, embracing Marxist dogma)? In fact, ideology plays very little part in Umbrian politics and, in any case, there is little in common between the pragmatic communism of Italy, which is really social democracy under a different name, and the discredited Soviet system of central planning.

Many an Umbrian will tell you that they originally voted Communist simply because the other lot (the Christian Democrats) had made such a mess of government that they

Umbria never experienced large masses of emigration or immigration and one rarely meets an Umbrian outside Umbria. Generally they are not keen on leaving their familiar surroundings and tend to be content with the small pleasures of life. For many families the extent of their travels is to pack a picnic lunch on a summer's day and take a trip to Lake Trasimeno.

The Umbrians are proud of their land and its bounties. You frequently see women combing the fields and meadows in search of field salad and herbs, the *caccialepre*, *rughetta*, *striguli,* and men with their dogs hunting for truffles, ugly-looking treasure as expensive as jewels. Or it might be the thin, green shoot of the wild asparagus that they are after. Everything that is taken from nature is honoured with a *sagra*, or festival, when whole communities gather at long tables for an evening of feasting, drinking and loud music. Every village in Umbria seems to have its own *sagra*, and the summer calendar is crowded with events, such as the Sagra della Berlingozza (cakes) in Gubbio in June, Lake Trasimeno's Sagra del Pesce (fish) in July, Pianello's Sagra dei Funghi (mushrooms) in August and Umbertide's Sagra della Castegna (chestnut) in October.

The Umbrians love to hunt anything which crawls or flies, from wild boar to robins. The

Umbrian. He works as a general purpose farmhand, but often pulls a large bundle of lire out of his pocket and says that he doesn't need the money anymore. He still takes an amorous interest in women, but his doctor has advised him to be a bit cautious lest he be overcome by a stroke in the middle of his passion; to compensate, his interest in St Rita of Cascia has increased. Liking to portray himself as a great sinner, he makes numerous pilgrimages to her, but the time he spends in the confessional is invariably short.

The more important aspect of these trips is the opportunity they provide for eating and drinking. After mass, Giacomino spreads a cloth over a table under the pergola of a bar

hunters hide in hunters' perches, camouflaged with leaves, and use small whistles to attract the birds. They rise before dawn, and when fishing is on the agenda they leave home in the dead of the night. Before daybreaks, the first rifle shots ring through the air, followed by the clattering of the motorised ploughs under the olive trees, the buzzing of the chainsaws, the banging of the mechanical threshing machine.

Umbrian character: Giacomino, 80 years old and still working, is an acrchetypal

Left, some of the delicacies on offer in Orvieto.
Above, in search of refreshment.

and unpacks his provisions: apricots, tomatoes, bread, ham, wine and a large knife. The only thing he orders from the waiter is a bottle of water, even though the first thing that Giacomino does in any restaurant is to lay his knife on the table and pull out his bundle of lire. Waving the money in front of the waiter, he cries, "There is no lack of funds here." This is his way of ensuring the best possible service. Throughout the course of this breakfast, his thoughts are occupied by the question of which would be the best venue for his noontime meal.

Giacomino carries a pistol with him when working in his secluded olive grove. He tells us that he was forced to take this precaution because of boundary disputes. He has often marked several of his trees with red paint, only to find them painted over with white by one of his neighbours. "He'll go on doing it until I shoot him full of holes," he claims.

There was the time when two carabinieri searched Giacomino's entire house looking for weapons. When he returned home that day, he found his wife sitting on the gutted mattress crying. The following Sunday, while he was at the barber, he saw the two policemen walking across the piazza. With the shaving cream still on his face, he ran after the men, took hold of one of them and bit a piece off his ear. "The Carabinieri searched

replaced by civil authority. Ever since time began, the people of Umbria have viewed the laws of the state merely as barriers which must be overcome.

A woman's place: Matriarchal law is the law of the land in Umbria and women are more influential than men. In the day to day matters of peasant life, just as in the economic realm, they play an important part. The woman's responsibility for the care of the domestic farm animals ensures her a limited, but secure, economic role; but it is her social role, as guardian of her family's morals, which gives her real power. If, for example, the wife of the carpenter suspects her son's fiancée may be a *putana* (loose woman,

for the piece," Giacomino relates triumphantly, "but I kept it in my mouth!" He quickly made friends with the prison director in Spoleto.

Although Giacomino usually has to fend for himself, normally the welfare of the individual is looked after by the family. Each member of the family finds therein support, comfort and advice. In earlier times, the village priest also offered concrete assistance: merely by means of his signature, he often arranged for the early retirement of some hard-worked labourer who could then draw a state pension. Although his authority has weakened in recent decades, it has not been

prostitute even), she will make enquiries. In former times, she would have gone to the priest with such a problem but today she is more likely to approach the *maresciallo* (superintendant) of the carabinieri for information (many Umbrians complain that modern priests are too keen on protecting the immoral elements in their society).

Today, 34 percent of the women in Umbria work. The effect this has had on the household structure is cushioned by the older generation. Grandmothers and mothers-in-law take care of the household chores and children. In any case, these days most families have only one child.

The families of the lower-middle class are willing to make great sacrifices in order to ensure that their sons and daughters receive a good education. They want their children to bank clerks or teachers, even though people in these professions earn less than skilled labourers and such jobs are by no means easy to come by. It may take years for the daughter to find a job working in an office. While she is waiting, she parades up and down the Corso with her friends, dressed in the latest fashions.

The evening *passeggiata* is a custom not unique to Umbria, but one that has a special significance here. In many Italian towns, and indeed in all countries bordering the Medi-

understood it, and little has changed in this centuries-old ritual other than the cut of the clothes and the fact that unmarried girls are no longer quite so closely chaperoned.

The Umbrians are considered considerate, gentle and old-fashioned people. This last characteristic is apparent in all sorts of ways – only in Bevagna, for example do parents give their children such unusual names as Ermogene, Oloferne, Tamiride and Eulogio; and Umbrians still harbour traces of Latin in their language, such as *amicu* instead of *amico, discurzu* instead of *discorso, acitu* rather than *aceto* and *capilli* instead of *capelli*. But that is not to say Umbrians don't have a darker side to their characters. Gubbio, for

terranean, it is an opportunity to put on expensive and fashionable clothing, to show off and establish, for everyone to see, that one has made it in the world. In Umbria there are further undertows running through the outwardly smooth current of the evening stroll; arm in arm, speaking in tones of intimacy, the participants are involved in courtship, political lobbying, business wheeling and dealing, and discussing issues of local and national importance. This is local democracy in action as the Greeks might have

Left, in midday meditation. **Above**, a warm smile from the Corsa dei Ceri in Gubbio.

example, occupies the tragic position of being the city with the highest rate of suicide in all of Italy.

Visiting Gubbio in summer it is hard to conceive why this chilling fact should be so; but in winter bitterly cold winds blast through the streets under a lowering grey sky and nobody stirs in this "City of Silence" – so-called by the poet d'Annunzio because it was once so remote that no traffic or noise other than human voices would be heard; then you may realise that what summer visitors see as a rural idyll is, for many in Umbria, a life of harsh, backbreaking toil that sometimes becomes too much to bear.

CERRETO'S REBELS AND CHARLATANS

The medieval and modern history of the Valnerina, the Nera Valley, is packed with conflict. Struggles between the emperor and the pope; battles between the various mountain communes; the machinations of the papal legate Albornoz; the perpetual wars between the Kingdom of Naples, the powerful city-states and the pope; the campaigns of the *condottieri*, and the war between Emperor Charles V and King Francis I have all influenced the lives of Valnerina residents.

Cerreto di Spoleto, once known simply as Cerreto, has always been the centre of such power struggles. During the high Middle Ages, it included eight *castelli* and 27 towns. In order to preserve its independence against powerful Spoleto, which was loyal to the pope, it flew the Ghibellene flag. As late as the 16th century, this town provided refuge for anti-Spoletan insurgents.

In 1221, the people of Cerreto surrendered to Spoleto. Soon thereafter - during the conflict between Emperor Frederick II and the pope – they fought again for their independence. In 1230, after the Treaty of San Germano, they were forced to accept papal supremacy. but this increased their grudge against the commune of Spoleto. And, although Cerreto had ceremoniously sworn allegiance to Spoleto in 1234, the town once again deserted to Frederick's side in 1240. In order to gain favour, Frederick endorsed Spoleto's territorial claims and forced the people of Cerreto to subject themselves to Spoleto. The seeds for the next insurrection were sown. In 1252, Cerreto, defeated, again had to pledge allegiance to Spoleto.

When the troops of Frederick's son, King Manfred, crossed through the region, a new rebellion began, one which ended deplorably in 1272: 12 families from Cerreto were forced to live in Spoleto as hostages. From these families comes the name Via dei Cerretani. Five years later, while Norcia was at war with the old ducal city, the Cerretani once again rebelled. They simply did not allow Podestà Messer Manenti, envoy from Spoleto, inside the city walls. But the Nursini suffered a bitter defeat along the Nera and the river "was coloured red with the blood of 1,200 rebels". As a result, the priors of Spoleto forced the inhabitants of Cerreto to agree to pledge their loyalty annually.

The rulers over the upstart town changed often. From 1255 to 1284, it was ruled by Ponte, a member of the mighty Varano family from Camerino. This family was loyal to the Pope. In 1425, Pope Martin V granted Norcia, which had tried earlier to conquer Cerreto, supremacy over the town. An uprising in 1431 failed. In 1438, Cerreto sided with the *condottiere* Francesco Sforza who was waging a war against the pope in the name of Milan's duke. However, when Sforza switched over to Eugene IV's side, Cerreto again fell under Norcia's rule.

From 1450 to 1453, when Spoleto and Norcia were engaged in battles for control of Triponzo, Pope Nicholas V intervened and placed Cerreto once again under Spoleto's authority. Things were not quiet for long. Two decades later, the citizens of Cerreto revolted once more, lost and came under the rule of Giulio Cesare Varano. His authority was endorsed by Popes Sixtus IV and Innocent VIII.

In the year 1499, Cesare Borgia started his liquidation of all of the old signors in the Papal States; once his time was up, however, Cerreto and Sellano once again came under the rule of the Varano family.

In 1522, the population of the Nera Valley staged their last revolt. The non-independent towns formed a league with the goal of ridding themselves of the papal yoke. The straw that broke the camel's back was when they were conscripted to fight against Siena. The entire valley rose up in protest. The focal point of the revolt was Cerreto and the revolution's leaders were Petrone di Vallo and Piccozzo Brancaleoni. On September 9, 1522, Don Alfonso of Cardon, Spaniard and papal representative in Spoleto, marched across the Forca di Cerro with a small band of men into Nera Valley.

He thought that by means of his position and office he would be able to bring the rebels to reason. Petrone di Vallo met him with 80 armed followers on the bridge near Paterno, but in the fighting, Don Alfonso was killed. In response, 7,000 soldiers were dispatched to fight against the Nera league. Petrone found refuge in a farm but his whereabouts were soon discovered. The farm was set alight and Petrone died in the flames along with his son. But this was not quite the end. The troops decapitated the revolt's leader, put his head on a pike and placed it in Spoleto as a warning for other would-be revolutionaries. In 1523, the uprising was ended: the last town to capitulate was Sellano.

Petrone came from Vallo di Nera, which he ordered plundered after it changed over to the side of the pope. Piccozzo Brancaleoni came from Scheggino, a town which was only briefly involved in the insurrection. A chronicle relates how on 23 July, 1522 the women of Scheggino successfully defended their town against the advancing troops of both military leaders. Cerreto's fate was scaled in 1523. The history of the town was marked by disputes over territorial and property boundaries, as well as taxes. After 1569, the *Prefettura di Montagna* in Norcia, an office set up by the Vatican in order to avoid quarrels among the mountain communes, regulated all of these matters. It was not until the year 1860 that Cerreto once again was granted independence.

Originally Cerreto lay further down the hillside than it does today, at the place known by locals as Cerreto Vecchio (Old Cerreto) and shown on maps as Borgo Cerreto. In the 13th century the new town of Cerreto di Spoleto was constructed above the former settlement and if you visit today you will drive to the town through a remote valley littered with the relics of past warfare.

Ancient towers and crumbling fortresses dot the landscape, especially around Ferentillo, at the head of the valley, where a miniature Great Wall of China, a curtain wall funnelling travellers through the bottom of the valley, straggles up the steep sides of the gorge. At Cerreto itself, the original fourfold division of the town, each with its separate gate, can still be traced. Remains of once proud palazzi bear the coats of arms of old families, such as the Alberici, Arrighi, Bonifazi, Ciucci, Maccioini, Nobili and Totti.

The town's fame does not ultimately lie in any of these resonant names, however, or in the town's history of rebellion. The reputation of Cerreto was spread throughout the land by the so-called Cerretani – travelling beggars who practiced nature healing. Their name lives on in the word charlatan. *Cerretano* was a term for a person without a "respectable" profession, for paupers who functioned under the guise of fortune-telling or as exorcists. They roamed through the countryside as astrologers, tightrope walkers, "eternal" pilgrims, herb salesmen or healers, earning their living in this manner.

The roots of this "profession" date back to the 15th century. At first, beggars were used by hospitals and leper colonies to sell healing remedies. The directors chose the Cerretani because of their reliability or cleverness – depending on which was required – and assigned them their own special territory, called a *baye*.

However, as time passed, this trade degenerated. Often the dealers, completely untrained – presented themselves as doctors or surgeons from Norcia or Preci. Chroniclers report that robbers and escaped prisoners joined the ranks of the dealers. The situation became so bad that in the mid-15th century St Antonius, bishop of Florence, complained about the Cerretani. "They are travelling about only to steal and deceive, rather than to beg," he said.

The poetic abbot, Gaetano Palombi from Cascia, characterised their cunning as follows: "Anyone who places his trust in this type of person commits a sin against his common sense and his honour. And yet the demented folk blindly puts its faith in the Cerretan who sells useless balsam for an ounce of gold at the square. The people value these wares as a treasure. They just do not see that it is merely the extract of pumpkins and onions which is contained within these jars."

In the year 1487, the pope sent the preacher Bernardino da Feltre to the Nera Valley in order to wipe out this scandalous swindle which was repeatedly recurring in the name of a hospital or of a saint. The pious man preached in Norcia and Spoleto. But his words had little effect. Thus, when we talk about swindlers, or charlatans, we are using, without realising it, the name of a small town in Umbria's Valnerina .

Umbrian painting has always displayed a strong religious influence. Assisi is the spiritual focal point of the region; it is here that the memory of St Francis is kept alive. Secular themes, so common throughout the rest of Italy during the early Renaissance, were unthinkable here. Even portrait commissions were rare.

In the 15th century, several of the great Florentine artists came to Umbria: Beato Angelico, Benozzo Gozzoli, Filippo Lippi. They left works in Todi, Orvieto, Narno, Foligno and especially in Montefalco. The people of the region were receptive to the sentiments expressed in art and, around 1460, artistic talents blossomed in Perugia. A spirited era began in Umbria, lasting for about 60 years.

During the Renaissance, Italy was a loose association of city-states, often with a tyrant at the helm, a tyrant whose power usually resulted from wealth gained through trade and bank dealings. Perugia was the largest and wealthiest of the Umbrian cities, which had long been a part of the Papal States. It had been independent since 1375 and was often the stage for extremely bloody battles between families competing for power. The victorious Baglioni family even battled within their own ranks, mounting the heads of the dead on the Palazzo Comunale.

At the same time, Perugino and Raphael were painting pictures filled with great sensitivity in Perugia.

Pietro di Cristoforo Vannucci, as Perugino was otherwise known, was born in 1445 in the Umbrian town of Città della Pieve. He came to Perugia as a child. There must have been at least 15 artists painting there at the time. Benedetto Bonfigli was their leader. He was the first one among them who dared to paint a realistic landscape behind holy figures.

The discovery of the so-called vanishing point during the Renaissance had such an

effect on the artists that they referred to it as the *divina prospettiva*, the divine perspective. It was the Florentine artists who were best able to capture space through perspective constructions. The Umbrian artists, on the other hand, were no great theoreticians. Aside from the geometrical linear perspective, their strength was the development, based on visual experience, of the atmospheric perspective – in other words, the colours becoming increasingly lighter and less vivid within the painting as it faded away

towards the horizon.

Bonfigli mainly painted banners, known as *gonfalone,* pictures which were carried round the city in great religious parades and designed to beseech the Virgin to assist the people in their battle against the plague or some other calamity. Works by Bonfigli are hanging in various churches in Perugia as well as in the Galleria Nazionale dell'Umbria. He and his rival, Fiorenzo di Lorenzo, introduced Perugino to painting. They painted with tempera colours; meticulous hatching and precision of lines were called for. It was not until 1493 that Perugino turned to oil painting. Between 1470 and 1472, he studied

Preceding pages: *The Adoration of the Magi* by Pietro Perugino. **Left,** fresco in Sant'Agostino church in Montefalco. **Above,** *Francis banishes the demons from Arezzo* –fresco by Giotto in the Basilica di San Francesco, Assisi.

in Florence which was, at the time, the centre of the artistic avant-garde. He was a willing pupil of Piero della Francesca and later of Verrocchio. It can be said with some certainty that he also met Leonardo da Vinci. He quickly established a reputation for himself as an artist. In 1478, the Pope personally requested that he come to Rome.

The papacy of Sixtus IV, a dark era in the annals of church history, was a golden age for art. Perugino painted the fresco *The Giving of the Keys to St Peter* in the Sistine Chapel. He depicted a few of his contemporaries among the saints; and he even painted his own well-nourished face. Perugino had reason to be content. He received more and

tures. The beauty of the lines, the perfect harmony of the figures, the heads bent in devotion in front of the expansive landscape, the glow on the faces – Perugino expresses the innocence of medieval piety at the threshold of the sceptical Renaissance.

Perugino bought properties in Florence and Perugia, but it was in Perugia that he finally settled in 1499, continuing to live and work there for 25 years. His art found followers beyond the boundaries of Umbria – in Florence, Bologna and Cremona. He passed his knowledge to other pupils from his home: to Gian Nicola di Paolo, to Giovanni di Pietro, known as Lo Spagna, and to Raphael.

At the peak of his career, Perugino re-

more commissions. By the end of the century he was reputed to be Italy's greatest painter. Perugino hired assistants to help fulfil all his commissions, and charged top prices.

By this time the art of painting was no longer considered as being entirely in God's service. Giorgio Vasari, first of the art historians, wrote, "Pietro had little religion and could never be convinced of the soul's immortality." However, he was able, as no other, to awaken religious feelings through his pictures. The "sweet angelic inspiration" of his figures has its effect even today. There are few artists who have so movingly incorporated such devout absorption in their pic-

ceived a commission from the leaders of the Cambio (Bankers' Guild) in Perugia. He was asked to decorate their Collegio (Money Exchange) with frescos. "No magistrate in the world sits in such a beautiful office as the judge of the exchange in Umbria," Jacob Burckhardt said in praise. A native scholar of the humanities recommended that the paintings be a mixture of Christian and pagan themes which would reflect contemporary tastes. The frescoes depict the Father with the prophets and Sibyls, classical virtues

<u>Above</u>, *The Annunciation* by Filippo Lippi in Spoleto cathedral.

THE BURRI COLLECTION

Alberto Burri, born on 12 March 1915 in Città di Castello, is one of Italy's most important abstract painters and collagists. His work is less concerned with constructive merit, as in cubism, or with shock value, as in dadaism. His main aim is to produce aesthetically pleasing objects. He uses a wide variety of other materials in addition to the traditional ones, including old boards, burlap (hemp or coarse canvas), metal plates and even melted plastic.

After studying medicine at the University of Perugia, he was an army doctor during World War II and was a prisoner of war in Texas from 1943.

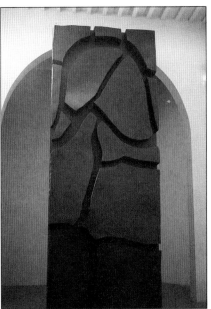

It was while he was in prison that he began his career as an artist, using a collection of discarded materials that he found around the prison to create his first composition.

At the end of the war, Burri returned to Italy. He had his first exhibition in the Galleria Margherita in Rome in 1947. In these years, when the art scene in Italy was embroiled in the controversy between abstract and realistic art, Burri's interest was in finding a new method of artistic expression. His innovative ideas consisted of combining contemporary painting with the use of new materials.

In 1951, along with Ballocco, Capogrossi and Colla, he founded the group called *Origine*. This group set itself the task of finding new techniques and combinations of materials for "anti-decorative forms". In that same year, two of his works were shown as part of a group exhibition in the Galleria dell'Obelisco in Rome. He used, for the first time in his work, white and black surfaces, thereby breaking one of the cardinal academic precepts of the time which shunned the use of these two "non colours".

The start of his most important phase, one which influenced all of his future works, began in 1952. Although he had been experimenting for years with worn out potato and mail sacks, his *sacchi* appeared for the first time in a large gallery in Rome in that year. These dominated all of the succeeding exhibitions which the artist organised in the important cities of Europe as well as over-

seas. The simple sack, which he had used in prison as a canvas, became an autonomous element. He painted over it with colours and varnish, he burned and tore holes in it and he stretched it over a basic surface, achieving a complex of different colours and forms which never allowed the structure of the original material to disappear into the background.

In the year 1957, Burri was a participant in the XXVI Biennale in Venice. This represented his international breakthrough as one of Italy's most popular artists. At exhibitions in Chicago and in the Guggenheim Museum in New York in 1953, his *sacchi* gained increasing recognition. They greatly influenced the young generation of American pop artists, including Robert Rauschenberg and Jaspar Johns.

In 1957, Burri introduced the "Combustioni", new works made of plastic and wood which he transformed, or deformed, with the use of fire. One year later, in Milan, he created his world renowned "Ferri Sculpture". With this he demonstrated that despite the difficulties inherent in working with iron, a chromatic ordering within the composition is still possible. During the following years, Burri organised exhibits throughout the entire world. In cities like London, Paris, Amsterdam, Berlin, New York, Houston and Pittsburgh, Alberto Burri attained an unbelievable popularity. The revaluation of simple materials as a result of his work, and the unpretentiousness associated with these materials, influenced an entire generation of young artists.

The Collezione Burri was opened in the Palazzo Albizzini in Città di Castello in 1981. This extensive collection, containing some of the most important works of the artist, is arranged in chronological order. It is open 10am–noon and 3pm–6pm Tuesday–Saturday, 9.30am–12.30pm Sunday and holidays, closed Monday.

Other modern art of note in Umbria is displayed in Terni's art gallery, housed in the 17th-century Palazzo Manassei (open daily except Monday 9am–2pm). Here you can see works by Wassily Kandinsky, Marc Chagall, Joan Miro and Orneore Metelli, a naive artist who painted local industrial landscapes, such as the steelworks of Terni, in vivid colours.

embodied in heroes of antiquity, the birth and transfiguration of Christ and, in between, the fat face of the artist with his large nose and stocky neck.

The work was completed in the year 1500. Three years previously, the 11-year old Raphael had become a pupil of Perugino. Raphael learned quickly and received his first commission, for an altar panel, at the age of 14. In 1502, Perugino painted a *Marriage of Mary*, which Raphael copied two years later for his *Sposalizio*. The depth of space evident in the work of Perugino characterised Raphael's work too.

Bernardino di Betto, born in Perugia in 1454 and teasingly called "Pinturicchio"

because of his small stature, was a contemporary of Perugino. In 1481, he arrived in Rome to serve as an assistant to Perugino. While there, he received several commissions, one of which was to decorate the papal apartments. In Perugia, he painted a fresco in the Sala del Consiglio Comunale, the Council Chamber of Perugia's austere Palazzo dei Priori, which now houses the Galleria Nazionale dell'Umbria, where several more of his paintings are displayed.

The Pinacotheca, a few floors above, contains several of his works. In Spello, he painted the Capella Baglioni in the church of Santa Maria Maggiore. Pintoricchio loved

the anecdotal and paid great attention to detail. The commission to decorate the Piccolomini Library in Siena was right in line with his story-telling talents. Here he painted a cycle of 10 frescoes relating the story of the humanist Enea Silvio Piccolomini, later Pope Pius II, one of the most eminent scholars of his age. Although he was plagued by illness and was anything other than bellicose, Pius II met his death leading a crusade against the Turks.

In 1502, Pinturicchio started out from Perugia, taking Raphael along to help with the sketches. It took Pinturicchio five years to complete the frescoes in the cathedral's library, frescoes with much attention to detail especially in the clothing. When he later went to Rome, people were no longer interested in his work. He died poverty-stricken in Siena in 1513.

Perugino, too, returned to Rome and was forced to accept the fact that his pupil Raphael was more in demand than he himself. Even his most loyal pupils discarded him as a model and turned to Raphael. In the second half of the 16th century, almost all the Umbrian painters followed a new idol: Michelangelo.

The Galleria Nazionale in Perugia houses Perugino's very first work, dating from 1473, scenes from the life of St Bernardino. This was the first time that a small section of landscape with a winding path meandering deep into the picture appears. In the area around Perugia, one finds Perugino's works – especially from his late phase – in the Bettona Pinacotheca, the church of St Mary in Corciano, the Nunciatella church in Foligno and in San Francesco in Montefalco.

Up until 1512, Perugino also painted for churches in Tuscany. Thereafter, he remained in Umbria. He painted his last work in 1523, at the age of 77. It was a fresco in the tiny church in the village of Fontignano. The Madonna with the child Jesus, and beside it an *Adoration of the Magi*, have been removed and now hang in the National Gallery in London. It is said that the artist refused to be given the sacrament of extreme unction on his death bed so that he could experience what happened to the soul of a non-believer.

Left, *Mary with Child* by Pietro Perugino. **Right**, *The Baptism of Christ*, also by Perugino, in Perugia cathedral.

UMBRIAN ROMANESQUE

The leading role played by Umbria in the development of Romanesque art was thanks to the dominant political role of Spoleto. The town had been the seat of a powerful duchy since the centuries of Lombardic rule, and Lombardic influence stretched far beyond the boundaries of Umbria itself; during the 10th century, when the papal government was embroiled in its most serious crises, Spoleto wielded more power than any other city in central Italy. Several of its rulers aspired to become emperors. Through their connections with the Roman urban aristocracy, they were even able to bring the papacy under their influence.

The unassailable autonomy that the town once possessed is reflected in the array of ancient buildings that can still be seen here. These are important from an art historical standpoint because they allow one to see, in an uninterrupted series, architectural development from late antiquity up to the early 13th century.

The sequence begins with the cemetery church of San Salvatore, just outside the city, which was built as a *martyrium* in the 4th century and demonstrates that the early Christian church had yet to develop its own architectural style. The facade of the church is not obviously ecclesiastical; indeed, it is one of the best surviving examples in Italy of what a late-Roman domestic house might have looked like at the time of Emperor Theodosius. The nave behind the facade is Carolingian in date, but still looks to Roman antiquity for its models, being essentially the same in form as the basilica or town hall, only with an altar where the judge would have sat on his throne of office.

Then there is the nearby church of San Pietro, the tiny churches of San Ponziano and San Gregorio as well as the cathedral of Santa Maria Assunta, whose completion approximately coincided with the end of Spoleto's golden age.

After the city was destroyed by Frederick

Barbarossa in 1155, the cathedral was rebuilt in Romanesque style, from 1175–1230. The magnificently decorative forms of the main portal, stemming from Gregorio Melioranzio, date from this era. These are in the same style as the capitals of the cloister of Monreale and draw liberally from the entire range of forms developed during antiquity and the early Middle Ages. With the fall of the Dukedom of Spoleto in 1198, artistic and architectural developments came under the direct influence of Rome. This fact is clearly demon-

strated by the huge rose window with its caryatids and symbols of the Evangelist, created in the early 13th century after the wonderful facade mosaic of *The Enthroned Christ between Mary and John* (1207) had been completed.

Manifestation of glory: The church of Sant'Eufemia, one of the rarest and most beautiful works of the 10th century, occupies the special position of being the most intimate example of the former glory of the town. The church, which is today encircled by the bishop's palace, has been lovingly restored during recent years. It was probably the court church of the Dukedom of Spoleto

Preceding pages: the Piazza Silvestri in Bevagna. Left, the cathedral of San Rufino in Assisi. Above, a caryatid adds support to the facade of Spoleto cathedral.

and thus provides evidence of the early medieval splendour of the city. It was built in the 10th century, although the vaulting was completed much later. The triple-nave basilica is of an imposing height, comparable to San Lorenzo in Verona. The reason for its striking stature is partly because it was based on late Carolingian style and partly because the expansive upper level was required for the royal court's use. This upper storey terminates, just as the corresponding aisles beneath, in the high side apses.

The abbey church of San Pietro in Valle, near Ferentillo, whose apse and campanile were renovated by Lombardic master craftsmen in the 11th century, is one of the oldest

talent for painting large dramatic scenes. Art historians regard them as among the first examples of an emerging Italian, as distinct from Byzantine, artistic style, and the powerful figures almost seem to be a premonition of Michelangelo.

Equally noteworthy is the extraordinary high altar in the apse of the 8th-century church, carved with foliage and totemic figures. It is inscribed with the name of the sculptor, Ursus, and the name of the patron, Iderico, the man who was Duke of Spoleto in AD 739.

There are two more wonderfully preserved churches in the Valnerina whose splendid facades were modelled on that of the huge

surviving churches in Umbria. It was constructed by the Lombardic duke, Faroaldo II from Spoleto, around 720 on a southern slope of the Valnerina Valley. The original church of the secluded abbey, built under Duke Hilderich in 739–40, still exists. It has a broad nave and three apses extending out of the transept. The campanile towering above the church dates from the 13th century and also has a Lombardic form.

The church is equally famous for its fresco cycle, painted by Roman master artists around 1190. The faded, half-restored, half-destroyed frescoes depict the story of Creation on a gigantic scale by someone with great

cathedral in Spoleto. These are San'Eutizio di Preci and San Felice di Narco, whose style is repeated in Piedivalle near Spoleto. The triangular gable of the facade is dominated by a double row of rounded arches framing a magnificent rose-window, the form which is typical of Umbrian lyricism.

The well-preserved work of two sculptor-architects, more than likely natives, can be seen in the neighbouring towns of Foligno and Bevagna. The architects Binelli and Rodolfo built the churches of San Silvestro and San Michele Archangelo, located directly across from one another in Bevagna. Along with the Palazzo Communale, they form a unified and noble structural entity. The exquisite side portal of the cathedral in Foligno also stems from these masters. The portal's relief depicts the bloody battle between Barbarossa and Alexander III.

Perugia, today Umbria's largest city, has only one remaining example of 12th century architecture. This is the portal of the suburban church of San Constanzo, a church whose original character has been largely destroyed through restoration work.

On the other hand, the Romanesque architecture of the cathedral of San Rufino in Assisi is overwhelming. In sublime severity, with absolutely no trace of Umbrian charm, the facade and campanile tower above the struction of an older structure, which he began in 1144. Between 1217 and 1228, the portal was further decorated. The three magnificent rose-windows, which dominate the overall character of the facade, date from the 12th century. The central window is borne as a mandorla (a kind of halo) by three figures (angels perhaps?) who are so well carved as to appear to be almost free-standing. Originally, the form of the facade had a broad horizontal emphasis. It was not until the pointed arch and the gable were added that it attained its present form, one which harmonises well with the weighty campanile.

The gruesomely plundered churches of Narni were also first-rate. Nearby, at Lugnano

church. But in the individual reliefs round the rose-window, borne by small caryatids, and in the three richly decorated portals, all stemming from different eras, there is clear evidence of the artists' great sense for plasticity, a sense whose roots appear to be based in the architecture of Ravenna and the eastern church. The sombre facade of this cathedral, the church in which both St Francis and the Emperor Frederick II were baptised, stems mainly from Giovanni da Gubbio's recon-

in Tevere, the church of Santa Maria Assunta is much better preserved. This is one of the most magnificent Lombardic vaulted basilicas in Umbria. and the beautifully carved marble pulpit and ambone again hint at the influence of Ravenna and the rites of the Byzantine church.

Sculptural highlights: Even richer than the Romanesque architecture in Umbria are the first-class sculptural works, dating from the same period. One of the oldest pieces, an ornate pillar built into Sant'Eufemia (Spoleto) as the *colonna santa*, is sometimes attributed to late antiquity, sometimes to the 9th century. In either case, it demonstrates the loy-

<u>Left</u>, facade relief on San Pietro church in Spoleto. <u>Above</u>, *The Martyrdom of St Blaise*, detail of a relief in the Museo Civico, Spoleto.

alty of art to tradition in Spoleto. Another example of this loyalty is the carefully executed copy in San Pietro of the 4th-century lintel of San Salvatore. This lintel is richly decorated with acanthus leaves.

At the foot of Monte Luco, just outside Spoleto, is the bishop's monastery church of San Pietro, originally settled by hermits and situated in the middle of a prehistoric burial field. It was founded in the 5th century and completed in the 13th century. The only original part remaining is the facade with several baroque supplements. The decoration of the Roman arch on the main portal is evidence of Armenian influence. The lower part of the sculptural decorations on the

portal and facade probably dates back to the beginning of the 12th century.

The lower part of the facade, either side of the portal, is decorated with 12th-century carvings of symbolic beasts; peacocks for immortality, a deer suckling her young and killing a viper, symbolising God's protection, and a ploughman in a tunic driving a pair of oxen, a delightful rural image reminiscent of Roman sacral sculptures and perhaps symbolising Adam's toil.

Ten larger panels flank the doorway depicting a mixture of Christian doctrine and popular story. In one panel, St Peter guards the bed of a dying man while an unhappy

devil holds a placard which says, in translation, "I am sad because the dying man was mine before" – a 12th-century strip cartoon treatment of deathbed repentance. In another scene, Reynard the Fox, disguised as a monk, pretends to study the Bible while eyeing his potential victim, a ram.

Also notable on the facade are the elegant stone decorations of the circular window. The museum in Spoleto possesses an earlier example of this form (a perforated round pane based on Syrian models).

The most beautiful plastic reliefs in Umbria were created around the turn of the 12th/13th century. One of these is the lavish ornamentation of the portal pillars of Spoleto cathedral, blessed by all of the good souls of antiquity and connected with the name of the master artist, Melioranzio. Other examples include the tenderly created reliefs of the facade of San Felice di Narco, the plastic reliefs on the churches of Foligno and Bevagna, both of which date from 1201, and the figures round the rose window on the cathedral in Assisi.

By stylistic comparison with the archivolt relief in Castel Ritaldi (1141), it has been possible to date Umbria's most important structural relief, the frieze depicting the martyrdom of St Blaise, as originating in 1170 (the relief was previously thought to be of Carolingian origin). This relief, whose drama closely resembles a group of Abruzzian works, can be found in the museum in Spoleto. Formerly part of an architrave in the church of San Niccolò, the relief relates the legend of St Blaise from Sebastea in Capadocia, beginning with his sentencing, continuing with the episodes of his martyrdom and ending with the reception of his soul by God. The saint is depicted with particular vividness in the scene where he is blessing and taming two lions that are about to attack him.

The introduction of so-called sculptural reliefs around 1200 signified the end of Lombardic style and of artistic autonomy for Umbria. This can not only be seen in the rose-window of the cathedral in Spoleto, but also in the pillars, signed by Pietro di Maria Romano, of the cloister of the Sassovivo monastery. Umbria was becoming a province of Roman art.

Left, the abbey church of San Pietro in Valle.
Right, the interior of Sant'Eufemia

Simplicity is the key characteristic of the Umbrian cuisine. The people who live here, many of whom are still closely tied to a peasant life, are no friends of culinary embellishments. Umbrians prefer their food to be straightforward and are proud of it: "That's just how we are," many Umbrians will say with satisfaction,and they may add a local saying; *piu se spenne, peggio se magna* (the more you spend the less well you eat).

As in neighbouring Tuscany, Umbrian cuisine rejects the use of too many different ingredients. Variation and flavour are more commonly provided by carefully chosen herbs, which must be absolutely fresh. Almost all grocery shops, however small, as well as many private individuals, sell freshly picked rosemary, thyme, marjoram and basil, sometimes with the roots still attached. The herbs are used sparingly, and not too many different kinds are employed in the same recipe.

Typical dishes, known here as *piatti tipici*, can be ordered in the region's numerous small trattorias and osterias, where the owner is also cook. Here the delicious *sugo* (sauce) for the *pasta* is prepared in the traditional manner in huge ceramic casseroles, and the meat is grilled over a charcoal fire. Many of the dishes in Umbria are *alla cacciatore*, a term meaning "according to the hunter's method", a mode of cooking which evolved when the dense woods covering the hills of the region were inhabited by an abundance of wild game.

There are plenty of excellent restaurants in which to sample local specialities. *Signora Lina Trattoria* near Perugia, for example, though quite unpretentious from the outside, offers a wonderful selection of gourmet meals *alla cacciatore*. The speciality of the house is rabbit stew seasoned according to Umbrian tradition. The rabbit meat is first fried with bacon and then allowed to simmer in red wine. Cloves, a sprig each of thyme and parsley, and a bay leaf are then added. Shortly before the meat is done, a roux is stirred in to

Preceding pages: cooking is an integral part of Umbria's culture. **Left** and **above**, smiles from the kitchen.

thicken the sauce and, to round out the flavour, a dash of vinegar is added.

Another delicacy is grilled fish brought fresh from Lake Trasimeno. It is especially delicious when accompanied by Umbrian asparagus. Lake Trasimeno is the source of eels (*anguille*), pike (*luci*) and carp (*carpe*), usually served in a tomato sauce or fried in olive oil and wine (*tegamaccio*). The clean, fast-flowing rivers of Umbria also yield fine wild trout and crayfish, both specialities of restaurants in the Valnerina.

Succulent pork: The real specialty of Umbria, however, is pork. Umbria is famous for roast suckling pig cooked on a spit or grill over an open fire. Amazingly, in some other regions, of Italy this delicacy is hardly in demand at all. Roast suckling pig (*porchetta*) can be bought from pork butchers, but is more traditionally sold from open-sided mobile vans parked in many an Umbrian main square or side street. You can buy slices of the tender, juicy meat to take home or ask for it with bread – in which case you will be given a *rosetta*, a large bread roll, filled with meat and crispy skin, sprinkled with salt and wrapped in waxed paper. This is a snack to be eaten at once, for the meltingly tender pork is best when still warm.

The pork butchers of Norcia are renowned all over Italy. A whole series of fine pork dishes bears the appellation *alla Norcia*. Although the widespread recognition of this label has caused prices of Norcia's pork products to escalate, the actual quality of the products has in no way been adversely affected by success.

The Norcian method of pork processing, viewed in the region as nothing less than an art, has its roots in a centuries-old tradition. In former times, the demand for the town's pork led butchers to expand into other towns. Everywhere they settled they formed frater-

talents lie in the salting and seasoning of fresh pork, processing pork into sausage, and in furthering developments in pig breeding.

Today, the term *alla norcina* stands in general for extremely fine-tasting dishes made with pork or bacon. Anyone who is fortunate enough to sample these dishes, especially ones which are delicately seasoned and accompanied by simply prepared vegetables, will quickly understand how these specialities came to be known as gourmet delights as early as Renaissance times.

Olive oil: Another important speciality of Umbria is its thick, aromatic olive oil. It is the pride of the entire region. Though usually used as a seasoning, it is also highly recom-

nities of *norcini*. Michelangelo's grandson once said of them, "Today's *norcini* live like they are in Utopia."

Norcian knife-wielders were once also very much in demand as surgeons (just as *norcino* is now synonymous in Italy with butcher, so *norsino* means doctor or nurse). Their speciality was castration, the fate inflicted on any poor mediaeval lad who showed potential as a falsetto singer in the church and court choirs. Perhaps that is why jealous detractors of the *norcini* liked to claim that they have only one real ability, namely that of knowing the proper time to castrate a boar. In reality their trade is highly skilled. Their

mended for frying meat, since it can be heated to extremely high temperatures without affecting the taste, and for making food easily digestible.

Umbrian olive oil, noted for its green shimmer, is said to be the best in the land, mainly because of its minimal acidity content and high proportion of oil substances. The product from around Spoleto is exceptionally fine, but oil from Foligno and Narni is also highly recommended.

Umbria's woods are, or rather were, rich in mushrooms, especially truffles, or *tartufi*. Because at one time they could be found in abundance, these truffles were used extensively in old recipes. Today, of course, truffles are extremely expensive and most of these recipes seem wildly extravagant to modern cooks.

The truffles from Acqualagna are particularly famous, but the black truffles from the area around Norcia are an absolute delicacy. A truffle dish which is as simple as it is delicious is *spaghetti al tartufo nero*. In this recipe, the truffles are finely chopped and left in a marinade of olive oil, garlic and anchovies overnight.

The crowning touch to an excellent meal with truffles is a dessert from Perugia known as *baci perugini*. The people of Umbria love to finish a meal with baked pastries and other

the long history of the Umbrian wine industry is proved by the numerous vases, wine containers and tools exhibited in the Museo del Vino in Torgiano (a town lying about 6 miles/10 km from Perugia). These date winemaking in the region to the time of antiquity. The exhibits demonstrate how the people of former times passed on their experience and "tricks" to succeeding generations of farmers and vintners.

At present, about 30,000 acres (12,000 hectares) are cultivated to produce registered wine. The amount of wine produced annually is about 1 million hectolitres. Although there are many fine Umbrian wines, there is one which is famous: the Orvieto

desserts. During the Christmas season, for example, sweet macaroni accompanies almost every festive meal. Marzipan cakes are also ubiquitous at this time.

Fine wine: As wine connoisseurs are probably aware, Umbria is once again a thriving wine-growing region. Loose, fertile soil and an especially mild climate, due in part to the hilly countryside, make for ideal conditions. Although the vineyards almost disappeared here in the recent past – because it had become so unprofitable to produce wine –

Left, *prosciutto* – an Umbrian delicacy. Above, a typical Umbrian *alimentari* (grocer's shop).

Classico. This discreetly elegant and versatile white wine can be served equally well as an aperitif or as an accompaniment to any course in a meal. The *secco* is especially good with fish or cheese, and the Orvieto Abboccato can be enjoyed with vegetable dishes.

For meat or game, whether grilled or stewed, the aristocratic Torgiano Rosso is the proper wine to choose. Anyone who wants to serve one wine with all of the various courses should try the red Colli Perugini. It is impossible to go wrong with this wine, no matter which of the region's culinary specialities is being served.

IN SEARCH OF TRUFFLES

In his trail to find Umbria's "black diamonds," its precious truffles, Peter Treutler went in search of Carlo Urbani in the small village named Scheggino in the Valnerina. Urbani is known as the "Truffle King" of the region.

Signor Urbani, accompanied by a shaggy little dog, is already waiting for us when we arrive in front of his farmhouse in Scheggino. Although he greets us heartily and at length, it is evident that both he, and his dog, are anxious to get going on their daily quest to find truffles. He suggests that we join him. Setting a brisk pace, Urbani leads us up through the under-growth and rocky terrain of the hills behind the farmhouse.

It isn't long before his dog picks up a scent. Pulling excitedly on his leash, the dog sniffs around the base of some small trees and starts digging wildly. He is allowed to go about his business for a time and then Urbino pulls gently on the leash. Reluctantly the dog stops digging and Signor Urbani completes the excavation himself, using his bare hands. Suddenly, he uncovers an object with a black, warty exterior and resembling a potato in shape. Knocking the soil off of it, he proudly shows us a truffle.

It is unlovely and emits a musty odour, but it is placed in the basket with all the care that might be lavished on a cut-glass goblet.

During the course of the morning the basket becomes fuller and fuller. Along the way Signor Urbani discloses the secrets of hunting for truffles. The *tartufi*, he explains, belong to the genus of mushrooms known as tuber, which attach themselves to the roots of trees, especially dwarf oaks. The quality of the soil and climate play an important role in the development of these mushrooms. There is a difference between the black and the somewhat finer white truffles. In Italy, truffles are found mainly in Piedmont and Umbria.

Back at the farm the truffles are taken to Signor Urbani's "treasure room", an extension on the side of the house which is set up like a laundry room.

Here the truffles are washed, brushed, dried and prepared for shipment.

Anxious that I should sample his truffles as well as hunt for them Signor Urbani invites me to dine with him that evening. The meal turns out to be a truffle extravaganza to which the entire family and several friends have been invited. The first course is duck liver paté served on *crostini* over which Mrs Urbani slices raw white truffles, completely covering them with paper-thin marbled slices. The next course is *carpaccio* with white truffles followed by dark black truffle sauce over spaghetti. The strong, musty odour of the truffles is transformed into a fine aromatic fragrance and the taste of the mushrooms evoke a wonderful memory of woods and nuts.

Signor Urbani did not always have it so good. He inherited stony, unfertile hillsides from his father. Like many other peasants from this region, he was forced to try to make his living collecting truffles. He scraped all of his money together and planted as many oak seedlings as he could on his worthless slopes. Then he waited 11 long years, not knowing if the parasitic mushroom would deign to attach itself to his oak trees.

Now, he can drink a toast of thanks to the *tartufi*. He has, he says, only one more wish – that everyone should have the chance to enjoy this incredible delicacy.

That wish is not so hard to achieve; in Norcia, the restaurants of the Grotta Azzura and the Posta hotels both feature truffle dishes on their menu, and you do not have to be especially rich to sample pasta garnished with shavings of the cheaper black truffle. The rarer *bianchetto*, or white truffle, is more expensive, but a little goes a long way; Signor Urbani's wife buries a truffle amongst newly laid eggs overnight and the perfume is sufficient to penetrate the shell, making for a breakfast of truffle perfumed omelette. In a restaurant it is more likely to be served combined with other wild mushrooms as a pasta sauce, or in an omelette that might also contain cheese and *prosciutto*. A last word of warning from Signor Urbani: sample your truffles in season (autumn and winter); out of season, they will have been preserved by freezing, canning or vacuum packing, with inevitable loss of flavour.

OLIVE OIL

It is difficult to say which has served mankind better, the olive tree or the grape vine. For 6,000 years the olive has competed with the grape for the honour. Olive trees were praised by poets, and presented to mankind by the goddess Athene as a source of nourishment, healing and bodily care. According to Homer, the gods rubbed themselves with perfumed olive oil

It was the Romans who put olive cultivation on an industrial footing. Plinius, the Roman scientist, said, "There are two things which are pleasing to mankind: wine for inside his body, and olive oil for outside. Both come from trees, but the oil is the more necessary of the two."

Today, of course, we know that the oil is also pleasing for the inside of the body. Olive oil is rich in vitamin E and easily digestible. Heart disease and arterial sclerosis are far less prevalent among the people of the Mediterranean region, the home of the olive tree, than in the regions lying north of the alps.

Within Italy, there is a constant debate as to which region produces the best quality olive oil – Tuscany, Calabria, Liguria or Umbria. Veronelli, one of the peninsula's famous gourmets, claimed that the best came from Liguria (needless to say, he came from Liguria!).

Others prefer the aromatic oil of Umbria – for instance from the groves of Terni or Magione, south of Lake Trasimeno. In reality, of course, preferences are a matter of taste.

Olive oil, whether dark or light, can be very aromatic or relatively neutral. As a general rule, if the aroma is intensive, the taste is also intensive, and it is fruitiest and most sumptuous when young. The very best oil comes exclusively from the *prima spremitura a freddo*, the first virgin cold pressing. The Italians call it *extra vergine*; the European Community guidelines classify it as "native" olive oil. The superior grades of olive oil can be as expensive as vintage wines.

Needless to say, the best quality oil is the most expensive to produce. Wages make up about 80 percent of the costs. The small green-violet fruits are hand-harvested (the season lasts from November to March) to prevent rupturing of the skin and contact with the ground, both of which could lead to fermentation setting in. Shaking the olives off the 10–16 ft (3–5 metre) high trees into nets spread out on the ground – a familiar sight all over Italy in season – is less work and therefore entails much smaller costs.

There are more than 50 different kinds of olives, and it takes 40 lbs (20 kg) to produce about a gallon (3-4 litres) of oil. Plenty of sunshine and a hot summer are needed to ensure a good harvest. The gnarled old trees also demand a certain amount of water. In times of drought a tree will not die but, in conserving what water it can, it will not produce any fruit.

Generally trees thrive in Umbria, the "green heart of Italy", but in 1985 catastrophe hit the olive groves of Umbria when the region was hit by frost in one of the severest winters it had ever suffered. Some sixty percent of the trees had to be radically pruned; 17 percent were totally destroyed. The result was an explosion in the price of quality olive oil. But necessity is the mother of invention, especially in Italy. With the help of colleagues in Spain and Greece, the Italian olive farmers were able to "stretch" their olive oil a little.

Fortunately the industry made a steady recovery from disaster. Today Italy produces 23 percent of the world's supply of olive oil. In Umbria, the plains surrounding Assisi and Spoleto are the major centre of the region's olive production.

If you would like to treat yourself to one of Umbria's best culinary delicacies, you should buy yourself a *Tartufo bianco a base di olio oliva*, a product combining olive oil and truffles, the region's most famous products. Poured over a simple salad of lettuce leaves or sliced mushrooms, it's delicious.

Of course, you can also enjoy whole olives – green (if picked when young) or black (if allowed to mature on the tree). They are particularly delicious when flavoured with an aromatic marinade containing herbs and preserved lemons. Many an Umbrian *alimentrari* (grocer's store) sells delicious sweet black olives prepared to a carefully guarded recipe.

When, around the year 1200, a well-dressed dandy by the name of Giovanni Bernardone, breezed into his father's shop in Assisi and announced that he was giving up all worldly goods, he was met with incredulity. Nothing in the boy's character suggested that he might be serious in his desire: he earned a good wage in the family business, trading in cloth, and appeared to relish spending it.

At the time, Giovanni (nicknamed Francesco, the "the little Frenchman", by his friends because of his French mother and his love of Provençal troubadour songs) probably did not understand his own motives. He knew only that he wanted to escape from his bourgeois existence. Perhaps a period in the army would knock some sense into him? So his father thought, and Francesco agreed, but on his way to join the Crusaders he fell seriously ill and returned home. Seeking clarification of his future through contemplation in the church of San Damiano, just outside Assisi, he heard a voice commanding "Repair my house, which you see is falling into ruin".

Francis took the injunction literally; he stole a bale of cloth from his father's warehouse and sold it to raise funds for the restoration of San Damiano. This time his father was not incredulous but extremely angry. Hauled before the bishop of Assisi, Francis was ordered to return home and see sense or renounce his inheritance. Francis took off all his clothes, raised his arms to heaven in a gesture of trust in God and chose the path to sainthood.

Tender character: Francis caused a stir wherever he went, not only because of the sensational renunciation of his inheritance, but also because of his appearance and unusual demeanour. Within time other people started to join him. One of them, Celano, wrote of the saint, "He was an unusually eloquent man with a pleasant countenance and kind expression, completely free of cowardice and arrogance. He was of short stature, had a relatively small, round head, a

Preceding pages: Francis preaches to the birds. Left, a portrait of St Francis. Above, his words are still heard today, and not only by the birds.

somewhat elongated face, a flat, low brow, dark innocent eyes which were not particularly large, dark hair… close, straight white teeth, thin and tender lips, a black, sparse beard, slender neck, straight shoulders, short arms, tender hands with long delicate fingers having somewhat prominent fingernails, thin legs, small feet, soft skin, he was very slender and wore rough garb…" The concept of tenderness predominates.

The "rough garb" was part of the uniform which he advised his "brothers" to don. It

comprised an inexpensive, coarse-textured habit with hood, trousers and, for those with cold feet, wooden sandals. Francis deliberately selected clothes which contrasted with the expensive garments of the wealthy. "With God's blessing, they can mend this garb with rough cloth and other rags. Because the Lord said, 'Those who wear expensive robes and live extravagantly are in the courts of the kings'." But he remained tolerant and allowed others more leeway than he allowed himself. He warned his followers not to judge those who dress and feast extravagantly, but "to judge themselves".

When Francis spoke, he inspired himself

as much as he did his followers. Celano described Francis preaching before Pope Honorius III:"He spoke with such fiery enthusiasm that he was beside himself. As he spoke, his feet began dancing, not out of insolence but rather because he glowed with the fire of God's love."

When he had gathered 12 brothers around him, he drew up a code of conduct for the group (1209), later ratified by Pope Innocent III, and sent them out into the world in pairs to serve as missionaries. They were destitute, just as the disciples of Jesus had been. He stipulated that they should possess neither silver nor gold, neither baggage nor luggage, nor bread.

society. Cities were gaining a measure of autonomy and the city fathers realised the expedience of harnessing the support of the so-called paupers, who now forced their way into politics. "Laws which apply to everyone must also be approved by everyone" was their slogan.

The "poor" craftsmen, traders and peasants formed groups later to become known as guilds or fraternities. Their members gained their new-found dignity not by right of birth but by means of their hard labour. This work, formerly a sign of lower class (the nobility did not "work" in this sense), was now given value. The idea of there being a right to work, as defended today by the labour unions, is

Francis of Assisi lived during a time of transition. In the Middle Ages the term destitute or pauper meant the opposite of potent (power), i.e."non-powerful, without authority". Even if someone possessed wealth as a merchant, he was a "poor man" if he had no political voice. Inevitably this important section of society began wanting a say in government.

Changing society: Thanks, in part, to the wealth and culture generated by the Crusades, the cities of upper Italy were far ahead of the rest of Europe in this development. The archaic feudal structure was disintegrating and the way was being paved to a modern

rooted here. "Fair" wages were discussed, according to the principle "to each his due". In reality, however, the day labourers were paid only the bare minimum needed to exist. And, for the first time, the question of fair prices was raised.

Nevertheless, this class system led to huge social inequities, here as well as in the regions of Europe north of the Alps, where the Franciscan monks had been going about their work since 1219. Up to 90 percent of the population of some areas relied on the welfare of others.

Francis became a spokesman for the poor. His followers settled in the most needy areas, such as leper colonies and hospitals for the acutely ill. Through their sermons, they engendered a sense of social responsibility and encouraged others to donate money to relieve suffering.

The wealthy were pleased to oblige: it eased their consciences, allowing them to continue living in wealth without feelings of guilt. The population in general was beginning to see the need to help those who could not help themselves, and the sense of virtue that might be gained from it.

Female influence: Francis of Assisi was part of a long tradition of religious movements in southern and southwestern Europe that pledged themselves to poverty and re-

Frederick Barbarossa, very nearly succeeded in creating a strong, unified Italy, free of papal influence, under his control between 1212 and 1246. He blamed St Francis for his ultimate failure to break the territorial power of the Church once and for all, because Francis and the Franciscan order had done so much to rekindle the faith of ordinary people in the Church. Macchiavelli, the Italian political philosopher of the Renaissance claimed that through St Francis the Reformation was postponed for 300 years.

Was the saint aware of the far-reaching political implications of his works? It was probably more important to him to have brought the destitute, plain human-like im-

form. As a rule, the mighty Church saw these "heretics" as a threat. For one thing, women – such as the Beguines and the Poor Clares (founded by Clara Sciffi, a childhood friend of Francis) – played a significant role in the movements.

It is all the more a tribute to Pope Honorius III, therefore, that he permitted the "Poverello" and his disciples free rein. He realised that Francis revitalised people's belief in the Church. Frederick II, grandson of

Left, Francis goes before Pope Innocent II. **Above**, Santa Maria degli Angeli near Assisi, a rather too grand memorial for such a humble preacher.

age of God closer to the people.

Francis died in 1226, aged 45, having asked to be buried in a pauper's grave on the Colle del Inferno, the Hill of Hell just outside Assisi where criminals were executed. His wishes were not carried out exactly. He was indeed buried there, but not until a splendid basilica, financed by the sale of indulgences, had been built on the hill. Thus, ironically, the saint who led a life of utmost simplicity came to be buried in one of the most sumptuous churches in Christendom – a building whose artistic treasures draw thousands of admiring visitors but whose pomp contradicts everything Francis ever stood for.

Johann Georg Seume hiked to Syracuse in 1802. Upon entering Umbria after crossing over the Apennines from the coast, he wrote "From this point on, every stone has a name." It was an apt observation for a land whose very rocks, springs, hills and mountains have been praised in literature by Virgil, Byron, Livy, Propertius and Goethe, to name but a few. Even for those who do not travel to this region with their luggage full of books by authors of the classics, the towns of Assisi, Orvieto, Spoleto and Perugia are usually on the list of sights they simply must see. And yet, the picturesque landscape of Umbria is just as noteworthy as its cultural attractions. The variety within the landscape pleases fans of the dramatic just as much as those who prefer the more gentle panorama of fertile rolling plains.

Conservation matters: Fortunately, the Italians are fully aware of the need to protect their "green heart", and conservation is now gaining more than a foothold in Italy. The green issue is provoking big interest in the media and the Green political party is gaining strength. The idea of establishing national parks as preserves for the flora and fauna of the region is being discussed, and even partially implemented. Four so-called "Parco Naturale Regionale" have now been established in areas of extraordinary natural beauty, away from the well-travelled routes. They are seen as offering environmental protection for wildlife while at the same time serving to attract tourists.

An important model for this type of park is the Abruzzi National Park, established in 1921. This park, in the neighbouring region of L'Aquila degli Abruzzi, has become one of the most important tourist attractions of Italy, and not just for friends of nature. The Abruzzi brown bear, the Abruzzi chamois and the Apennine wolf are just a few of the species that have settled here, and they draw plenty of visitors wanting to see them in their natural habitats. Consequently, the area is served by good roads and hotels and the

Preceding pages: the Eremo delle Carceri hermitage, near Assisi; a field of poppies. **Left,** rural idyll. **Right,** Umbrian panorama.

infrastructure for winter and summer sports is well established.

Though not as famous or as large as the Abruzzi reserve, Umbria's national parks have the advantage of being visited by fewer and more discerning tourists and thus remaining true wildernesses. Even the tourist offices within the region cannot provide detailed information about the parks (some tourist office staff appear not to know of their existence). In fact, the Umbrian parks are located in areas which are easily reached via

short detours from the well-travelled routes leading to the region's main cultural and historical sites.

The national park at the foot of the Monti Sibillini mountain range, which at an impressive 7,900 ft (2,400 metres) is the second-highest group of peaks in the Apennines, is gradually gaining renown. Its location is superb. The park stretches eastward from the village of Norcia, the birthplace of St Benedict and his twin sister, St Scholastica (480), and the entire surrounding area of this ancient town, known under the Romans as *Nursia*, retains much of its historic authenticity. The industrialisation of the Italian plains at the turn of the century did not affect this region. Its Piano Grande, with an altitude of 4,124 ft (1,257 metres), is a popular sports area, providing extensive opportunities for hang-gliding in summer and skiing in winter. An added attraction is its flocks of wild mountain goats and herds of deer. For nature lovers, though, the main appeal of the region is its alpine meadows. The Piano Grande itself, which is where Franco Zefferelli made his film about the life of Saint Francis, *Brother Sun, Sister Moon*, is a mass of wild flowers during spring and the footpaths leading out of the village of Castelluccio will take you to slopes rich in alpine flora.

This region has been repeatedly rocked by

nature served on a platter will especially enjoy the town, which is famous for its salami, *prosciutto* and truffles.

About 12 miles (20 km) to the southwest of Norcia is Cascia, the home of another saint. St Rita was born in nearby Roccaporena in the year 1381. Her birthplace is a popular, though extremely rural, place of pilgrimage, a pretty hamlet in a magnificent setting below impressive limestone crags. From Roccapovenna, and the nearby hamlet of Capanne di Collegiancone, there are numerous footpaths threading through the alpine pastures of the region.

For those who have the time to linger for a while in Norcia, a journey to the east over the

earthquakes (Norcia suffered severe damage in the last quake of 1979), the traces of which can still be seen. If anything, however, the quakes have enhanced rather than detracted from the landscape; they underscore the rugged beauty of the mountainous terrain, giving a preview of the Abruzzi range, the wildest part of the Apennines.

Saints and pork butchers: The town of Norcia itself is also worth exploring. The village has more to offer than just its impressive landscape or the fact that it was the home of the founder of the Benedictine order and of the monastery of Monte Cassino near Naples. Those who appreciate the finer things of

snaking road toward Ascoli Piceno (in the Marches) is recommended. The traveller is confronted again and again with surprising panoramas, perspectives which one would never expect in this part of Italy: for example, to the north, the peaks of Monti Sibillini, snow-covered even in summer, and to the south, the Gran Sasso massif. The most beautiful panorama can be seen from the top of the Forca Canapine Pass just before the road starts its equally winding descent down to Arquata dell Tronto. At this point, one is already in the Marches.

A region of unspoiled virgin nature, offering no organised activities designed to attract tourists, can be found to the north of Norcia. The pines of the national park stretch all the way to the regional boundary. Travelling over steep and often winding roads for about 15 km (9 miles), one reaches the monastery of San Eutizio at the foot of Monte Moricone (4,688 ft/1,429 metres). Three miles (5 km) further along, the road turns into a rather better thoroughfare, on N209. This leads southwest to the town of Terni, following along the western flank of a second regional park.

Dramatic wilderness: Much of this park is covered in dense and impenetrable ilex forest and you need local knowledge or a very detailed map to find your way through this

almost every visitor to Umbria, however uninterested in religion, makes a bee-line for his former home. But in addition to the magnificent church complex in Assisi, the nearby Eremo delle Carceri on Monte Subasio is well worth discovering.

This small hermitage, wildly romantic, situated in a holm-oak forest between rugged cliffs, is probably much more in line with the simple views and teachings of the saint than the splendid monumental church in Assisi. This secluded retreat is where Saint Francis would often come with his followers to pray and contemplate.

Another regional park is currently being established all around the hermitage in order

huge area of upland which is home to wolves and wild boars and which has a massive complex of unmapped caves and potholes. Even so, you can acquire a feel for the dramatic beauty of the park just by driving down the little-used N209, which follows every twist and bend of the fast flowing river Nera; here and there you are likely to see shepherds on horseback tending their flocks with the help of white-haired mountain dogs.

Umbria is a land of saints. Francis of Assisi is, of course, the most prominent and

Left, Monte Vettore near Norcia. **Above,** cattle grazing the high pastures.

to preserve the idyllic setting. The most beautiful view of the entire region can be had by taking the metalled road through this park, from the hermitage. After 5 miles (8 km) the read reaches the flat peak of Monte Subasio (4,230 ft/1,290 metres). A pleasant hike of 6 miles (10 km) takes you down to the village of Collepino at the eastern limit of the park.

The last Parco Naturale lies in the north of Umbria, near Gubbio. To the east of the N3 (the Via Flaminia, one of the region's busiest roads) steep cliffs rise to the summit of Monte Cucco (5,138 ft/1,566 metres), and the park stretches north from here to the border with the Marches and south towards Gualdo Tadino. Despite its high altitude, Monti Cucco can be reached easily by car by taking the road heading eastward out of Sigillo. After 6 miles (9 km) this scenic road gives out near the summit, a popular picnic spot in summer.

A short walk back down the same road, at Ranco di Sigillo, is an entrance to the extraordinary cave system that penetrates deep into the mountain, reaching to a depth of over 3,000 ft (920 metres). On several occasions during the summer one of the more accessible caves, the Grotta di Monte Cucco, is open to the public.

Further north, the N360 out of Scheggia

climbs through the park along the Sentino valley to Isola Fossana. In this village a winding by-road leads through beautifully wooded countryside until, after about 2 miles (3 km), you reach the semi-ruinous Abbazia di Santa Maria di Sitria, with its restored 11th-century church sitting on top of a 6th-century crypt.

Continue on for another 6 miles (10 km) and you will reach an even more remote abbey, the Eremo di Fonte Avellana. This hermitage, surrounded by oak woods and mountain pasture, was founded in AD 980. Off the graceful Romanesque cloister you can visit the original monastic cells, one of

which gave shelter to Dante around 1310 when he was wandering in exile from his native Florence and composing various forms of poetic torture to which he condemned his enemies in Hell. The hermitage was an important medieval centre of learning and the Dante Alighieri Library, named in honour of the poet's visit, occupies the former scriptorium where manuscripts were laboriously copied by hand.

In addition to these four designated parks, there are many other areas of Umbria in which you can enjoy unspoiled nature; the area around Lake Piediluco near Terni, for example, or the scenic N79bis road between Todi and Orvieto, which passes through a varied landscape of bare rock, cut by deep ravines, and woodland full of jays and red squirrels.

By chair lift: One of the region's most accessible hills for walking is Monte Ingino, which rises steeply above the city of Gubbio. Well-defined paths lead from the town to the summit, but if you are not fit enough to make the climb there is also a chair lift. The panoramic view from the 2,972 ft/906 metre summit is splendid. When you have recovered your breath from the climb, be sure to visit the Basilica di Sant'Ubaldo to see the huge ceremonial *ceri* (candles) which are kept here for most of the year. They feature in one of the region's biggest festivals, the Corsa dei Ceri (15 May), when teams of runners race from Gubbio up to the summit of Monte Ingino carrying these weighty wooden poles on their backs.

Umbria, aside from its national parks, has numerous other scenic attractions. The inhabitants of the "green heart" are finally realising how important it is to protect their natural landmarks – and not just to ensure the preservation of the waterfowl on beautiful Lake Trasimeno for the hunters of the region. Even so, nature has occasionally been relegated to a back-seat role, as in the case of the famous waterfalls, the Cascata delle Marmore near Terni, an attraction which has drawn visitors for over two millennia. Today this grandiose natural wonder can only be visited on weekends and holidays; on other days, the water is tapped for Terni's industrial needs.

Left, a descendent of the Lombard chargers? **Right**, the harvest is in.

As the Italian art historian Attilo Brillo has pointed out, the paths which early pilgrims took to Christianity's major points of pilgrimage were usually designed to take in various minor shrines along the way. That way the pilgrims were able to draw spiritual sustenance as they went. The same reasoning applied to the more secular routes travelled during later epochs. The "Grand Tour", the path of the aristocrats of the 18th century, the "artists' trail" of the Romantics and even the heavily travelled routes used by tourists of today were all designed to lead to Rome, but not before taking in a number of other interesting sites en route.

All roads, as the saying goes, lead to Rome, and the choice of route depended on the amount of time travellers wanted to take, the reason for their journey and personal preferences. Some travelled by ship (the mode chosen by the German painter Anselm Feuerbach in 1855); others by land. To begin with the most popular land route was via the old "Francigena" which led through Tuscany, Siena and Viterbo; but over time this became plagued by robbers and brigands. The alternatives were to travel via Perugia, Spoleto and Terni, a route favoured by the French author Stendhal, or to travel along the Adriatic coast, visiting towns along the way, in particular Loreto, before crossing over the Apennines.

Both of these routes converged in Umbria, so almost every traveller passed through this central Italian province. Various auxiliary roads leading off this main route encouraged travellers to visit sites off the beaten track, such as Foligno, Assisi or the Cascate delle Marmore, the picturesque waterfalls located just outside Terni.

For many who travelled to Italy – for example Johann Wolfgang Goethe – it was their first encounter with the architecture of classical antiquity. The Umbrian countryside, with its gentle rolling hills, towering mountains and overgrown, picturesque ruins offered a wealth of motifs especially for the

romantic painters, who were influenced by Giovanni Battista Piranesi.

But an astounding number of travellers on their way to Rome barely noticed the many attractions along the route. The letters, drawings and travel journals of these early tourists recount an almost breathless excitement at their first glimpse of the eternal city but little about the journey along the way.

The worship of relics: Another factor which clouded the vision of those travelling through Umbria was that, at that time, the green heart

of Italy still belonged to the Papal States and many of the artists and writers who passed through were Protestants and outspoken critics of the Church. They saw in Umbria the negative effects of Church rule – poor roads and highway robbery, inadequate lodging facilities, widespread poverty and mendacity. The aspects of the region which most impressed the travellers were the Umbrians' astonishing belief in miracles and worship of religious relics.

Many travellers made unfavourable comparisons between Umbria and the neighbouring province of Tuscany. Whereas the comments about Florence were always of a

Preceding pages: 19th-century romantic landscape. Left, peering down to the Cascata delle Marmore. Right, in the Nera Valley.

highly laudatory nature, objective travellers, such as Michel de Montaigne or Karl Philipp Moritz, found no shortage of relatively critical words to describe Umbria. Stendhal, a passionate fan of Italy – he even referred to himself in his epitaph as a son of Milan – noted this negative view of Umbria : "An English priest piously raised his eyes toward heaven as we left Perugia and prayed that the earth might open up and swallow the entire population of Rome and Naples. And he was completely serious thereby. Why not just admit that civilisation ends in Florence?"

For some tourists, however, the journey to the Italy of classical times did not actually begin until they reached Umbria. Byron, for

Claudius among them – to more recent times. Corot was one of several artists who have painted the spot. The springs are dedicated to the Roman god Clitunnus, famous for his oracle. Umbrian white cattle, bred near Bevagna, were blessed at this spring before travelling on to Rome where they formed an essential component in any major sacrifice to the gods. Byron wrote of nymphs bathing in the crystal clear waters and:

The finny darter with the glittering scales,
Who dwells and revels in thy glassy deeps;
While, chance, some scatter'd water-lily sails
Down where the shallower wave still tells its bubbling tales.

example had his imagination kindled by Lake Trasimeno and the narrow valley leading to the lake's shore where Hannibal's army slew 16,000 Roman soldiers at dawn on 24 June 217 BC, a victory that sent a chill through the heart of all Romans at the thought that little now stood between Hannibal and the conquest of Rome itself. Byron looked upon the scene and wrote of rivers swollen to torrents by the blood of slain soldiers and deplored "the absorbing hate when warring nations meet". On a happier note he was lyrical about the tranquillity of the Fonti di Clituno, just south of Trevi, a spot that has charmed visitors from antiquity – Virgil, Caligula and

The nymphs have been scared away by the number of visitors who come to the spring by the coachload today, but it remains as charming a spot as ever.

Waxing lyrical: The Cascate delle Marmore, near Terni, have long been another traditional attraction for travellers to Italy. The 525-ft/160-metre falls are in fact a man-made creation, but nonetheless spectacular for that. They were created by the Romans to channel the waters of the rivers Nera and Velino so as to drain the surrounding marshes. Even in antiquity they were regarded as one of the wonders of the world. For numerous artists, particularly those of the Romantic school, they were a favourite motif. Henry Mathews, in *Diary of an Invalid* (1820), said of the Cascate delle Marmore "No description can give a more lively idea of the impression which the first sight of it makes upon the spectator, than the exclamation of Wilson the painter, overheard by Sir Joshua Reynolds, who happened to be on the spot. Wilson stood for a moment in speechless admiration and then broke out, with, – 'Well done, Water, by G—!'."

William Hazlitt, in 1826, found the falls too slender – "the Doric, or at any rate the Ionic, among waterfalls" – but his remarks didn't deter others from seeing for themselves. Dickens travelled to the falls and

than to be awakened before day-break" he noted while in Terni). By the way, the father of this famous poet, Johann Caspar Goethe, had also made the journey to Italy about 50 years previously and collected innumerable Latin inscriptions and the most absurd examples of the people's belief in miracles. Compared to his father's dry descriptions of the country, the writings of J.W. von Goethe were much more colourful. He may have noted the "peculiarity" of the geological formations, the weather and the farming methods, and, in typical Teutonic fashion had a suggestion as to how each could be improved, but, on the other hand, he viewed his journey to Umbria as a very personal

Stendhal wrote extensively about his visit there. They are no less dramatic today, and the modern visitor has the benefit of seeing them dramatically spotlit at night.

The most famous of the authors who wrote about Italy, J.W. von Goethe, did not visit the falls. Instead he hastened past them on his way to Rome ("because, out of impatience to proceed toward my goal, I sleep fully clothed and can imagine nothing more wonderful

Left, Johann Wolfgang von Goethe wrote extensively of his travels in Umbria at the end of the 18th century. Above, the Cascata delle Marmore.

voyage of discovery.

Goethe followed the classic route from Perugia ("The location of the city is beautiful, the view of the lake very pleasing. I have stored these impressions in my memory") to Foligno, Spoleto and Terni.

Assisi made an extremely deep impression on him, though, as a classicist, he only had eyes for the works of antiquity and deplored the great medieval churches that he encountered. With extraordinary bias, he dismissed the great Basilica di San Francesco with its Giotto frescoes as the "unbelievable substructures of the Babylonian churches piled on top of one another, where St Francis lies". He was much more impressed by the far from complete remains of the Temple of Minerva: "Finally we reached the old town: and the most laudable of works stood before me, the first complete monument of ancient times that I had ever lain eyes upon... a humble temple, completely appropriate for such a small city; and yet so perfect, so exquisitely conceived that it would be considered a jewel no matter where it was located." Today's visitors might not be so impressed, or so blind to the defects of this temple, consisting of little more than six time-worn Corinthian columns forming the porch to today's church dedicated to San Filippo Neri, of which even the official town

guidebook candidly admits that "the baroque ornamentations of the interior are a real disappointment."

Goethe's description of his journey so impressed his contemporaries that many other northern Europeans followed in his footsteps. It opened up a new and more romantic picture of Italy, vastly different from that which had been painted previously. The focal point was no longer the collecting of impressions with the help of a travel guide, no longer the urge to visit all of the important sites. The new order of the day was to experience individually the unique charm of this land as well as its monuments and artistic

works, despite the hardships of inadequate accommodation and real, as well as figurative, highway robbery.

Perhaps the best example of the effects the landscape had on the visitors from "the far north" is provided by the romantic description which Erwin Speckter, an artist and book iluustrator, noted in his journal. He wrote in December of 1830, as he came down from the Apennines: "It lay before me and below me and all around me like an open book. This springtime, this fullness of life, magnificence and splendour lay before me as if placed there by magic. It was like a midsummer night's dream or a winter's tale. I rubbed my eyes and could not believe that I was seeing correctly... I was surrounded by beautifully formed mountains, small green foothills and a shining valley through which small shimmering brooks wound their way. On all the mountainsides and throughout the entire valley, we saw small towns, villages, villas, fortresses, monasteries, etc. which appeared as jewels glittering in the sun which had been sewed onto the colourful cloak of a sorceress."

Such ecstatic descriptions have drawn more and more travellers to Umbria. For some, the goal is still Rome, and all they see of the region, before speeding south in their air-conditioned coaches, is Perugia and Assisi (Michael Adams, a modern writer, on Umbria quotes a conversation with the Director of Tourism in Assisi. Watching the queues of coaches at the Basilica di San Francesco, Adams asks "How do you find room for them all?" "It's just another little miracle on the part of Saint Francis," came the reply).

However, many more now come as gentle respectful pilgrims, seeking inspiration in the life and works of St Francis, even if they are not Christian or even religious, such is his contemporary relevance. Mercifully, highway robbery, uncomfortable accommodation and primitive superstitions no longer characterise the region and today's visitors can still enjoy all the sights that charmed Byron and Goethe – Virgil and Propertius even – in considerable comfort whilst absorbing what one old traveller described, with only slight exaggeration, as "a little piece of heaven fallen to earth."

Left, baroque grotesque. Right, *passegiata* in Orvieto.

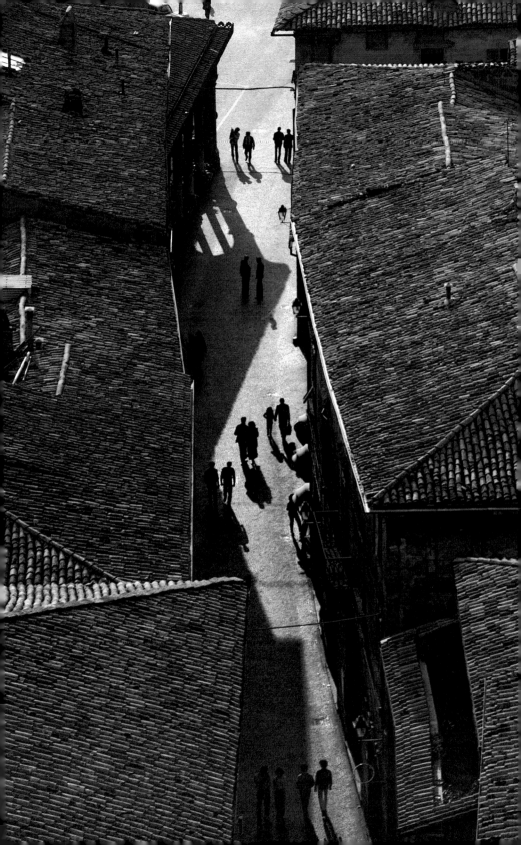

When people speak of castle-filled regions, they are usually referring to the Rhine Valley or the Loire. Not many people would think of the heart of Italy. Just by glancing at a map of Umbria, however, the visitor will learn how many castles there are dotting the landscape.

For instance, travelling on the N219, which follows the Assino river and leads from Gubbio to Umbertide, you pass an entire chain of castles which are just waiting to be discovered. There is the well-preserved Castello di Carbonara, not far from Mocaiana,

and the picturesque ruins of the Castello di Monte Cavallo, once the property of the Gabriellis of Gubbio, perched above the abbey of Campo Reggiano. Others include the Castelli di Serra Partucci and di Civitella Ranieri, and the Castello di Poggio, situated where the N219 joins the N3.

Converted castles: Castelli di Serra Partucci and di Civitella Ranieri can be reached by following the old road toward Umbertide. Shortly before the N219 crosses over the Assino, the road to these castles branches off to the right. The remainder of the way is well signposted. Both of these building complexes represent "converted" castles. They have been transformed into residences, incorporating parts of the original edifice.

The renovated Castello di Civitella Ranieri, with its two square gate towers and dual cylindrical *torri*, dates back to the 15th–16th centuries. Once the seat of the aristocratic Ranieri family of Perugia, it is today reputed to be one of the most beautiful combinations of a fortress complex and castle grounds in the entire upper Tiber Valley. The Castello di Serra Partucci is almost equally beautiful. A huge four-cornered *torre* dating from the 14th century stands in harmony with a cylindrical tower which was built about 200 years later. The battlements surmounting the castle wall performed more of a decorative function than a defensive one. Both *castelli* are situated on small mounds facing one another. From the terrace at the rear of the Serra Partucci, there is a marvellous view across the entire breadth of the Tiber Valley and a beautiful, though now slightly weathered, sculpture of a nude.

Almost every town in Umbria has its *rocca*. Strictly speaking, these were never actually a part of the town; they were generally built on the highest point within the town area, but separated from it by forbidding walls, to stand sentinel over the houses and churches such, for example, is the case in Narni, Spoleto or Assisi.

Spoleto's monumental rocca is undoubtedly the most dramatic fortress in the region, mainly for the spectacular Ponti della Torri aqueduct which spans the gorge between the fortress and Monteluco on the opposite bank. The aqueduct was built before the fortress, in 1345, but incorporated into it to provide a reliable water supply in the event of siege and an escape route from the city *in extremis*. The fortress itself, built in 1355 under the direction of Cardinal Albornoz, was the base form which papal representatives subjugated the region. Later it was converted into a luxurious palace for Lucrezia and Cesare Borgia, before serving as a maximum security prison. Soon it will reopen after conversion to a museum and arts centre.

Unlike the seat of the powerful Lombardic dukes in Spoleto, the *rocce* of Narni and Assisi normally pass unnoticed by tourists visiting these towns. The thought of going to see the *rocca* rarely crosses the minds of those visiting Assisi, even though the route to it is actually very simple: from the cathedral of San Rufino, situated about 230 ft (70 metres) lower than the castle, it is a 20-minute walk, passing San Lorenzo on the way. The *rocca* can also be reached by car: drive to Porta Perlici in the northeastern part of the city, from where the N444 leads to Gualdo Tadino. Before reaching the city gate, follow the Via di Porta Perlici uphill in a westerly direction. Driving by San Lorenzo, one reaches the walls of the castle after about half a mile (800 metres).

Emperor Frederick I (Barbarossa) stayed the emperor until 1198, when Conrad from Urslingen, imperial representative in the Duchy of Spoleto since 1177, capitulated to Pope Innocent III in Narni. He promised that the emperor's troops would retreat and that the three largest fortresses would be relinquished. One of these was Assisi, a fortress in which Emperor Frederick II had spent several years of his childhood under the custody of Conrad. But before the castle could change hands, Assisi's citizens – among them perhaps the young Francis – stormed the grounds, threw out the occupants and completely destroyed this symbol of imperial oppression.

It is said that the *rocca* lay in ruins for over

in the independent *comune* of Assisi more than once during his lifetime. After the curtain wall of the *rocca* was constructed in 1171, this became his principle stronghold in the region. When the town rebelled against Barbarossa, his troops, led by Archbishop Christian from Mainz, conquered the *comune* in 1174 and an administration loyal to the emperor was instituted in Assisi.

Symbol of oppression:The town remained under the administration of forces loyal to

Preceding pages: the Rocca at Spoleto. **Left**, the bastions of Assisi's Rocca Maggiore. **Above**, the Castello di Civitella Ranieri.

150 years. The state of affairs did not change until 30 June 1353, when Cardinal Gil d'Albornoz was named by Pope Innocent VI in Avignon as the vicar general for Italy and the Papal States. The Spanish cardinal was in Italy twice, from 1353 until the end of 1357 and from December of 1358 until his death in August of 1367. His mission there was to attempt to bring to an end the desolate situation in *Patrimonium Petri* and to lend authority to the papal claim to power.

By the end of 1357 he had achieved his aims. The Papal States were, with the exception of a few cities in Emilia Romana, once again under the control of the pope – thanks to military power and the establishment of mighty fortresses. One of the master builders, Ugolino di Montemarte, drew up the new plans for the *rocce* of Narni and Assisi. Their completion, however, was something that the cardinal did not live to see. It is said that the *rocca* of Narni was completed shortly before 1370, and that the so-called Rocca Maggiore of Assisi was finished towards the end of 1367.

Built on the site of Barbarossa's former castle, the Rocca Maggiore has a trapezoidal curtain wall with angle towers; this encloses the four-sided fortress keep surmounted by a square tower. Construction of a polygonal tower was begun in 1458 in the northwest

Subasio with the Eremo delle Carceri on its slopes. Whether the *condottiere* Cecchino Broglia decided to make Albornoz's rocca into his headquarters in 1398 because of its panoramic view is open to doubt, but when he received a tempting and lucrative offer from Florence to represent that city on the battlefield, he preferred to take over as ruler of Assisi. While he haggled with the Florentines, he collected "protection" fees from all the *comuni* which he and his soldiers could threaten from the Rocca Maggiore.

Fairy tale fortresses: Lake Trasimeno is not all that far from Assisi. It is a castle landscape *en miniature*. Ever since the time of the Romans, this region around Italy's largest

corner. Completed under Pope Pius in 1458-60, it is connected with the keep by a battlemented parapet. Sixtus IV ordered its restoration, and in 1535, Paul III ordered the entrance secured by means of a cylindrical and pinnacled "battery tower". Construction was completed three years later.

If you visit the Rocca Maggiore, you will be admitted by the *custode*. Inside, you can see the inner ward, the kitchen, a spacious hall, the sleeping quarters and the tower of Pius II. There is also a spectacular view from here to the north across the Tescio Valley, to the south across the city and the Basilica di San Francesco and eastwards to Monte

lake was a strategically important area. And it remained so for centuries. The line of defence through Tuoro, Castiglione del Lago, Piegaro and Città della Pieve protected the route to Rome as early as the time of the Ostrogoths, Byzantines and Lombards. The region was a deployment zone for imperial as well as papal troops, and it was Perugia's most important bulwark against cities such as Orvieto, Cortona, Arezzo and Florence. Thus it is no wonder that here a dense ring of fortresses is found around the lake. Rocca Bagliona Zocco, Sant'Arcangelo, Salci, Castel Rigone, Montecolognola, Passignano and Monte del Lago are just a few of the many *castelli* here. Magione even has two fortresses: the Torre dei Lombardi and the Castello dei Cavalieri di Malta. Both have a long history.

The Torre dei Lombardi, said to have been built around 1200, was originally called the Torre di Pian di Carpine, coming from *carpine* (meaning hornbeam). It probably owes its modern name to the noble Marcello Lombardi from Passignano who was killed nearby in 1688. His family owned the *torre* at the time. In earlier times, around 1370, Cinolo Montesperelli, who had been banished from Perugia, was the occupant and used it as a base for military endeavours against the regime of the Raspanti. In 1800 the tower was turned into a nunnery and was severely damaged by an earthquake 46 years later. This was a fate which was often to befall the tower.

The nuns moved into the Castello dei Cavalieri di Malta. This was a fortress designed by Fieravante Fieravanti of Bologna and constructed around 1420. In the 11th century it was a plain hospice of the Templars. After their conquest, it fell to the Order of St John, later known as the Knights of Malta, which still administers the *castello*. In October of 1502, powerful families met in one of the halls to draw up secret plans. The lords of Bologna, Siena, Perugia and Fermo joined in a pact against Cesare Borgia, a pact which failed dismally.

One of the mightiest fortresses of the Trasimeno region is situated between Torre di Pesci and Borghetto. This is Castiglione del Lago, a village which was already settled during the Paleolithic age. It was later Etruscan and Roman and was known as *Castrum Clusini*, a name it was to keep until the 13th century. It was then a part of the Byzantine line of defence and fell under Tuscan influence during the time of the Lombards and Carolingians. In the year 996, Emperor Otto III granted sovereignty over it to the margrave of Tuscany. In the year 1000, Perugia began to fight for control over the lake region in a series of wars which lasted throughout two centuries. In 1247, Emperor Frederick II had the *castello* destroyed and ordered its reconstruction in a form which, with a few minor exceptions (for example

the passageway to the Palazzo Comunale), has remained unchanged to this day. Frederick also renamed the castle Castello del Leone, a name which which was later shortened to Castillonem and then Castiglione.

With the aid of the pope, the "castle of the lions" once again came under the control of the city of Perugia and continued to play an important role in papal as well as municipal interests. Around 1500, the *condottiere* Gianpaolo Baglioni, a descendant of one of the mightiest families of Perugia's aristocracy, lived within its walls. He entertained such important guests as Niccolò Macchiavelli and Leonardo da Vinci. Castiglione's golden era began after Pope

Julius III granted sovereignty over it to Giacoma della Corgna, also a member of one of Perugia's most important families. She turned over the duties of administering the castle to her son Ascanio who, 13 years later, was named *Marchese di Castiglione del Lago* as well as governor of Città della Pieve by Pope Pius IV.

Ascanio della Corgna was one of the last of the great *condottieri* of Italy. He was a brilliant swordsman and strategist. At the age of 21, he had already served under the king of France, taken part in the siege of Genoa and lost his right eye at Casale Monferrato. Barely three years later, in 1538,

Left, "My home is my castle" –a mini-castle near Lake Trasimeo. **Above**, the more forbidding Rocca at Castiglione del Lago is not far away.

he entered into the service of Venice as a commander of an infantry company, gained great renown fighting against the Turks and subsequently served in the papal forces.

But Ascanio did not remain long in Italy. He changed over to the side of King Francis I of France, fought along the Spanish border and just a few months later – in his heart and soul a true *condottiere* – fought on the side of Emperor Charles V against France. Returning to Italy, he consolidated his reputation as a swordsman.

Continuing in the service of Charles V, he fought in Germany against the Protestant reformers as well as against the rebels in the Spanish Netherlands. In 1550, one of his

uncles was enthroned as Pope Julius III. At the time Ascanio was already *governatore* of Ancona. With the help of his powerful uncle, he was able to rise even further. He became administrator of the territories of Castiglione as well as Città della Pieve and finally *Custode della Santa Chiesa*. That meant that he was a viceroy of Rome.

With the election of Pope Paul IV, however, Ascanio's fortunes took a downward turn. He fled to Naples and fought with the rank of general against this new evil-minded pope. For this act he was promptly excommunicated. The appeal from Spain's King Philip II could not have come at a more

opportune time. Philip, the son of Charles V, made Ascanio commanding general of his fortresses in Flanders and the other provinces of the Spanish Netherlands.

Upon the election of Pope Pius IV, Ascanio regained all of his former titles and offices, and was promoted to *marchese*. An adventurer of his calibre, however, is not long content off the battlefield. He fought for the Maltese Knights against the Turks and later played an important role in the decisive battle of Lepanto by developing the successful plan of attack. In December of 1571, Ascanio della Corgna died in Rome, aged 57. And a short time later, the once so influential Marquisate of Castiglione was also dead.

In the year 1617, under Fulvio della Corgna, the region was raised to the status of a duchy. But the last male descendent of this famous family was a man who "never carried a weapon except for during the hunt". In a scandalous act, Fulvio della Corgna passed control over Castiglione to the duchy of Tuscany.

It came about thus: during a war between the pope and the Duke of Parma, who was allied with Venice, the Duke of Modena and the Duke of Tuscany, Tuscan troops advanced against Castiglione del Lago. And, although the bastions were strengthened and the town was being defended by 2,000 soldiers, Duke Fulvio surrendered the city to the enemy after a mere three days of siege. He then immediately fled to the court of the enemy in Florence. It was not until the 18th century that Castiglione del Lago once again came under papal rule, a status it retained until the unification of Italy.

Still today, as in the time of Frederick II, Castiglione's fortress is known as La Rocca del Leone. It has an irregular pentagonal form, with four angle towers and a triangular main tower with a height of 128 ft (39 metres). Although it is enclosed by the town's ring wall, it is independent of the town. It has its own inner curtain wall, constructed so that it could be defended even if the town was conquered. As late as the 16th century, the *rocca* was considered one of the most invincible in Europe.

Left, despite the weathering of centuries, this lady still ennobles the park of the Castelli di Serra Partucci. **Right**, the Eremo delle Carceri near Assisi.

Travellers to Umbria have a choice of three major roads through the region. The first is the N71 which circumvents Lake Trasimeno with brief as well as more lengthy detours into the surrounding countryside, for instance to Città della Pieve. The second route, the N3*bis*, follows the Tiber Valley, passing through the cities of Città di Castello, Umbertide, Perugia (the capital of Umbria), Todi and Orvieto.

The third route follows the N3, the Via Flaminia, a major thoroughfare since the time of the Roman Empire, starting in the south in Narni and ending at the Scheggia Pass in the north. It passes through the towns of Terni, Spoleto, Trevi, Montefalco, Bevagna, Foligno, Spello, Nocera Umbra and Gualdo Tadino.

One last, shorter route, the N209, leads from Terni eastwards, past the Marmore waterfalls and through the Valnerina, where you can visit the venerable abbey of San Pietro in Valle. This road continues up into the most remote region of Umbria, to Norcia and the far-reaching Piano Grande plateau.

The region has numerous noteworthy hilltop cities – more than you could do justice to in a short visit. Assisi is perhaps the crowning glory, with its double basilica dedicated to St Francis, its Giotto frescoes and an atmosphere, quite unusual for a pilgrimage town, of youthfulness, freedom and gaiety. Its noisier, brasher neighbour, Perugia, hums with life, partly because of its large student population; besides the impressive ensemble of the cathedral, the Palazzo dei Priori and the Fontana Maggiore, it also has the best shopping in the region.

Spoleto's Romanesque cathedral, with its frescoes by Fra Filippo Lippi, is one of the outstanding buildings of the region, and the Ponte delle Torri (Bridge of Towers) aqueduct has to be seen to appreciate its full dramatic impact. Orvieto, built on a volcanic plateau and surrounded by vineyards, has some of the most accomplished carvings of the Romanesque era on its cathedral facade and Signorelli's Apocalyptic frescoes within.

These are just a few highlights of a region in which almost every hilltown, no matter how small, hides some gem of art and architecture; not to mention an unpretentious trattoria offering a table in the shade, a glass of local wine, a hearty meal and an opportunity to reflect on your experiences of a region that has seen so much violent history but which has now settled into calm and gracious tranquillity.

Preceding pages: the countryside around Todi; the Torre del Comune and Temple of Minerva in Assisi; over the rooftops of Orvieto; Umbria is famed for its fine wines. **Left**, old traditions live on.

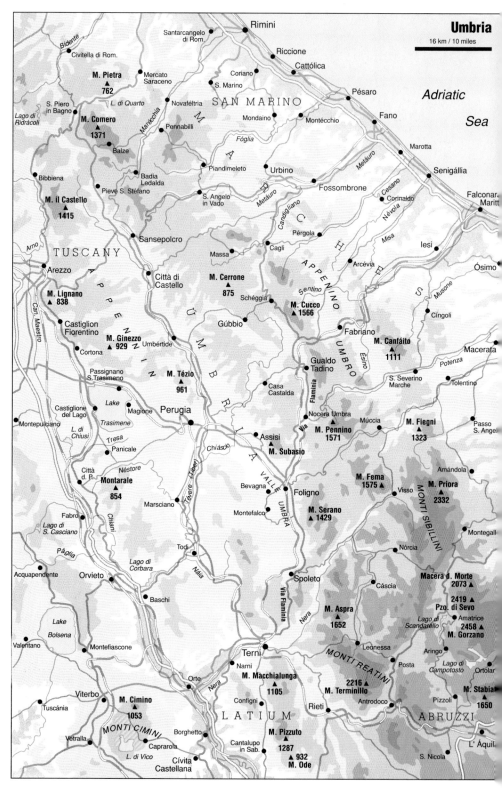

Umbria

16 km / 10 miles

Bidente
Civitella di Rom.
Santarcangelo di Rom.
Rimini
Riccione
Cattólica
M. Pietra 762
Mercato Saraceno
Coriano
S. Marino
Pésaro
Adriatic
S. Piero in Bagno
L. di Quarto
Novaféltria
SAN MARINO
Mondaino
Montécchio
Fano
Sea
Lago di Ridrácoli
M. Comero 1371
Maréchia
Pennabilli
Fóglia
Marotta
Balze
Badia Ledalda
Piandimeleto
Urbino
Metáuro
Senigállia
Bibbiena
Pieve S. Stéfano
S. Angelo in Vado
Fossombrone
Corinaldo
Cesano
Névola
Falconar. Maritt
M. il Castello 1415
Metáuro
Candigliano
Pérgola
Misa
Iesi
Sansepolcro
Massa
Cagli
Arcévia
Ósimo
TUSCANY
Arezzo
Città di Castello
M. Cerrone 875
Schéggia
APPENINO
Musone
Cíngoli
M. Lignano 838
Sentino
M. Cucco 1566
Fabriano
M. Canfáito 1111
Macerata
Castiglion Fiorentino
M. Ginezzo 929
Umbértide
Gúbbio
UMBRO
Potenza
Cortona
Esino
S. Severino Marche
Tolentino
Passignano S. Trasimeno
M. Tézio 961
Gualdo Tadino
Flaminia
Castiglione del Lago
Lake
Magione
Perugia
Casa Castalda
Nocera Umbra
Múccia
M. Fiegni 1323
Passo S. Angel
Montepulciano
Trasimene
Tresa
Panicale
Chiáscio
Assisi
Via
M. Pennino 1571
L. di Chiusi
M. Subasio
Amándola
Città d. P.
Néstore
Montarale 854
Bevagna
Foligno
M. Fema 1575
Visso
MONTI SIBILLINI
M. Priora 2332
Fabro
Marsciano
Tévere (Tiber)
Montefalco
UMBRA
M. Serano 1429
Montegall
Lago di S. Casciano
Chiani
VALLE
Nórcia
Páglia
Todi
Nália
Lago di Corbara
Spoleto
Cáscia
Macera d. Morte 2073
Acquapendente
Orvieto
Baschi
Via Flaminia
2419 Pzo. di Sevo
Lake Bolsena
M. Aspra 1652
Lago di Scandarello
Amatrice
2458 M. Gorzano
Valentano
Montefiascone
Nera
Leonessa
MONTI REATINI
Aringo
Ortolar
Viterbo
M. Cimino 1053
Orte
Terni
Narni
M. Macchialunga 1105
Posta
Lago di Campotosto
2216 M. Terminillo
M. Stabia 1650
Tuscánia
MONTI CIMINI
Borghetto
Configni
Rieti
Antrodoco
Pízzoli
ABRUZZI
Vétralla
Caprarola
Cantalupo in Sab.
M. Pizzuto 1287
LATIUM
L. di Vico
Cívita Castellana
932 M. Ode
S. Nicola
L' Áquil

152

ASSISI

Assisi draws people from all over the world, many of them coming to retrace the steps of St Francis. They want a sense of the surroundings in which this popular saint, made patron saint of Italy in 1939, and of ecology in 1979, lived and worked. More than 800 years after his death, the stories of St Francis's humanity still move people, whether they are Christian, atheist, Buddhist or any other religion. Few visitors come just to see the town's beautiful churches or the magnificent works of art.

Assisi is located on a rolling hillside below Monte Subasio, a mountain which has supplied the stone that characterises the city's buildings for centuries. The soft colours of the fine-grained, almost plastic, Subasio limestone, ranging from light pink to ivory to ochre brown, endow Assisi with a special charm, creating a synthesis between the buildings and the natural landscape which makes it an especially fitting birthplace for St Francis, whose doctrine was based on the harmony between man and nature.

Although Assisi is often crowded with visitors, obtaining a hotel room, even without making a reservation, is not a problem. It is best, however, to visit on a weekday rather than a Sunday or religious holiday. The town provides all categories of hotels as well as ample bed and breakfast accommodation. Most of the restaurants offer good quality regional cooking rather than unappealing tourist fare.

The holy convent: The history of St Francis is widely documented, not least by the local tourist office. The travelling preacher Giovanni Bernadone, as Francis was originally called, had at first only a handful of faithful followers. Within just a few years, however, the number of people seeking conversion by him had swelled into thousands.

The Basilica di San Francesco is perched like a fortress on the western slope of the city, rising above the distant plains. Construction of this gigantic monastery was begun two years after Francis's death in 1228, the same year that Francis was canonised in a ceremony led by Pope Gregory of such pompous absurdity that Francis himself would surely have laughed. He always enjoined his followers to "avoid being sad and gloomy like hypocrites, but rather be joyful in the Lord". Contemporary accounts of the canonisation ceremony relate that the assembled cardinals were so moved to tears by the long list of miracles attributed to St Francis since his death that "their vestments were wet and the ground soaked".

The Church, of course, had a vested interest. The sale of indulgences to finance the building of the basilica brought in so much money that work proceeded at an extraordinary pace. So fast, in fact, that the work was not done properly and the whole ensemble needed underpinning in the 1470s; the majestic series of 53 arches that you see beneath the basilica as you approach Assisi was the result, installed to shore up the subsiding structure.

The basilica was nearly complete by

1230 when St Francis, who had been temporarily laid to rest in the church of San Giorgio, was given his official funeral. Once already a raiding party from Perugia had attempted to steal the body – a mark of just how financially lucrative was the medieval pilgrimage trade. To ensure that no further attempts at saint snatching could succeed, the actual day of the funeral took an unusual turn of events. Vast crowds of onlookers gathered to watch the funeral cortège, drawn by white oxen and covered in bouquets of wildflowers, approach the basilica. Suddenly an armed guard snatched the saint's coffin, bolted the cathedral doors and the body was interred in secrecy.

Not even the pope was expecting such an unceremonious event, but the ploy succeeded. The exact location of St Francis's tomb remained undiscovered until 1818, and then it took two months of excavation to find it. Today you can walk down from the lower basilica to the crypt built as the site of the saint's last resting place. Here, in a grave made of rock, lie the remains of St Francis, secluded and withdrawn from the world.

The soul of St Francis lives on. The walls of the large double church are covered in paintings depicting stories of his life. No space is left unpainted. In the dome, golden stars stream from a background of deep blue.

The frescoes: The walls of the upper church are covered with motifs from the gospels and the Old Testament. Below each biblical scene is a corresponding scene from the life of St Francis (probably no other person in history has so unquestioningly followed the path of Christ). Most of the frescoes were painted by Giotto between 1296 and 1300. When he began this work he was about 30 years old. Giotto emphasises man, with his various attributes, and depicts his relationship to the landscape and architecture. His success at portraying emotions is perhaps the most exceptional aspect of the frescoes. Joy, anger, awe and sorrow are all superbly illustrated. Just as Francis diverged from the hell and brimstone philosophy of medi-

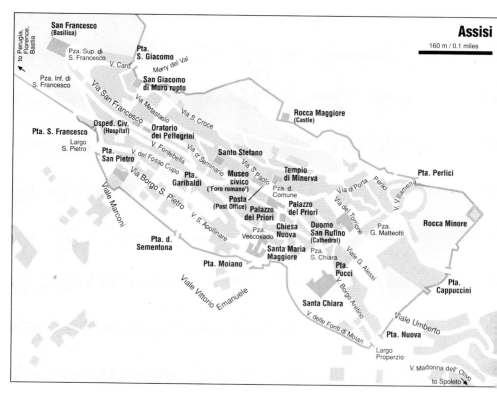

eval religion, Giotto set new standards by reaching out beyond the impersonal and cold severity of Byzantine art. This ability made him one of the forerunners of the Renaissance.

Brother Jim, a Franciscan from England, is one of the many guides who show visitors round the basilicas, and he never loses an opportunity to draw some moral lesson or universal truth from this cycle of pictures. Understanding is greatly enhanced by his explanations. Picture number 15, for example, depicts St Francis preaching to the birds, each of which is painted differently. As Brother Jim points out, this is because Giotto – in keeping with the allegory – is really portraying us, mankind, with our widely differing characteristics.

The pictures of the Giotto cycle which merit particular attention are:

Picture number 4: In front of the crucifix in the church of San Damiano. From this cross, Christ spoke the following words to him: "Francis, depart from here and bring my house in order once again. It is disintegrating."

Picture number 5: Francis gives his clothes and all his other worldly goods back to his father (note that Giotto has painted the face of St Francis's father in livid yellow to symboise his rage) and the bishop covers Francis's naked body with his cloak. The Austrian poet Rainer Maria Rilke, deeply moved by this scene, wrote the following lines:

Oh where is he who sacrificed time and worldly goods in order that he might gain such strength in his poverty that he could shed his robes at the marketplace and appear naked before the bishop.

Picture number 7: Pope Honorius III's verbal sanction of the regulations of the order. Giotto has decorously counterpointed the pomp and majesty of the pope and cardinals with the poverty and humility of St Francis and his followers.

Picture number 8: The saint appears to his companions in the form of a vision on a chariot of fire in Riverto.

Picture number 10: The banishment of the demons from Arezzo.

Picture Number 11: St Francis tries to convert the Muslims of North Africa to Christianity. In the course of his trav-

els, Francis set sail from the Italian port of Ancona in 1219 and sailed up the Nile delta to seek an audience with Sultan Malek-al-Kamil, with whom the Crusaders were then at war. The Sultan enjoyed the company of this earnest but good-humoured little friar, and Francis emerged alive from the encounter; in this scene he is shown walking unharmed through a blazing fire to prove the truth of the gospels to the Sultan.

Picture number 13: St Francis institutes the first Christmas crib; in 1223 St Francis set up a living tableau in a cave near Greccio, complete with live animals and child, to teach the illiterate local shepherds the message of the Gospels. Ever since, and to this very day, many a church in Umbria follows the custom of mounting a living tableau on Christmas Eve.

Picture number 14: The Miracle of the Spring. Vasari, the Renaissance art historian, considered this scene to be one of Giotto's finest works because of the striking realism of the thirsty peasant, bending to drink from the spring

Corinthian columns of the Roman temple of Minerva in Assisi.

that St Francis caused to flow simply by praying.

Picture 15: The Sermon to the Birds is one of the most celebrated scenes in the cycle, even though it has lost much of its force through the deterioration of the pigments.

Picture number 23: in this beautifully composed scene, the last in the cycle by Giotto (the rest are the work of pupils and the anonymous "St Cecilia Master") St Clare pays her respects to St Francis as his funeral cortège passes by the church of San Damiano, just outside Assisi, which St Francis gave to the Poor Clares as their mother convent.

The frescoes by Cimabue in the apse of the Upper Church seem unusually obscure. Because of the gradual oxidation of a certain white pigment in the paint, the pictures have been transformed into negatives, but even so the drama of his Crucifixion, in which the brutality of the crowd on the right is counterpointed with the grief of the onlookers on the left, still has force.

In contrast to the bright and colourful spaciousness of the upper basilica, the lower basilica is enveloped by a cave-like darkness. Some interpret this symbolically as the meditative penetration of Francis into the inner depths, the undiscovered, the transcendental: again and again during his lifetime, he retreated into caves in order to pray. The walls of the lower basilica, too, are completely covered with frescoes. The colours stream from the darkness and address onlookers directly. The picture of Francis, painted by Cimabue on the wall of the lower basilica's right-hand transept, is particularly interesting. Cimabue's portrayal corresponds very closely to the description of Francis by his first biographer, Tommaso da Celano: "black eyes, normal height and a simple appearance... soft, crisp and penetrating speech... he is thin, dresses simply, sleeps little and is generous. With unparalleled humility, he demonstrates his goodness and understanding to all by approaching them in a wise and appropriate manner. A saint under saints as well as being an equal under sinners."

At Assisi's Calendimaggi● festival.

156

On the wall beside this is a portrait of St Clare, the first successor to Francis. Of the five saints seen in this fresco, she is the fourth from the left. The subtle colours and the lightly-drawn sketch by Simone Martini reflect the sensitive and tender character of this woman, the founder of the order of the Poor Clares.

Impressive, too, is the picture cycle by Simone Martini depicting scenes from the life of St Martin. This is found in the chapel nearest the entrance to the lower basilica. The cycle concretely emphasises the importance of brotherhood and compassion among people of different ranks and positions.

More frescoes by Giotto are found in the transept. In the arches over the high altar are frescoes by the "Maestro delle Vele" depicting allegories of the three principles on which the Franciscan order was founded: Chastity, Poverty and Obedience.

Interestingly, these frescoes are the only ones in the basilicas to stress the self-imposed torments of ascetism, fasting and self-flagellation for which the

Franciscans were later renowned. In one scene, Poverty is portrayed as a bride being given to St Francis in marriage, walking barefoot on thorns, her way impeded by a barking dog and a scornful, stone-throwing youth; St Francis, in his wanderings, frequently encountered just such ridicule. In the next scene, Obedience is portrayed as a seated figure placing a yoke round the neck of a friar while in the foreground, a centaur, representing sexual passion, is being driven away.

These pictures contrast with the gaiety and vivacity of Giotto's frescoes upstairs. Goethe compared this genial medieval painter to his contemporary Dante: "The sensuous, metaphorically significant geniality also governed his works. He envisaged the object so squarely in his imagination that he was able to reproduce it nearly perfectly. This is why we are able to see before us the most abstruse and curious things, drawn, as it were, according to nature."

A walk around town: Goethe did not head straight for the Sacro Convento

ancis casts his clothes from otto's sco cycle the silica di n ancesco.

and Giotto on his visit to Assisi. He preferred instead to trace the tracks of the old Romans. He visited the **Piazza del Comune** and its **Temple of Minerva**: "Before me stood that laudable building, the first complete monument of ancient times that I had ever lain eyes upon," he wrote. "A modest temple, completely appropriate for such a small city; and yet so perfect, so exquisitely conceived that it would be considered a jewel no matter where it was located."

The Minerva temple was transformed into a church in 1539. This was the best way to save it from destruction. The Piazza was once the site of the **Forum Romanum** of the old *Asisium* of Roman times. Today the forum remains can be seen in an underground museum complex (Museo Civico, Via Portico 2).

There are several other noteworthy buildings located on this gorgeous piazza. These include a medieval tower, the **Palazzo del Podesta** and, across from that, on the other side of the square, the **Palazzo dei Priori** whose vaulted arcade is decorated with grotesque frescoes. If you pass through the arcade you will come to **Oratorio di San Francesco**, the house in which St Francis was born.

In the town of Gubbio, just a short distance away, the citizens erected the Palazzo dei Consoli in the 14th century as a manifestation of their new-found freedom and democracy. Here in Assisi, citizens fighting for their freedom in the 12th century destroyed the castle, the **Rocca Maggiore**, built by the German emperor. The revolt began in 1197, with the death of Henry VI. The citizens drove out the nobility, which had pledged allegiance to the emperor and embodied the old order of power and suppression, and established the republic of Assisi. In 1367 the castle was rebuilt and served the Papal States as a fortress. From the castle's tower, one has a wonderful panorama of Assisi as well as a scenic view stretching across the Tiber Valley.

Every year, from 29 April to 1 May, Assisi celebrates the knights of old in a festival called Calendimaggio. An age-

Assisi's mai square, the Piazza Comune.

old dispute between the upper and lower parts of the city is again brought to life. The citizens don period costumes and warriors, lords and servants and religious and secular figures from history, roam the streets. Everyone joins in.

Eremo delle Carceri: An ideal way to experience the Umbrian-Franciscan landscape is by taking a stroll either along the stony path leading up to Monte Subasio or a more comfortable trail ending at the Eremo delle Carceri, an old cloister where, according to legend, St Francis preached to the birds. The saint and his followers often came here to pray and meditate. The cloister buildings with their small simple chapels, located in a romantic holm-oak forest, are in perfect harmony with the picturesque mountain landscape.

All those who make the approximately 2½ miles (4 km) long hike there and back may need a bit of refreshment after their journey. The restaurant La Stalla is to be found about half-way along the route, and it's an ideal place to rest. Dishes cooked over an open fire are served the guests as they relax under shady trees.

Assisi's cathedral, dedicated to **San Rufino**, lies at the upper part of the town, where few visitors penetrate. Yet San Rufino has the most outstanding Romanesque facade in all of Umbria, a sculptural masterpiece, partnered by the massive and stately Romanesque campanile. Before the canonisation of St Francis, the town's principal saint was the early Christian martyr, San Rufino (d. 238). The crypt which held San Rufino's tomb can be entered through the door on the right side of the cathedral square (signposted "Accesso al sotteraneo"). San Rufino himself was translated to a grave beneath the cathedral's main altar, but his 3rd-century marble sarcophagus, carved with reliefs illustrating the myth of Diana and Endymion, is displayed in the crypt.

The principal attraction of the cathedral, however, is its marvellous facade. The lunette of the central portal is carved with a charming scene, rustic in its execution but nonetheless expressive. In the centre Christ is seated in Majesty between the sun and the moon. San Rufina stands to the right, in vestments, while to the left the Virgin suckles the infant Christ.

Two red marble lions crouch either side of the portal, the stone polished by countless generations of children who, despite the ferocity of the lions' features, have climbed upon their backs. Inevitably the interior of San Rufino will come as a disappointment, failing as it does to fulfil the promise of the exterior. At the back, though, to the right is an iron-bound marble font, originally from the town's first cathedral, which was used to baptise three future saints – Francis, Clare and Agnes – and the future Holy Roman Emperor, Frederick II, who was born prematurely outside the town in 1194.

Just south of the cathedral is the Basilica di Santa Chiara, begun in 1257, five years after St Clare's death, and modelled on upper church of the Basilica di San Francesco. The interior was once gorgeously frescoed with scenes from the life of St Clare but,

e Eremo
lle Carceri.

sadly, the frescoes were covered with whitewash in the 17th century to deter visitors who were disturbing the contemplative life of the nuns.

The best of the surviving frescoes are found in the transepts and in the Cappello del Crocifisso you will find the 12th-century painted crucifix which, according to Franciscan legend, spoke to St Francis in the ruined church of San Damiano, commanding him to rebuild the church. The remains of St Clare herself are displayed in the crypt beneath the high altar, a rather ugly neoclassical edifice. Clare's body was rediscovered in 1850 and, as you would expect of a saint, her body was found to be perfectly preserved when her coffin was opened. She did not long survive exposure to the open air and deteriorated rapidly until human hands intervened to produce the saintly sleeping figure that lies in the crypt today.

San Damiano church lies amidst olive groves just outside the city walls. St Clare spent most of her life within the tranquil walls of this simple building of rough unadorned stone and the spot where she died, in the dormitory, is always marked by a small vase of white flowers. The chapel contains a remarkable crucifix carved in 1637 by Innocenzo di Palermo. The head of Christ has three different expressions – anguish, death and tranquillity, depending on whether you view it from the left, right or centre. A door leads off the flower-filled cloister to the refectory of the Poor Clares, a low room with smoke-darkened ceiling and its original 13th-century rough tables and benches. Few other places so well evoke the life of utmost simplicity and poverty that St Francis and St Clare chose in their rejection of the richness and pomp of the Church of their time.

Farewell in Porziuncola: Visible from afar, the church of **Santa Maria degli Angeli** rises from the plains near the motorway, the old Via Flaminia, about 4 miles/6 km west of Assisi. The monumental baroque structure was built over a small chapel which had great significance for St Francis. It was here that he

The Rocca Maggiore.

founded the very first Franciscan friary.

It was here, too, that he was brought when death approached. Blind and weak, he directed his monks to lay him in the dust As he lay dying, he added a further verse to his *Canticle of the Sun*: "Praise be to Thee, my Lord, for our sister, bodily death, from whom no living man may escape: woe to those who die in mortal sin."

Santa Maria degli Angeli was begun in 1569 but reconstructed after an earthquake in 1832. Its great bulk (it is the seventh largest church in Christendom) makes it seem like the memorial to some emperor rather than that of the humblest of saints. Beneath the great dome of the echoing nave is a rustic church, preserved in its entirety. It is known as the Porziuncola (literally "little portion"), a reference to the small clearing in the woods where the church was built at the centre of the first Franciscan community. The friars originally lived in timber huts in the surrounding woods.

To the right of the Porziuncola is the Cappella del Transito, standing on the sight of the original infirmary where St Francis died. Frescoes on the walls, painted in 1516 by Lo Spagro, depict Franciscan saints and there is an ascetic figure of St Francis in glazed terracotta above the altar, the work of Andrea della Robbia. More of della Robbia's work can be seen in the crypt; his bas reliefs of the Nativity and the Adoration of the Magi are considered to be amongst this Renaissance artist's finest work.

A corridor from the right-hand transept leads to the Rosary, a tiny garden tucked beneath the basilica walls. Legend has it that St Francis threw himself naked one winter's night into the rose garden to chastise his flesh, whereupon "white and red roses, wonderfully perfumed, sprang up and blossomed on all sides". Moreover, the thorns dropped from the rose stems, and they remain thornless to this day, their leaves streaked with markings the colour of blood. Many consider this tiny garden a more fitting memorial to St Francis than the monstrous basilica alongside.

manesque ulptures on e facade of e San fino thedral.

LAKE TRASIMENO

If you approach Umbria, as many visitors do, along the Florence to Rome motorway, the A1, you will reach the shores of Lake Trasimeno not long after you leave the motorway at the Montepulciano intersection and head for Castiglione del Lago, the principal town on the lakeside.

As you approach by means of the winding road over the wooded and vine-covered hills, later passing through the grain-producing plains, will see the town from afar, built on a spur of land jutting into the lake. This route provides you with adequate time to adjust to the slower pace of rural roads and get in the mood for the phenomenon known as *"Il Trasimeno"*. Lake Trasimeno is the last of the large prehistoric Umbrian inland lakes and it is still Italy's largest. The surface of the lake is 846 ft (258 metres) above sea level.

Julius Caesar and later Napoleon both had ambitions to drain the lake. Caesar planned to parcel out pieces of the 50 sq. mile (128 sq. km) land-lake area as remittance to his legionnaires, who had served him so well for so little reward; Napoleon wanted to turn the lake into another duchy. The Romans dug the "Emissarius" canal in order to protect the shores from flooding during heavy rains, and the mercenary leader Braccio da Montone, called *Il Fortebraccio* (Strongarm), governor of Perugia from 1416–24, later tried to improve the drainage canal, albeit with relatively little success. In recent years it was feared that the lake might dry up without human assistance because the rainfall was so low. In the summer of 1990 alone the water level sank about 3 ft (1 metre). Since the maximum normal depth is only 26 ft (8 metres), that is quite a significant drop.

Castiglione del Lago: The town's **cathedral**, with its dome and belfry, and **castle**, with its mighty triangular donjon and pinnacle, compose an impressive silhouette on the skyline. Before exploring the town proper, it's a good idea to take in the view from the top of the castle walls overlooking the shimmering blue waters of the lake. Anyone making this journey on a hot summer day will be pleased to discover the bathing beach and cool meadows.

The circuit for a walking tour of the town starts in the castle courtyard, the venue for outdoor plays throughout the summer. The castle's long covered passageway leads to the **Palazzo Comunale**, the town hall. In former times, the della Corgna dukes resided here. One can see the frescoes, all depicting heroic and mythological scenes, that they commissioned to glorify their family name. They were painted in the 16th century by Giovanni Antonio Pandolfi (d. 1581) and Salvio Savini (16th–17th century). In the **Castle Chapel** next door, which is now part of the hospital, the fresco of the *Madonna della Rosa* by Giovanni Battista Caporali (*circa* 1476–1560) is worth a visit.

Interesting, too, is an evening stroll from the castle through the main street of the city to the cathedral of **Santa**

ceding es: reed-ued Lake imeno. the view ss to tiglione Lago. t, signano, ven for ors.

Maria Madalena (with an altar-piece previously attributed to Raphael until a bill of sale provided evidence that it was a work by Eusebio da San Giorgio, 1465/70–post 1540, a contemporary of Perugino). The café terraces of the small square, the **Piazza Mazzini**, provide a lovely setting for an aperitif. And for dinner, continue a few steps further to the old Hotel Miralago. Dinner is served under the trees, with a view of the lake, vineyards and cornfields beyond; the menu offers first-class specialities of the region.

Those who arrive in mid-June will find themselves, along with the 13,000 residents, in the midst of the *La Fiera del Rigattiera*, a regatta lasting an entire weekend. The festival, attracting boating enthusiasts from all over Italy, is a colourful spectacle.

You will drive 60 km (40 miles) if you do a complete circuit of the lake. Near **Borghetto**, the Tuscan border reaches almost to the shores of the lake. The tower provides a landmark for the motorist, making it easy to find this peaceful fishing village. Here, at the northern end of the lake, those travelling by car are offered the choice between the motorway and a more pleasant country road. The railway line from Florence to Perugia follows the shore at intervals, distracting from the panorama of the lake, until it reaches **Torricella** where it disappears into a tunnel.

Ancient battleground: The town of **Tuoro** is divided into the old town on the mountain (with a marvellous panoramic view) and the lido with its beaches. Here, during the normal working week, tourists are pretty much alone. The town is famous for the Battle of Lake Trasimeno (217 BC), in which Hannibal, on his way to Rome, defeated the Roman general Flaminius. The cry of alarm, *"Hannibal ante portas!"* (Hannibal at the gates!), which spread throughout ancient Rome now echoes through Latin classes thanks to Livy's dramatic account of the battle in his history of the Punic Wars. The Roman Empire was the centre of the world at the time and this was its first defeat at the hands of a

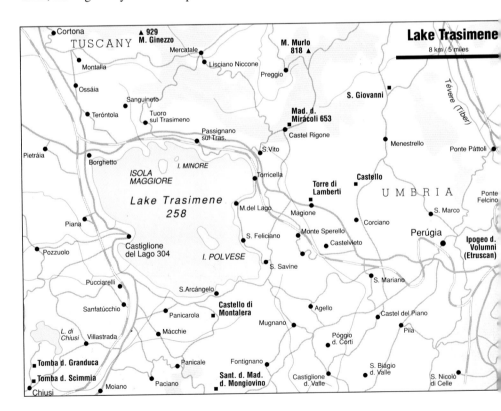

non-European enemy. Rome eventually conquered this "son of Baal" (the translation of the name Hannibal) after 13 years.

The people of Tuoro like to view themselves as the descendants of these heroic legionnaires and to think that the courage of the ancients has passed down to them (even though Tuoro did not even exist at that time); in summer, they stage a Roman chariot race *à la* Ben Hur. They have set up a "learning trail", which tells visitors all about the battle of "Sanguineto", a name referring to the fact that the stream running into the lake at this point was coloured red with the blood of the battle's victims. The trail also provides interesting topographic information; for example, at the time of the battle, the lake's waves washed all the way up to the hills of today's city, and until the end of the Middle Ages the town was a fishing village.

The regatta of the fishermen of **Passignano sul Lago** (on the last Sunday of July) is firmly rooted in the folklore of the region. However, the inhabitants of this picturesque village can no longer live from eel-fishing, its traditional work; industry and tourism are now the mainstays of the local economy. A factory building seaplanes and a school for pilots have been in existence here since the beginning of the 1960s. When the white cruiser departs for the **Isola Maggiore** or **Polvese**, the seaplanes perform impressive manoeuvres.

Passignano, strung out along the lake's northern shore, is a centre for all types of water sports, from swimming and diving to sailing regattas. In the main holiday season, the waters overflow with tourists; off-season, however, it is altogether more civilised and a good place to enjoy the relaxed Italian lifestyle.

Continuing the journey around the lake in a clockwise direction, you pass two churches, both reached by a short climb uphill. The first, **La Madonna dei Miracoli** in **Castel Rigone**, is known throughout Umbria as a destination for pilgrims. Construction was begun by Lombardic master craftsmen in 1494

e old
tifications
Castiglione
l Lago.

and the building has a Tuscan style despite its awkward 19th-century campanile. The tower was built to replace the original one which was destroyed by an earthquake, and the portal was designed by a pupil of Michelangelo. The works of Umbrian painters such as Domenico Alfani (*circa* 1480–1553) and G.B. Caporali, as well as their Tuscan guild brothers Roselli and Pappacello, are noteworthy here. The history of the Rigone castle can be traced back to the turbulent times of the 6th century when Totila's Goths were terrorising this part of Umbria.

The second church, **San Vito** (halfway up, beside the road to Rigone), is quite a defiant Romanesque structure, dating from the 13th century. It is reminiscent of church architecture in the Ticino. The bell-tower, off to the side and built on four angular legs, looks like the work of a peasant builder. Inside the church is a fresco from the school of Fiorenzo di Lorenzo (*circa* 1440–1525).

Because it is very difficult to get to the lake through the dense crop of reeds lining the shoreline, any path down to the water is a welcome sight for the hot and weary traveller. **Torricella** is a bathing area with a village character. It has a small modern hotel of the same name. For dinner, the young proprietress usually recommends the local, though not particularly cheap, fish (the lake still supplies plenty of fish, but the recent lack of rainfall threatens to deprive them of sufficient oxygen). One of her best is the *persico reale*, a perch-like fish with tender meat. Other favourites are the eel and the *tinca*, similar to a tench. The latter, prepared with many herbs, tastes quite exotic. Another recommended dish served in many places around the lake is made of a large number of small deep-fried fish.

Beside the hotel is an ice cream parlour. This appears to exert a magnetic effect on the youth of the area at sunset, toddlers included.

On the road between Torricella and **San Feliciano**, a stout six-sided tower stands guard. From here, a tiny narrow street leads up to the village of **Monte**

The marina a Passignano sul Trasimeno.

168

del Lago. With its 14th-century fortress it looks just like a stage setting for an opera. Indeed, the composer friends Pietro Mascagni and Giacomo Puccini were guests in the Villa Palombaro, located on this steep peninsula. In the early years of their acquaintance, before they could afford to do otherwise, they lived together. Puccini was a great lover of the duck hunt, a passion which was easily fulfilled on Lake Trasimeno.

San Feliciano – dedicated to St Felix, the happy one – is a village where the people have traditionally worked as fishermen, using virtually the same methods now as centuries ago. The rows of posts on which the eel-pots are attached stretch far out, perhaps up to about 1 mile (2 km) into the shallow water. In the shade of the trees, the old fishermen repair their nets, while a helper, often an elderly woman, cuts up bait. It's a picture that is both melancholic and full of energy. Inevitably the younger generation demand a faster pace of life – a speed boat, for example.

The mainstay of tourism here, in ad-dition to the small marina, is the dock from which the boats servicing the islands, especially **Isola Polvese**, depart. The short promenade is somewhat spoiled by the inevitable trappings of tourism; signs on the newsstands make it clear that foreign-speaking guests are common hereabouts.

San Arcangelo could be called a sister town to San Feliciano. It is only about 5 miles (8 km) as the crow flies across the bay. On the shoreline road, however, the distance is about twice that, through yellow fields of sunflowers. In San Arcangelo, everything is a bit larger than in the village of San Feliciano and the pier here is more robust. A well-maintained campsite nestles among the trees; it provides every imaginable service including entertainment. Motorists without intentions of camping are also allowed to use the beach here, though not without a hefty charge. When the sun beats down and the temperature climbs to 100°F (38°C), you may feel tempted. In fact, it isn't as inviting as it looks. The sign announces

"Attenzione! Acqua Profonda!" (Warning! Deep water). In reality, the lake here is more like a weed-infested village pond.

Island touring: A journey on the lake is refreshing, so investigate the routes covered by the Servizio Provinciale Navigazione. They include trips to **Isola Polvese**, located in the southeastern corner of the lake, which has a surface area of 54 hectares (133 acres) and is the largest of the lake's three islands. This is more than just a peaceful bathing island; it has been beautifully landscaped with countless trees, olive groves and orchards. After a refreshing swim in the lake, tuck yourself into one of the numerous shady spots to relax and digest the day's impressions.

It was Charlemagne that presented this island, and indeed the entire lake, to the Vatican. Until 1624, it was inhabited by monks of the order of the Olivetans, who shared it with fishermen. In 1139, the *Civitas Perugia* declared the lake, with its rich supply of fish, a part of Perugia and the island thus also came under that city's rule. The governor resided in the castle whose ruins are now a part of the landscape.

Popes were sometimes guests in the abbey. Although this no longer stands, its relics and paintings can be found in the church of Santa Francesca Romana in Rome. In addition to the castle and the abbey, there were also five other religious structures here – a somewhat excessive number when one considers that in 1887 there were only 27 inhabitants on the island. The exodus was complete when the island was sold to a private owner who used it as a hunting ground. In the 1980s, it was taken over by a Polvese syndicate which has been able to bring some prosperity back to the island. Agriculture and limited tourism is flourishing.

The shortest route to **Isola Maggiore** is from Tuoro, but the most popular one is from Passignano. The latter route leads by the **Isola Minore**, an island which looks like the moss-covered shell of a turtle, which is privately owned and not open to visitors. The Isola Maggiore,

A day out for nuns.

only 27 acres (11 hectares) in size, is also covered with dense vegetation. The angular tower of the castle-like **Villa Isabella**, named after the original owner's wife, a certain Marchese Gulielmi, dominates the island. The 19th-century villa is built on the foundation of a monastery of the Observantine monks, originally constructed in 1328. A round tower protects the southern point of the villa facing the nearby shoreline.

The highest point of the island is claimed by the church of **San Michele Arcangelo**, built in the mid-14th century. Here one finds 14th to 16th-century frescoes and a painted crucifix by Bartolomeo Caporali (*circa* 1420–1503/05). On the western side, where the ships dock, the old fishing village with its cobblestone street is worth exploring. The street is lined by two small palaces, a 16th-century house and three medieval churches. The 12th-century church of **San Salvator**, with its interesting fragments of a 15th-century fresco cycle by Sano di Pietro of Siena, towers over its north end.

St Francis of Assisi once viewed this island as an ideal place for contemplation. In 1211, he spent 42 days fasting here. A bronze sculpture by G. Zaneti on the eastern shoreline pays tribute to his visit. A chapel was formerly located on this site, inside which was a stone worn smooth by the many hands of pilgrims. And speaking of hands, those of the lacemakers living in the village are rarely still.

The surrounding countryside: A short tour of the peripheral area of the lake leads first to **Magione** (population 11,000) with its landmark **Torre dei Lombardi**. This tower, erected in about 1200, is clearly visible from afar. A short climb to the park at its foot is worth the effort, though the tower itself is currently being restored.

Among the famous sons of Magione is a predecessor of the explorer Marco Polo. John of Plano Carpini was sent as an ambassador by Pope Innocent IV in 1225 to the ruling emperor of the Mongols. It was an incredible journey, all the way across Central Asia and through

_azing in the
sun.

the Karkorams. In the **Palazzo Comunale** is a fresco depicting the pious friar as he kneels obediently before the desert ruler.

The Maltese castle occupies the site of a 13th-century pilgrim's hospice built under the protection of the Knights of St John. In the 15th century, the architect Fioravante Fioravanti of Bologna, in a surprising act of defiance, converted it into the **Castello de Cavaliere di Malta**. However, the pilgrims' chapel with its frescoes from the school of Pinturicchio was spared from destruction. Today's structure, with its corner towers and bastions, knight's hall of honour, and multi-level arcades, looks like a castle straight out of a storybook.

Panicale, easily reached via the southern plains, is well worth a visit. Its high elevation provides a magnificent panorama of the surrounding countryside. A further attraction here is the *Martyrdom of San Sebastiano*, a painting by Perugino in the church of San Sebastiano.

In the centre of this symmetrically constructed fresco dating from 1505 is the graceful figure of the saint, naked except for a loin cloth. He stands on a pedestal, totally calm (as demanded by Seneca), awaiting his punishment and looking up humbly towards heaven. The four executioners, lined up as if choreographed for a ballet, prepare their weapons, aiming them at their victim. The Swiss historian Jacob Burckhardt says of Perugino that he drew excellently when he *wanted* to, that "the luminosity of his colouring and the finely defined individual segments in some of his pictures show what he could have done if he had *wanted* to." In Panicale Perugino clearly *wanted* to. It is a very moving experience to move from the plain exterior of the church of San Sebastiano to the inside and the magnificent fresco. As so often in his work, Perugino includes the Umbrian landscape.

A picture by Giovanni Battista Caporali from 1519 hangs in the **Collegiate Church of San Michele**, in the third chapel on the left. It depicts the Nativity, set in an Italian background.

An Umbrian farmer.

Panicale possesses an unequalled medieval character. Even those with very little time should visit **Piazza Umberto I** and the **Rocca del Podestà**, dating from the 14th century.

In the area along the border between Tuscany and Umbria, rising out of the Chiani valley is the elegant town of **Città della Pieve**. The town was founded on the site of a Roman settlement which, in turn, was built on the site of an Etruscan village. In the centre of this episcopal town are the **Piazza Gramci**, formerly the Piazza del Plebiscito (Square of Plebiscites), the **Cathedral**, **Palazzo Bandini**, **Palazzo Mazzuoli** (formerly owned by the dukes of Corgna), frescoes by Salvio Savini and the **City Tower** (Torre Pubblica) rising to a height of 125 ft (38 metres). Construction began on the latter in the 12th century.

Home of a great artist: The city is chiefly famous as the birthplace of Perugino, whose real name was Pietro di Cristoforo Vannucci, who is regarded as the greatest of the Umbrian school of artists. Vannucci House, the place where he was born in 1445, is in the main square; it is marked by a bronze portrait.

The cathedral of **Santi Gervasio e Protasio**, founded in the 12th century, was completely rebuilt in 1600. It is decorated with several interesting works of art. To the right of the first altar is a *Crucifixion* by a German artist of the 16th century; above the high altar is a *Madonna in Glory* by Perugino, depicting both patron saints of the cathedral, painted in 1514; to the left of the first altar is *The Baptism of Christ*, also painted by Perugino, in about 1510. Another painting by Perugino with this same motif is found in the Museum of Art History in Vienna.

Perugino continued painting until the ripe old age of 75 or perhaps even 78 years. He died of the plague in 1523 in Fontignano near his home town, where he was carrying out a commission. Many say that Perugino continued painting for 10 to 20 years too long, but one must remember that he was already a famous and revered artist at the age of only 30.

His apprenticeship began at the ten-

der age of eight. He then went to train in Florence, then the centre of all that was new and exciting in art, studying under Andrea Verrachio along with Leonardo da Vinci. He was totally dedicated to his work, according to Vasari, who says "he knew no other pleasure than exhausting himself in the practice of art". That dedication paid off. By 1480 he was in such demand that he was invited to paint the east wall of the Sistine Chapel in Rome along with other contemporaries such as Botticelli and Ghirlandaio. His fresco there, *Christ Giving the Keys to St Peter*, is one of the most marvellous pictures he ever painted and it displays his characteristic skill at painting the beautiful, limpid landscapes of his native Umbria.

Perugino's greatest work is the fresco cycle in the Collegio di Cambio in Perugia, where he was assisted by, and had an enormous influence on, the young Raphael. The view that Perugino continued painting too long is based on the decline that set in in his latter years when, unable to paint all the works that were commissioned from him, he would put his name to second-rate works executed by various pupils. He also lost his innovative edge and was content to paint works to a formula that lack spontaneity or conviction.

Perugino's most significant work in his home town is the *Adoration of the Magi* in the church of **Santa Maria della Mercede** or **Santa Maria dei Bianchi** (Via Vannucci; if locked the custodian is at Via Vannucci 29). It depicts the adoration of Christ by the three kings from the Orient. The picture is symmetrically constructed: the worshippers are positioned theatrically to the left and right of the Virgin and child. In the middle of the background are the shepherds with their flocks. Knights on horseback with their followers appear out of the hills to the left and right. The idea behind this symmetry is that the tidings of the miracles of Christ are spreading and showing their first effects. Deep in the background, the watery light from Lake Trasimeno radiates from the picture.

Left, outside a café in Citt della Pieve. Right, dressed for Sunday Mass

THE BATTLE OF LAKE TRASIMENO

Rome did not make any special efforts for its military campaign of the year 217 BC. The Senate justifiably viewed the situation as not particularly serious, despite recent defeats in battle. Aside from the troops along the coast which were dispatched to Sardinia, Sicily and Tarentum, and the reinforcements which were delegated to Spain, the two consuls Gaius Flaminius and Gnaeus Servilius were provided with only enough troops to bring the four legions back up to their full strength. Their job was to protect the northern border and they thus set up their forces along the two roads leading north from Rome, the western one ending near Arretiserum and the eastern one ending near Ariminum. One was the responsibility of Gaius Flaminius and the other of Gnaeus Servilius.

But Hannibal had no intentions of defending the Po Valley. He was well aware that, despite his glorious victory on the Trebbia, he was in a weak position. He also knew that his ultimate goal, the humiliation of Rome, could only be attained by conquering that proud city. It was crystal clear to him that the Italian confederacy was far superior both from a standpoint of political stability and from that of military equipment and supplies. After all, Hannibal received only erratic assistance from the home front and in Italy he could only count the unreliable and fickle Celts among his allies.

With this in mind, there were two basic premises which influenced Hannibal's strategies in Italy: to fight the war in an adventurous manner, constantly changing both the plans of operation and the sites of battle, and to make the goal of the war not a military victory, but rather a political conquest resulting in the weakening and finally the destruction of the Italian confederacy. This strategy was imperative because the only trump card that Hannibal had, with so much going against him, was his military ingenuity. This exerted its maximum effect only when he was able to bluff his opponent by means of unexpected moves, keeping him constantly guessing. He knew that, without such a strategy, the war was lost before it begun.

Hannibal arrived at this plan after noticing that although he was able to defeat the generals in every battle, he could not defeat Rome; and after every new battle, the Romans still held the upper hand just as surely as Hannibal held the upper hand over the Roman generals. That Hannibal never allowed himself to be deluded by his luck is more amazing than his most stunning victories.

This is also the reason why Hannibal vacated his newly won base of operations and moved the scene of the battle to Italy. But first he paraded his prisoners of war. He singled out the Romans from among these prisoners and had them chained as slaves – the story that Hannibal had all Romans who could bear arms massacred is grossly exaggerated. Actually, he freed all the Italian soldiers, without ransom, so that they could return to their homes and spread the world that Hannibal was at war only with Rome, not with Italy, and that he would guarantee every Italian community their former independence and secure borders.

Because winter was drawing to an end, Hannibal left the Po Valley in order to seek a route through the treacherous Apennine mountains. Gaius Flaminius was stationed with his Etruscan army near Arezzo; from this strategic point, weather permitting, he planned to proceed as far as Lucca in his mission to secure the Arno Valley and the Apennine passes. But Hannibal was there first. The crossing of the Apennines was accomplished with little difficulty by travelling as far to the west as possible, that is, at the furthest point away from the enemy.

The only problems arose in the swampy lowlands between the Serchio and the Arno which had been made even wetter by the melting snow and the spring rains. Here, the army had to march through water for four days and the only dry place to sleep at night was on top of a pile of baggage and dead mules. The troops suffered badly, especially the Gallic infantry marching behind the Carthaginians over the swampy trails. Their complaints were loud and there is no doubt that they would have deserted in great numbers if the Carthaginian cavalry, led by Mago and bringing up the rear, had not rendered escape impossible.

The horses, suffering an epidemic of foot-and-mouth disease, died in droves; other epidemics spread through the troops; Hannibal himself lost an eye as the result of an infection. Nonetheless, they reached their goal: Hannibal set up camp by Fiesole while Gaius Flaminius was still waiting at Arezzo for the routes to become passable so that he could block them. But now Hannibal's men had bypassed the defences and, although the consul would probably have been strong enough to secure the mountain passes, he did not feel that his troops were capable of fighting Hannibal on an open field. Thus, the only sensible thing for him to do would have been to wait for reinforcements from the troops in Ariminum which had now become superfluous.

However, Gaius Flaminius, convinced of his military genius, reached a different decision. He cited his successful campaign against the Insubrians in 223 (in reality a prime example of efficient soldiers managing to save the day when an incompetent general bungled) as unmitigated proof that, under Flaminius's command, Hannibal could easily be defeated. Such claims had brought him his second consulate and such hopes had also led a large number of men thirsty for booty to enlist in his forces – historians claim that their numbers were larger than those of the legionnaires.

Hannibal's plan was based in part on these facts. He made a wide detour around these troops, with no intention of attacking them. He let the large cavalry and the Celts, who had much experience in plundering, ravage the surrounding landscape. The complaints and bitterness of the masses, plundered right under the eyes of the hero who had promised them such rich bounties, as well as the enemy's apparent unwillingness to take any action before reinforcements arrived, put Gaius Flaminius in a difficult position. He knew he had to develop a foolproof strategy in order to teach a lesson to this rash and arrogant enemy.

This was exactly what Hannibal expected, and never was there a plan which functioned so perfectly. In great haste, the consul followed the march of his enemy, passing by Arezzo, through the Chiana Valley in the direction of Perugia. He caught up with him in the area around Cortona, where Hannibal, well informed of the march of his foe, had had plenty of time to select a field of battle. It was a defile between two steep mountain walls; one exit was guarded by a high hill and the other by Lake Trasimeno. He secured the hill with the core of his infantry; the light infantry and cavalry hid along both sides of the defile.

Unsuspecting, the Roman columns entered the pass; a thick morning mist hid the enemy troops from view. Just as the vanguard of the Roman forces neared the hill, Hannibal gave the signal to begin the fighting. Suddenly Hannibal's troops poured out of the hills, surrounding the Romans on all sides, and they, unprepared for the attack, had not time to organise themselves into fighting formation. In the panic that ensued, it was every man for himself, and, as Livy tells us, "so great was the fury of the struggle, so totally absorbed was every man in its grim immediacy, that no one even noticed the earthquake which ruined large parts of many Italian towns, altered the course of swift rivers, brought the sea flooding into estuaries and started avalanches in the mountains".

To this Wagnerian accompaniment, the Romans were massacred; many drowned in the lake in their haste to escape.

The main part of the column, inside the pass, was destroyed almost without resistance and the troops, including the consul himself, were slaughtered. The vanguard of the Roman army, 6,000 footsoldiers, was able to push through the enemy infantry; but with no leadership, they marched without direction. The next day they were forced by a section of the Carthaginian cavalry to surrender.

Gaius Flaminius's army was destroyed. Some 15,000 Romans had been killed and an equal number had been taken prisoner. Hannibal's forces, on the other hand, suffered few casualties – 1,500 men, most of them Gauls. To add insult to injury, the cavalry of the Ariminian army under Gaius Centenius, 4,000 men-strong and sent by Gnaeus Servilius to aid his comrade, was surrounded shortly thereafter and defeated by the Carthaginian troops. Many were killed and the rest were taken prisoner. The Roman army had suffered the greatest defeat in its history and Hannibal could continue his march towards Rome unhindered.

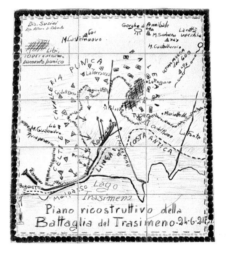

Piano ricostruttivo della Battaglia del Trasimeno·24·6·217

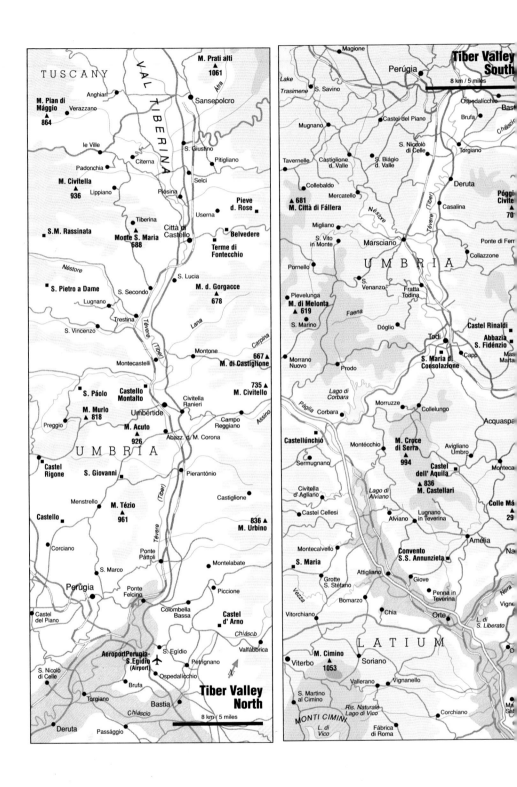

TUSCANY

VAL TIBERINA

M. Prati alti 1061
Afra

Anghiari
Sansepolcro

M. Pian di Mággio 864
Verazzano

le Ville
Citerna
S. Giustino
Pitigliano

Padonchia

M. Civitella 936
Lippiano
Piósina
Selci

Tiberina
Userna
Pieve d. Rose

S.M. Rassinata
Città di Castello
Belvedere

Monte S. Maria 688
Terme di Fontecchio

Néstore
S. Lucia

S. Pietro a Dame
S. Secondo
M. d. Gorgacce 678

Lugnano
Trestina
Lana

S. Vincenzo
Carpina
Montone
667 ▲ M. di Castiglione

Montecastelli

735 ▲ M. Civitello

S. Páolo
Castello Montalto
Civitella Ranieri

M. Murlo ▲ 818
Umbértide
Campo Reggiano
Assino

Preggio
M. Acuto 926
Abazz. d. M. Corona

UMBRIA

Castel Rigone
S. Giovanni
Pierantónio

Menstrello
M. Tézio 961
Castiglione

Castello
Corciano
Ponte Páttoli
836 ▲ M. Urbino

Montelabate

Perúgia
Ponte Felcino
Piccione

Castel del Piano
Colómbella Bassa
Castel d' Arno

Chiáscb

Valfábbrica

AeroportPerugia-S.Egidio (Airport)
S. Egidio
Pétrignano

S. Nicolò di Celle
Brufa
Ospedalicchio

Tiber Valley North

Torgiano
Bastia

Chiáscio

Deruta
Passággio

8 km / 5 miles

Tiber Valley South

Magione

Perúgia
8 km / 5 miles

Lake Trasimene
S. Savino
Ospedalicchio
Bas

Mugnano
Castel del Piano
Brufa
Chiáscl

Tavernelle
Castiglione d. Valle
S. Nicolò di Celle
Torgiano

S. Biágio d. Valle

Collebaldo
Mercatello
Deruta

▲ 681 M. Città di Fállera
Néstore
Casalina
Póggi Civite ▲ 70

Migliano
Már' Tévere (Tiber)

S. Vito in Monte
Marsciano
Ponte di Ferr

UMBRIA
Collazzone

Pornello
S. Venanzo
Fratta Todina

Pievelunga
M. di Melonta ▲ 619
Faena
Dóglio
Castel Rinaldi
Abbazia S. Fidénzio

S. Marino
Todi
Capp
Mas Marta

Morrano Nuovo
Prodo
S. Maria di Consolazione

Lago di Corbara
Morruzze
Collelungo
Acquaspa

Páglia
Corbara

Castellúnchio
Montécchio
M. Croce di Serra ▲ 994
Avigliano Umbro

Sermugnano
Castel dell' Aquila ▲ 836 M. Castellari
Monteca

Civitella d' Agliano
Lago di Alviano
Lugnano in Teverina
Colle Má 29

Castel Cellesi
Alviano

Amélia
Na

Montecalvello
Convento S.S. Annunzieta

S. Maria
Attigliano
Giove

Grotte S. Stéfano
Vezza
Penna in Teverina
Nera
Vigne

Bomarzo
Chia
Orte
L. di S. Liberato

Vitorchiano

LATIUM
O

M. Cimino
Soriano
Viterbo 1053

Vallerano
Vignanello

S. Martino al Cimino
Corchiano
Ma Sai

MONTI CIMINI
Ris. Naturale Lago di Vico

L. di Vico
Fábrica di Roma

THE TIBER VALLEY

Ninety minutes' drive east of Florence, 4,265 ft (1,300 metres) above sea level, on the road up to **Monte Fumaiolo** vehicles wind their way through the clouds, their windscreen wipers invariably hard at work. A scratched-up sign: *Sorgenti del Tevere*, marks a sharp left. Soon afterwards, a playground, campground, souvenir shop and a whole series of restaurants come into view. Everything, however, is closed and boarded shut.

The muddy trails continue on up the mountain, through an oak forest. A streamlet ripples through small stone channels. The forest recedes and a semicircular terrace around a white four-cornered pillar comes into view. An inscription on the side of the pillar reads: "This is the source of Rome's holy river of fate." No name is given, but everyone knows that this tiny clear trickle of water bubbling out of the opening in the wall is the source of the famous river Tiber.

It is worth spending some time up here. The 18th and 19th-century visitors endowed the river with all kinds of superlatives, including "Holy river of culture" and "the Nile of western civilisation". Normally, when one spoke of the Tiber, one meant Rome. In the eulogies of the eternal city, the Tiber was always given its due credit.

National shrine: But what would the Tiber be without Rome? The river has a length of merely 250 miles (400 km). Mussolini was the first to get the idea to appropriate the river at its source, both for Rome and for himself. Ever since the beginning of time, Monte Fumaiolo had been in Tuscan territory. In the year 1934, Mussolini decided to move the border of his home province, Emilia Romagna, so that it formed a kind of noose around the mountain. He declared the spring a place of patriotic devotion. Ever since that time, it has been a kind of national shrine to which everyone, at one time in his life, makes a pilgrimage. The Romans, especially, like to fill their thermoses with its water to prove to people back home that the water of the Tiber is actually drinkable.

The god of the Tiber was, in former times, notorious for his mercurial temper. In cycles of 25 years, the river flooded its banks, placing half of Rome under water and popes would throw consecrated wax lambs into the flood waters in a bid to avert the floods. When the Tiber eventually receded, the plague would break out. It was an age-old problem: Julius Caesar formed a committee of experts to examine the possibilities of re-routing the Tiber around Rome.

Unfortunately their final report was not finished before he died, and the Tiber continued to rage. More recent victims of the river lie in the Protestant Cemetery at the Cestius pyramid. The tombstones tell their stories:"Carl-Philipp Fohr, German painter. Drowned in the Tiber"; "Lady Badhurst, taken from us in the best years of her life. Her horse shied and she was thrown into the turbulent river".

As a waterway, however, the Tiber

ceding
ges: the
ttle
tours of
upper
er; in the
unds of the
azzo Vitelli
Città di
tello.
ht, early
rning near
ugia.

was indispensable. At the height of the Roman empire a whole fleet of ships busied itself transporting grain and wine from Tuscany to the capital. *Otriculum* (now Otricoli), on the border between Umbria and Latium, was the Roman oil port – from here, the coveted Umbrian olive oil was shipped to Rome. It would have been impossible to transport over land the huge quantities of goods which ancient Rome needed for its daily bread.

Today the village of **Otricoli** is located on a hillside, having retreated to this position during the Middle Ages, just as all river-side towns were forced to do for strategic reasons. The ancient Otriculum, though, with its population of 30,000, must have been a thriving harbour, with amphitheatre and vast warehouses. Sheep now graze on pastures between the red ruins.

Huge amounts of wood, used as fuel and for construction in the empire's capital, were rafted down the river from the woods of the upper Tiber Valley. Because the upper part of the Tiber in those days did not have much more water than it does today, sluices were built at regular intervals in order to dam the water. After eight or nine days, the sluices were opened and the boats and rafts floated along on small, constantly regenerated tidal waves. Michelangelo later used this method to bring the long logs he needed to construct the scaffolding up to the dome of St Peter's. His father was the mayor of Caprese in Tuscany, a village located not far from the Tiber.

Strategic value: The Tiber has served as a border during certain periods of history. When the Etruscans arrived, the Umbrians, a folk of moderate temperament and humble demands, retreated to the east banks of the river. By occupying **Perugia**, the Etruscans gained an important centre along this border. After the fall of Rome, the Lombards pushed their way to the western banks of the Tiber. The eastern banks were occupied by the Byzantines whose centre of operations was in Ravenna.

Unaffected by the important movements of history, the relationship of the

Canoeing on the Tiber.

people to their river remained the same right up until the middle of this century. The children, whenever possible, were *sul Tevere*, catching frogs and fish with their bare hands. For the poor, this provided an additional source of income.

The river was also a means of income for millers and washerwomen, rush collectors and basketweavers. The generation of Umbrians now in their forties had their first swimming lessons in the Tiber and drank its water to the magic words taught them by their parents: *L'acqua corrente, la bebe el serpente, la bebe il nostro Dio, la posso bere anch'io*. (The snake drinks from the flowing waters just as our God does, and thus, without a care, I too now drink). Today, no magic words in the world would save anyone who drinks the waters below the source. For the past 30 years farms with tens of thousands of animals pump their untreated waste water directly into the river. This has had catastrophic consequences. The younger generation knows the river under the name "the untouchable".

On the other hand, the beauty of the Tiber landscape has remained unchanged and you can follow its route, along the N3bis, from Città di Castello in the north, through Umbertide and Perugia, through the pottery town of Deruta and on to Todi, one of the oldest of the ancient Umbrian border towns. From there the Tiber swings westward to Orvieto and is channelled into a narrow gorge; the N448 road clings to the mountainside high above, affording spectacular views of this most beautiful river landscape. The river then swings southward, accompanied by the noisy A1 Florence to Rome motorway, but you can continue along the eastern bank high above the river passing through Guardea with its watchtowers and Lugnano in Tevere with its jewel of a Lombardic church. Finally you can seek out Otricoli and the ruins of the Roman Ocriculum river port, right on the southern boundary of Umbria, bidding goodbye to the river as it flows down through an uninterrupted chain of hills to the famous seven on which Rome was built.

nglers prefer more placid waters.

CITTA DI CASTELLO

Città di Castello is located on an intensively farmed plain, one of Italy's leading centres for tobacco growing and production, and is ringed by industrial estates, an unpromising introduction to the town. A glimpse, though, of sand-coloured towers, set against the blue sky, suggests that there is more to see within the medieval core.

A bridge leads over the Tiber into the town. Invariably the deep green river is packed with canoeists. For Dottore Gildoni, the president of the local canoe club, nothing has brought more fame to Città di Castello than his canoeists. They are the vice-champions of Italy. A high point of the club life is the annual *Discesa a Roma*, a canoe trip to Rome held every April, lasting eight days and enjoyed by canoeists from around the world.

Those who want to discover more of the city than its famous canoe club should do so on foot. Just like all towns along the Tiber, Città di Castello is narrow and winding. It is a pedestrian town in which every automobile is a disturbance. Behind the town wall, with its mighty gates, is a village of 25,000 residents. Città di Castello does not bother to curry favour with visitors, as a short stroll through the town will prove. There are the churches and palaces about which every travel guide writes, but the churches prove to be unspectacular, and the yellow-grey facades of the palaces are crumbling.

Culinary centre: That said, Città di Castello is a town which deserves to be explored. First, join the men who gather on the **Piazza Matteotti**. They call themselves Tifernati, after the Latin name of their city, *Tifernum Tiberinum*. As noon approaches, these Tifernati suddenly forsake the square for the long-established Tifernum restaurant, where the food is said to taste better than anywhere else along the Tiber. The reason for its culinary superiority might have political reasons. It seems that Città di Castello could never seriously compete with its

A room with a view.

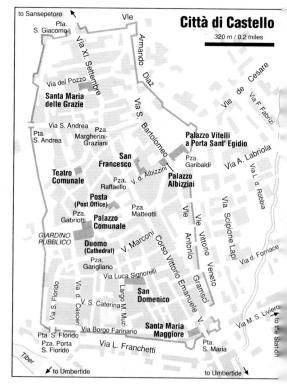

traditional antagonists, Florence and Perugia (it was conquered by both of these cities), so it found another outlet for its aspirations in food. In the vaulted cellars of the Enacoteca, the local wine bar, one again sees some of the Tifernati. This is a wonderful place to sample real Umbrian cuisine; for instance fettucini with rabbit stew, tortellini in duck sauce, wild boar with polenta – and truffles. Città di Castello has shops selling nothing but truffles, and every year in November, a mushroom and truffle market is held here.

Rustic museum: In the kitchen of his farming museum, the **Centro delle tradizioni populari**, Livio dalla Ragione occasionally prepares meals based on recipes which he has collected from all over Umbria. Any visitors lucky enough to be in the museum at the time are invited to share the meals. The museum is located in a venerable old manor on the road to Umbertide. It contains a collection of almost every imaginable implement and tool that a working farm of former times needed in order to survive: spinning wheels, oil presses, looms, tools for working in the fields and in the vineyards, tools for making shoes, furniture and hats, baroque farm machinery from the early days of mechanisation, sieves, pitchers and barrels which still smell of the liquids they once contained. For thousands of years, a large portion of man's practical intelligence went toward the pursuit of agricultural affairs.

Some of the craftsmen's shops in Città di Castello do not look so different from Livio dalla Ragione's museum. There are cabinetmakers, for example, who specialise in rescuing doors and beams from houses which are being torn down. From these they fashion new furniture, modelled in the classical Umbrian style, unique pieces with their own mysterious history.

The family palace of the **Cappellettis** is located directly beside the farming museum. The last of the Cappellettis had a passion for trains. The restless earl spent his entire life building exact scale models of locomotives, and the result is

Città di Castello rooftops.

a palace filled with trains. Everywhere you look, along the walls, on the parapets and galleries, there are trains. And behind the French doors leading to the salon are rail lines on which tiny trains travel round and round. Nestled among them are the busts of his ancestors, cardinals of former times.

In the afternoon, the centre of activity in Citta di Castello moves from the Piazza Matteotti to the *boccia* lanes near the city wall. A look inside the **Tela Umbra** on the **Piazza Costa** is definitely to be recommended. The atmosphere is one of relaxed concentration as the weavers work like sisters of an order, always in pairs.

The Laboratorio Tela Umbra is the most famous example of the region's craft traditions. At the beginning of this century, illiteracy and malnutrition were prevalent across this countryside. The women, though skilled weavers, were forced to spend their lives as washerwomen along the Tiber. In 1908, the American philanthropist Alice Hallgarden Franchetti founded the Tela

Umbra where about a dozen women were provided with looms on which to weave. Their children were cared for in a kindergarten integrated into the workshop. Today, towels woven on the looms of Tela Umbra are used in the Vatican.

Art of the highest order: The highlight of the town for art lovers is the Pinacoteca Comunale, housed in the Palazzo Vitelli, in Via della Cannoniera. The once powerful Vitelli family were great art patrons and Raphael's *Crucifixion*, now in the National Gallery in London, was commissioned by them. It is said that one of the Vitelli daughters, Laura, was in the habit of throwing rejected lovers to their death from the windows of this palace.

Today, the collection here is regarded as the best in Umbria, after the Galleria Nazionale in Perugia. Masterpieces include Signorelli's magnificent *Martyrdom of St Sebastian* and Ghirlandaio's *Coronation of the Virgin*. If modern art is more to your taste, the Collezione Burri (*see feature on The Burri Collection, page 89*) is housed in the Palazzo Albizzini, not far away from the house where Dottore Alberto Burri, considered one of Italy's best living artists, lives and paints.

The cathedral, with its unfinished baroque facade, is no beauty, but you should seek out the museum in the sacristy where the Tesore di Canoscio are displayed, a precious hoard of early Christian silver communion plates and spoons, thought to have been made in Constantinople in the 6th century. They were found in Città di Castello in 1935 and, like so many treasures, approriated by Rome until the local bishop appealed succesfully to Mussolini for their return to the town.

A visit to the town's theatre is an ideal way to get to know the Tifernati. It is a real jewel-box, with deep red carpets and bow-fronted golden balconies.

One last architectural highlight is the palace at the end of the **Vitelli Park**. The ceiling of the entrance hall depicts a scene of unbridled appetites. Here, obese gods are seen tearing off hunks of meat, fish and fruit in a display of carousing mythological greed.

Left, playing *boccia*. **Right**, the Umbrian hills seen from Monte Santa Maria Tiberina.

UMBERTIDE

Motorists making a bee-line from Citta di Castello to Umbertide can arrive there in as little as 20 minutes. However, it would be a mistake to rush the journey. When travelling between Città di Castello and Perugia, a detour is often the shortest way to a discovery.

In the hills above the western bank of the Tiber, for example, lies **Monte Santa Maria Tiberina**, the home of the former noblewoman of the same name. In the Middle Ages, the inhabitants of this area of high ground enjoyed the dubious privileges of being able to mint their own currency, declare war and carry out bloodletting duels in order to settle a point of honour. A duelling ground, of which there are only three in all of Europe, is found beside the church of **San Agostino**. Here, the citizens of former times were allowed to fight a duel to the "last drop of blood" without fear of punishment.

Visitors to this region may be surprised to see a whole cheese flying through the air. Be prepared – it may be followed by a few more cheeses, each weighing several pounds. The 20 to 30 men who appear in hot pursuit are playing a game called *la Ruzzola*, the cheese game. With great animation, they discuss the distances which the cheeses have covered. Then, one of the men will grab a cheese, wrap a leather band tightly around it, and with a running start, a deep breath and a loud bellow, fling it, as with a sling-shot, 350–500 ft (100–150 metres) through the air. Originally, or so we are told, this game was the weekend entertainment of farmers.

On certain days in the area around **Trestina**, the smell of tobacco used to waft deep into the surrounding valleys. Its source was the high, windowless building from whose roofs thick gusts of smoke would stream. These buildings, still visible today, were the smoke houses for tobacco, a crop which arrived here in 1880.

The upper Tiber valley is still Italy's

The defiant battlements of Umbertide

mbol of
iperial
wer.

largest tobacco-producing region. The warm moist climate during the summer months provides ideal growing conditions for the sub-tropical plant. The leaves were originally dried over open fires in the smoke houses, a technique that was later replaced by a sort of central heating system. Today, these smoke houses are nesting places for pigeons; since the 1970s the tobacco leaves have been brought to a central collecting point where they are then dried and processed, for example in the Azienda di Tabaco in Trestina. A cigarette purchased in Italy is likely to have a Tiber tobacco content of 60 percent.

The people of Città di Castello tend to regard **Umbertide**, with its population of 15,000, as dull in the extreme. But this town has a number of good points. No other town along the river rises so picturesquely from the floodlands of the Tiber, no other has such a lovely reflection in the river at sunset. And the fact that every nook and cranny of Umbertide, including its **Rocca** dating from 1385, and the church of Santa Croce containing a *Deposition* (1516) by Signorelli, can be explored in less than an hour means you will have plenty of time to relax on the terrace of the justly popular Trattoria Apennino. It's worth taking a look in the kitchen of this restaurant to see the wide variety of pasta that is made.

Umbertide is a good base for excursions into the nearby countryside. On the N219 road to Gubbio there is the Castelli di Serra Partucci to see, and its neighbour, the impressive 15th-century Castelli di Civitella Ranieri (*see Castles feature, page 134*). You can walk off lunch by driving southwest for 3 miles (5 km) to the village of Montacuto and walking along relatively easy paths to the summit of Monte Acuto 3,038 ft (926 metres) for panoramic views. Alternatively you can drive north to the well-restored hilltown of Montone, birthplace of the condottiere Fortebraccio (*see feature on The Rise and Fall of Andrea Braccio, page 60*), where the church of San Francesco has important frescoes by Antonio da Ferrara.

THE POLIDORI VINEYARD

About 3 miles (4 km) south of Umbertide, an asphalt road to the right leads down to the village of Pierantonio and to the Tiber. Here, to the left, a small dirt road leads up into the vineyards. The turn-off is marked by a notice saying "Agriturismo Colle del Sole".

The dirt road winds its way through the chicken yard of a farm, becoming increasingly steep. At the the top of the hill is an ageing but venerable hacienda, a massive grey stone house nestled amidst a grove of olive trees. Aside from the usual noises of an Umbrian summer evening, absolute stillness rules here.

The proprietress of the Agriturismo Colle del Sole is a small, lively woman called Romana Polidori. She can offer guests a spacious bedroom, hall and bath and a characterful kitchen complete with an open fireplace.

Agriturismi, meaning holiday on a farm, is a widespread and popular form of holiday in Italy. Every tourist office can provide visitors with a list of farms offering such quarters. The vineyard, Polidori, however, offers more than most. In addition to flats for small groups, the entire upper storey of the main house, with space for eight persons, can be reserved. What's more, sampling the product of the vineyard is an integral part of one's stay here.

It is the perfect spot for a relaxing holiday in the countryside. The tranquillity up here is as idyllic as the view, which changes according to the hour of the day. At dawn the Tiber is covered by a blanket of white fog spreading out over the river valley.

In the evenings, the Tiber reflects the last shimmer of the setting sun and the vine leaves take on an antique gold colour. This is the best time to enjoy a glass of Polidori wine

Romana, who has made an art of anticipating the wishes of her guests, is usually on hand with three bottles for tasting – a red, a white and a rosé – courtesy of her vintner husband Carlo. After an hour or so of chatting at the wooden kitchen table in the dim light of the lamp, sipping wine and enjoying some tasty local sheep's cheese, it may become just cool enough to justify lighting a fire.

The Polidori vineyard is the only vineyard in the region which follows the principles of organic farming. The labels on the bottles proudly announce *coltivazzione agrobiologica.*

The vineyard is an old family concern (Carlo's mother, 99 years old, still occupies a chair by the fire in the farmhouse kitchen, a fact which Carlo proudly attributes to the salubrious effect of his wine), but the precise origins of the vineyards on the hill are lost in time. Carlo's grandfather grew wine here trained on maple trees, just as the Romans did 2,000 years ago. He can still remember the donkeys at harvesting time carrying barrels of grapes to a cellar which resembled a cave. At that time, the family produced the wine only for its own needs. When any was sold at all, it was only to guests and neighbours.

Carlo's father, a construction worker by trade, began commercial production on a part-time basis in the 1930s. By the 1960s the family was confident enough to expand production.

It took time and patience to build up the business. To begin with, Carlo travelled to northern Italy and Germany with a suitcase full of wine bottles. He knew hardly a word of German and had no knowledge of marketing, but he set up shop in the lobbies of hotels and in exhibition centres and offered samples of organically-grown wine from Umbria. Serving salmon canapes with the white wine, bread and salami with the rosé wine and small steaks with the red wine, against a blown-up picture of the vineyards and villa, he cut a *bella figura.*

However, fed up with such gruelling legwork and feeling like a travelling salesman, he was struck by the idea of inviting potential buyers to visit the Polidori vineyard and see the benefits of organic wine-growing for themselves. It was the best thing he could have done.

In 1978, the Polidori product was given a DOC classification, a mark of quality. Today business is thriving. Though using organic techniques means that the yield is 10 percent lower than intensive viticulture, Carlo finds a ready market for all his products. Being additive free, as you will discover if you visit the vineyard, customers are rarely plagued by a morning after hangover.

PERUGIA

The route from Umbertide to Perugia is 25 miles (40 km) and makes for one of the most interesting journeys in the region. For one thing, it passes the elegant castle of **Ascagnano** (5 miles/8 km south of Umbertide on the west bank of the Tiber). The castle has its own tale to tell visitors – this time one of romance.

At the beginning of the 19th century, a ball was held in Rome for members of the upper nobility. Although not officially invited, the beautiful 16-year-old Marianna Florenzi from Ascagnano was talked into attending. The hostess greeted Marianna's arrival with sarcasm, drawing attention to her country origins: "My dear child, perhaps it is the custom in Perugia to come uninvited to a ball. But we are in Rome."

At this obvious snub, Marianna wanted to leave, but several of the men present had already noticed the beautiful girl from Ascagnano. One of them stepped out of the crowd, took her hand and partnered her in the opening dance. The young man was the crown prince of Bavaria and duke of Perugia, later to become King Ludwig I. For 30 years he was devoted, though not necessarily faithful, to his Marianna. Today visitors to Ascagnano castle can conjecture on the purpose of a secret stairway leading from a wardrobe in Marianna's room.

Balls still take place every weekend in this region, most spectacularly in a popular club known as Brooklyn near Perugia, on the road to Gualdo Tadino. They are popular events; every Saturday evening, crowds throng here as if to a soccer match, despite the 15,000 lire entrance fee. Things are done in great style – violins provide the music, waves of perfume ascend from acres of décolletage, waiters weave through the crowds as on a slalom course with bowls full of olives on their outstretched arms – and yet it is firmly a family occasion, in which everyone participates. As the evening lengthens the violins are replaced by saxophones playing such tunes as *Arreviderci Roma*, children fall asleep on banks of coats, and on the dance floor high-heeled girls twirl with white-bearded men and teachers with mechanics. There's nowhere like it outside Italy, and it is well worth experiencing if you are passing through at the weekend.

The capital of Umbria: Perugia, stretching across several hills, looks out over the valley of the Tiber. At one time, this city was the most powerful member in the league of cities of the Etruscans, a people whose culture was so thoroughly suppressed by the Romans that today it is a mere footnote in history. It could be argued that the conflict between the Romans and the Etruscans was based on the need for legitimacy. For reasons of propaganda, the Romans legitimised their conquest of the Hellenic world by pointing out that the Etruscans had maintained close ties with the Greeks. Perugia was a flowering Etruscan community up until the conquest by Octavian in the year 40 BC. This was due partly to its clever politics based on making the right treaty at the right time and partly to its unconquerable defensive walls.

eceding
ges:
rugia, a city
eeped in
story.
ft, a detail
the facade
the Oratario
San
rnadino.
ght, the
urch of San
etro.

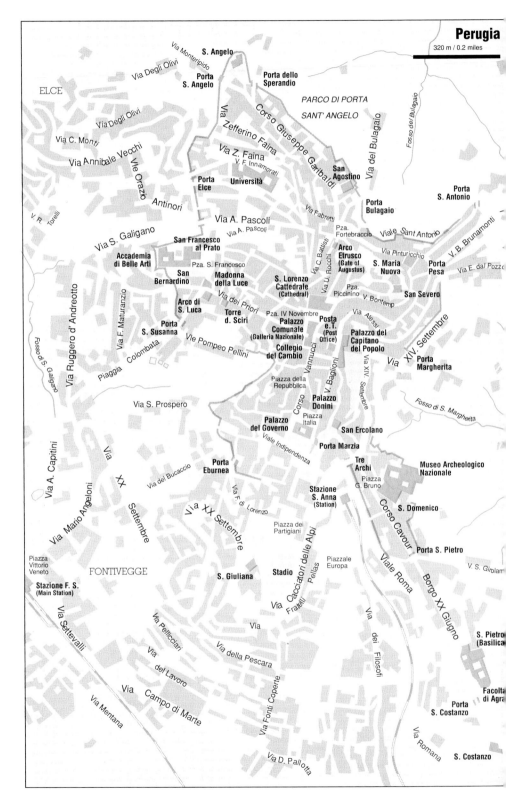

Perugia

320 m / 0.2 miles

ELCE

Via Monteripido

S. Angelo

Porta
S. Angelo

Porta dello
Sperandido

PARCO DI PORTA
SANT' ANGELO

Via Degli Olivi

Via Degli Olivi

Via C. Monti

Via Annibale Vecchi

Vie Orazio

Antinori

V. R. Torelli

Corso Giuseppe Garibaldi

Via Zefferino Faina

Via Z. Faina

V. F. Innamorati

Porta
Elce

Università

San
Agostino

Via del Bulagaio

Fosso del Bulagaio

Porta
S. Antonio

Porta
Bulagaio

Via Fabretti

Via S. Galigano

Via A. Pascoli

Via A. Pascoli

Pza.
Fortebraccio

Viale Sant Antonio

Via Pinturicchio

V. B. Brunamonti

San Francesco
al Prato

Accademia
di Belle Arti

Pza. S. Francesco

San
Bernardino

Madonna
della Luce

Arco di
S. Luca

Via dei Priori

Torre
d. Sciri

Pza. IV Novembre

Arco
Etrusco
(Gate of
Augustus)

Via C. Battisti

Via U. Rocchi

S. Maria
Nuova

Porta
Pesa

Via E. dal Pozzo

S. Lorenzo
Cattedrale
(Cathedral)

Pza.
Piccinino

V. Bontemp

San Severo

Fosso di S. Galigano

Via Ruggero d'Andreotto

Via F. Maturanzio

Porta
S. Susanna

Vle Pompeo Pellini

Colombata

Piaggia

Palazzo
Comunale
(Galleria Nazionale)

Collegio
del Cambio

Posta
e.T.
(Post
Office)

Via Alessi

Palazzo del
Capitano
del Popolo

Vannucci

V. Baglioni

XIV. Settembre

Via XIV.
Settembre

Via

XIV. Settembre

Porta
Margherita

Via S. Prospero

Corso

Piazza della
Repubblica

Palazzo
Donini

Piazza
Italia

Fosso di S. Margherita

Palazzo
del Governo

Viale Indipendenza

San Ercolano

Via A. Capitini

Via Mario Angeloni

Via

XX

Settembre

Via del Bucaccio

Porta
Eburnea

Via F. di Lorenzo

Via XX Settembre

Porta Marzia

Tre
Archi

Piazza
G. Bruno

Museo Archeologico
Nazionale

Corso Cavour

S. Domenico

Stazione
S. Anna
(Station)

Piazza dei
Partigiani

Porta S. Pietro

V. S. Girolam

Piazza
Vittorio
Veneto

Stazione F. S.
(Main Station)

FONTIVEGGE

S. Giuliana

Stadio

Cacciatori delle Alpi

Pellas

Piazzale
Europa

Viale Roma

Borgo XX Giugno

S. Pietro
(Basilica

Via Settevalli

Via Pelliccari

Via
del Lavoro

Via Campo di Marte

Via Mentana

Via della Pescara

Via
Fratelli

Via

Via Fonti Coperte

Via dei
Filosofi

Facolta
di Agra

Porta
S. Costanzo

Via D. Pallotta

Via Romana

S. Costanzo

The former city fathers now lie in a vault below the walls. *Ipogeo* is the Italian name for such a subterranean gravesite. Like most of the archaeological sites of this country, the **Ipogeo dei Volumni** is difficult to find. It is safely hidden in a small yellow pavilion which is located just after a sharp right curve along the road which leads from Ponte San Giovanni (in the southeast) up to the old town.

From the car park at the **Piazza degli Invalidi** in the southern part of the city, an escalator carries visitors up to a setting of sublime unreality, the **Rocca Paolina**, the fantasy of a baroque-era pope. Visitors are immersed in a world of mighty halls, gates, ramps and vaults in a yellowish twilight, a labyrinth of passageways, occasionally occupied by a fountain or a stove and chimney. In places water drips down the walls and in others passageways disappear into dark caverns. At the most remote point of this eerie underworld there is a small plaque. On it is written, "In consideration of the fact that the castle of Perugia was built by the popes in order to tame the arrogance of the people of Perugia, the following decree is issued: the castle of Perugia is declared from this day on as the property of the city. Issued on 15 October, 1860."

Italy's largest fortress: The "arrogance of the people of Perugia" was a phrase coined by Pope Paul III. The assertion was based on their unconcealed aversion to papal authority. It was not until 1540 that Perugia succumbed to the rule of the pope (three years after Florence). Immediately thereafter, Paul III ordered his chief builder, Sangallo, to construct a castle from which the city could be defended as well as kept in check. An entire section of the city, including a church and monastery, was torn down in order to realise this project. Three years later the Rocca Paolina, Italy's largest fortress, was completed. The citizens of Perugia accepted this domination for three centuries, but destroyed the fortifications in 1860. The exit from the remains are through a massive gate; those who turn around for a last look

e Corso
annucci.

will recognise the heads of the gods on the Etruscan **Porta Marzia** overhead.

The distinguished **Corso Vannucci** cuts a broad pathway across the top of the hill on which the centre of the old town is located. It starts on the **Piazza Italia**, above the Rocca Paolina. The most beautiful time of day here is at sunset when the last rays of the sun shining on the white tower of the **Church of the Dominicans** endow it with a rose-coloured hue. The Corso, lined with palaces and banks, bars and sidewalk cafés, stretches as far as the Piazza IV Novembre, dominated by the cathedral, the Palazzo dei Priori and the Fontana Maggiore and the heart of Perugia. During the murderous conflicts that broke out in the city, the blood of the massacred was said to flow through the sloping alleyways to the left and right of the Corso – through "Witch Alley", "Moon Alley" and the "Street of Wisdom". One of the bloodiest conflicts was between the rival Oddi and Baglioni families. When the Baglionis eventually won, they set about killing each other. It was

to put an end to this massacre that Pope Paul III annexed the city and abolished all forms of self-government here. The builder Sangallo incorporated the **Baglioni Palace** into his Rocca Paolina. Later, Julius III allowed the Perugians a limited amount of autonomy.

Sermons of the saints: While the nobility was immersed in its power struggles, the ordinary people were preoccupied by religion. The citizens congregated at the **Piazza San Francesco** to hear the sermons preached by the poverty-stricken Francis from neighbouring Assisi. They witnessed the self-flagellation of the hermit Ranieri on the square in front of the cathedral, an act which met with such enthusiasm that soon thereafter hundreds of thousands of people in Europe sought salvation in the lash. St Bernard of Siena addressed this restless power-hungry folk from the heights of the small outside pulpit beside the portal of the cathedral on the **Piazza IV Novembre**.

Today the steps of the cathedral serve as a gallery for visitors from around the

The heart of the Umbrian capital: Piazza IV Novembre and the Font Maggiore.

world. If you join them, seated with your back to the cathedral, you can take in the details of the Fontana Maggiore, an outstanding monument to that most humble, but essential of commodities, water. The fountain dates to 1277 and is covered in sculptures carved by Nicolo Pisano and his son Giovanni: biblical scenes, the Labours of the Months, Roman mythology, scenes from Aesop's fable, the lion and griffin symbol of Perugia – they are all here carved in masterful detail, along with statues representing Lake Trasimeno (a woman holding a fish), Perugia (a woman holding a cornucopia) and Euliste, the mythological founder of the city.

Opposite are the various buildings that comprise the Palazzo dei Priori. Perugians claim this to be the most beautiful ensemble in Umbria; you may not agree, but it is not wise to voice your opinion. Externally sombre, the interiors are, however, gorgeous. Facing the cathedral is the entrance to the Sala dei Notari, the lawyer's chamber, reached by a fan-shaped flight of steps and frescoed with coats of arms of leading Perugian families. Round the corner, in Corso Vannucci, is the entrance to the Sala del Collegio della Mercanza, the Merchant's Guild, decorated with carved poplar and walnut panelling.

Next comes the entrance to the Collegio del Cambio (Exchange Guild), containing Perugino's finest work. His frescoes follow the humanistic idea that the ancient philosophers, including Socrates and Plato, expressed ideas that were close to Christian ethical and moral principles, and the paintings draw parallels between pagan and Christian ideals. Here too Perugino painted a self-portrait of unabashed realism; he frowns from beneath his red cap, a plump-featured man with double chin and heavy black eyebrows. Finally, the main portal of the palazzo leads to the offices of the local authority that governs the *comune* of Perugia and a lift takes you to the upper floor housing the Galleria Nazionale dell'Umbria. Here many of the acknowledged masterpieces of the Umbrian Renaissance are on display.

Left, altar painting by Bernadino Pinturicchio. Right, the subterranean Via Bagliona below the Rocca Paolina.

Highlights include Fiorenzo di Lorenzo's lovely *Adoration of the Magi* and two paintings by Perugino: an early work, the *Adoration of the Magi* (1475) and a mature work, *Christ Entombed*, a stark and expressive painting of the dead Christ.

From Piazza IV Novembre, the Via dei Priori leads down to the stunning Oratorio di San Bernardino. This small chapel stands on the side of a large square where students from the nearby Academy of Art kill time between lectures. Alongside is the vast and ruinous church of San Francesco al Prato, which was built on unstable ground and began collapsing as early as the 15th century. San Bernardino's facade is covered in swirling, dancing angels, singing and playing musical instruments, carved by the great Florentine sculptor, Agostino di Duccio, in 1451. The richly intricate figures, in their diaphanous drapery, are reminiscent of Alphonse Mucha's art nouveau posters of the Four Seasons.

The oratory was built to honour one of Umbria's more unusual saints. Bernardino not only preached peace and reconciliation, trying to stop the constant in-fighting between rival Umbrian towns, he also helped to draw up statutes for towns like Perugia intended to regulate local government and put an end to despotism and strife. Bernardino recently suffered the indignity of being declared patron saint of advertising in recognition of his persuasiveness.

Quiet refuges: Having seen the major sights of Perugia, there is a choice of places to go to escape the heat and noise of the city. One of the best is the church of **Sant'Angelo**, a simple circular structure dating from the 6th century lying about a 15-minute walk up Corso Garibaldi, between meadows and vineyards. Relax here for an hour or so and then continue to the monastery of **Sant'Agnese**. The nuns boast a fresco by the renowned Perugino and are more than willing to show it to visitors, albeit with the necessary precautions. As soon as a visitor enters the monastery, a bell starts ringing and continues incessantly while two nuns escort the guest to the picture. The nuns' attitude to the picture is one of deep reverence, as though the painting could work miracles. The impartial observer merely sees a Madonna between two saints. In the hand of the saint on the left is a small bell, and at his feet a small pig.

In the opposite direction, Corso Cavour leads to the church of **San Domenico**, little visited despite the fact that it contains the exquisite tomb of Pope Benedict XI, hailed as the finest example of Gothic funerary art in Italy. The next door cloister contains the **National Archaeology Museum of Umbria** and you can loose youself for an hour or more enjoying the fine views from the gallery windows as you wander amongst case after case of Etruscan and Roman pottery and bronzework.

Finally, don't miss **San Pietro**, further out along the same road. The armrests of the choir stalls, carved in 1525, form a complete bestiary of lions, ducks, crocodiles, dragons and dolphins, and a door at the rear of the church leads to a tiny balcony with a memorable view right across the Tiber valley to Assisi.

Left and right, Perugians young and old.

TODI

Todi is everything one could hope for in a medieval Italian town. It is steeped in history and patently looks the part. It was here that in 1310 the Perugians finally won control of the region.

Looking down on the Tiber from **Montemolino Castle**, you can make out the former battlefield on the other bank. Beyond, Todi perches on the mountain. The town's location is often compared to that of an eagle's nest, and probably accounts for the legend that Todi was founded on the spot where an eagle let a napkin drop that it had seized from an Etruscan banqueting table. According to this story, all the members of the founding generation would have fitted around one large table.

On a typical Umbrian morning, misty in the valley bottom and bright above, Todi appears to the approaching traveller much like the heavenly Jerusalem – bathed in celestial light. Crossing the modern Tiber bridge, you will notice, in the distance, the iron construction of its predecessor. Bridges often contribute substantially to the beauty of a river, but most bridges of the Tiber cannot be said to add anything very scenic. The exceptions are those in Rome and the old hanging bridge here. It was brought from Florence in 1942; before then there was only a ferry crossing here.

The first thing visitors to Todi notices is the church of **Santa Maria Consolazione**, a handsome domed Renaissance building nestling among trees. The people of Todi, always in the shadow of Perugia, like to claim that this church was designed by Bramante, the architect of St Peter's in Rome,because there are many similarites between the two churches, but no proof supports the claim. The church evokes mixed emotions. It is an elegant structure with a dome-topped cubic nave, and tall polygonal apses off each face of the cube. Seen from afar, set against its background of wooded hills, it is a pleasing building, though not, as some have **Relaxing in the grounds of the Rocca Montemolino**

Todi

160 m / 0.1 miles

Pta. Perugina

San Francesco

S. Prassede

Palazzo Vescovile

Santa Maria (Cathedral)

Pza. d. Popolo

Palazzo del Capitano

Palazzo del Popolo

Posta

Pza. (Post Office)

Pta. Orvietana

Palazzo dei Priori

Garibaldi

San Carlo

Pza. Iacopone

Pza. Oberdan

Via Ciuffelli

Fonte Cesia

Mercato Vecchio

Pta. Marzia

San Fortunato

Via S. Fortuna

Via Roma

Rocca

Pza. IV. Novembre

Pta. Libera

Pta. d. Catena

Via Matteot.

Via della Vittoria

Pta. Aurea

Santa Maria in Camuccia

Via d. Consolazione

Pta. Amerina

Santa Maria della Consolazione

Borgo Nuovo

Muraglia

Via del Duomo

Via Cesta

Viale di S. Fillippo

dubbed it, Italy's finest Renaissance church. Inside, though, all pleasure stops; the nave is marred by huge and lifeless baroque figures of the Apostles and a dreadful fresco of the Virgin.

The houses of the town are crowded together behind the church. The narrow passageways and thousands of steps wind between walls which tower like cliffs. The town's highest point is the majestic **Piazza del Popolo**. The palaces here are restrained and yet grand, bearing witness to the chivalrous medieval spirit that prevailed before the Renaissance.The square has changed little in appearance since the 14th century. The main buildings are the Palazzo dei Priori, now serving as the town library with shops below, completed in 1369, the Palazzo del Capitano, dating to 1292 and fronted by a fine staircase, and the Palazzo del Populo, with its Ghebelline fishtail battlements, begun in 1213 and one of the oldest surviving civic buildings in Italy.

The cathedral, at the opposite end of the square, incorporates Romanesque,

Gothic and Renaissance features. The square columns of the nave have capitals carved with Biblical scenes; the outstanding woodwork of the choir stalls is under restoration, but you may catch glimpses of the exquisite intarsia work panels made in 1530. The crypt dates to pre-Roman times, for the cathedral was built on top of an Etruscan temple.

The well-preserved city walls provide evidence of the three phases of the city's development. Starting as a small Umbrian border village, it grew into a Roman town liberally endowed with baths and theatres and went on to become a prominent medieval city with its own university. The town's archaeological museum, in the Palazzo del Capitano, is unfortuantely closed for the forseeable future for restoration.

In the absence of the museum, Don Mario from the church of Santa Maria in Camuccio is said to be the best authority on the history of Todi. His answer to this claim is "In the kingdom of the blind, the person with one eye is the king," and goes on to explain that the museums in

e Piazza
l Popolo
d cathedral
Todi.

Todi have been closed for the past 20 years, because they simply could not cope with the sheer number of art treasures and historical artifacts. Don Mario is the one person trying to bring order into this chaos.

The difficulties of his job is illustrated by the fact that a sculpture of the Virgin and Child was recently stolen from here. This particular statue had a curious history. In the 15th-century Augustinian priests sawed off the head of the Virgin because they found it too stern and replaced it with a friendlier face. The expressions of the figures had caused controversy as early as the 12th century, when the sculpture was used as an argument by the church in its conflict with the German emperor. It was argued that the Virgin had a severe look because she represented the church, and the child on her lap had a praying countenance because he symbolised the German emperor. This ruler, it was pointed out, received his authority from the church and was only allowed to use it under supervision. In other words, it was perceived as a political sculpture.

This work has since been retrieved and is now in Perugia being restored, but it will probably remain there. The Ministry demands certain security precautions and Todi cannot afford them.

Before you leave the piazza, look again at the layout. Note that there are only four narrow exits from the square, one at each angle. Originally there was a gate at each of the corners so that the whole piazza could be sealed off and defended in the event of an attack.

For lunch the restaurant Umbria, hidden behind the Palazzo del Capitano, is strongly recommended, especially for its wild boar with red wine. Afterwards, walk off the effects by exploring the upper part of the town, reached through streets filled with flowers and with views over unspoiled countryside, the reason why so many wealthy Romans have bought second homes here. The church of San Fortunato, built at the end of the 13th century, stands at the highest point of the town, It is dedicated to the appropriately named bishop of Todi who led the citizens in succesful resistance to an attack by Totila the Goth. The magnificent portal was added in 1436. It is an exquisite work, crowded with figures and vivid vignettes; naked figures cavort amongst vine leaves between the sterner figures of Church fathers.

The echoing airy interior is, for once, not a disappointment. Sunlight pours in through the windows lighting the slender columns of the nave. The walls are painted white or stripped to bare stone, so the few surviving frescoes shine out with colour; the best fresco, in the fourth chapel on the right, is Masolino da Panicale's dreamy *Madonna and Child*.

The crypt contains the huge baroque mausoleum of Saints Cassianus and Callixtus. A much more modest memorial marks the burial place of the Franciscan poet Jacapone, who composed the *Stabat Mater*. As a critic of Pope Boniface VIII he spent five years in prison for leading a Franciscan revolt against Church corruption. Perhaps that is why one of Italy's great early medieval poets was not given a more imposing memorial.

Left, the interior of Santa Maria della Consolazion **Right**, the same church viewed from the outside.

ORVIETO

Beyond Todi, the Tiber begins its difficult search for a new valley. The mountains are closer together and the river widens into the **Corbara Reservoir**. High above this body of water, perched on a cliff, is **Civitella del Lago** and on the other side is **Orvieto**.

In a geographical sense, Orvieto is not really one of the Tiber cities. It actually lies on the Paglia which flows into the Tiber just south of the city. But seen from an historical perspective, Orvieto is definitely a city of the Tiber. Ancient Orvieto's harbour at *Palianum* was the river's northernmost port for large ships.

Livy mentioned a port at this site where ships stopped on moonless nights, and Pliny the Younger reported that he had his belongings brought by ship from Rome to Città de Castello where he had purchased an estate. Undoubtedly the goods would have had to be transferred to smaller ships in Palianum. The port must have still been in operation in the Middle Ages because the marble used for Orvieto's cathedral was brought by ship from Rome, a distance of almost 120 miles (200 km) along the Tiber.

Of course, the large ships of antiquity were smaller than those of today and the Tiber and Paglia were also rather mightier, but even with these considerations in mind it is difficult, when standing on the overgrown peninsula between these two shallow rivers, to imagine that there ever could have been heavy ship traffic here. However, archaeological digs in the 1920s uncovered large numbers of coins between the foundations of the grain storage buildings and those of the harbour, and exploration in the area leads to some surprising discoveries, for example an ancient archway behind a curtain of ivy.

The city of Orvieto, with an elevation of 490 ft (150 metres), is situated on the plateau of a volcanic plug. Sheer cliffs fall to the valley floor beneath its walls. The soft, easily eroded tufa of the plateau has been eroded by weather and quarrying activities for the last 2,500 years. Even in Roman times the cliffs were unstable and laws prevented houses from being built round the cliff edge, called the *rupe*. In 1977 there was a major landslide that threatened to demolish parts of the city. The vibration from heavy traffic contributes to the erosion and a plan, yet to be implemented, has been devised to protect the city from further destruction. The cliff will be supported from all sides and the sewer and water supply systems must be totally renovated. The surrounding area is to be declared an archaeological zone and all automobile traffic banned from the city. New tunnels and shafts will be bored in the brown tufa and escalators and elevators will transport people from a large car park into the pedestrian city.

As early as 1888 an amazingly simple and clean transportation system was introduced here – the water-mountain-railway. Two carriages, connected with a cable and having large water containers under their floors, plied their way

eceding
ges: Orievto
dominated
the
thedral of
nta Maria.
e exquisite
thedral
ade. Left,
ve groves
the
untryside
und
vieto.

Orvieto

320 m / 0.2 miles

between the terminus in the valley, at Orvieto Scalo, and the upper town. The container of the wagon at the upper end of the line was filled with water and that of the wagon in the valley was emptied. When the wagon on the mountain started down, it pulled the substantially lighter valley wagon up. Today, an electrically-powered train travels this route.

Etruscan places: On the main road from Orvieto **Scalo** to the upper town you will notice small yellow signs with the inscription *Tombe del Crocifisso del Tuffo*. Behind these is hidden an Etruscan necropolis where entire networks of streets have been uncovered. The Etruscans built the first roadways up to the plateau, settled there and established a second town below for their dead. Their burial practices were elaborate. Corpses were wrapped and stretched out on benches, and objects needed for daily life as well as weapons were placed nearby. Each room was shared by two bodies. Further traces of the Etruscans are found in the upper town at the edge of the **Piazza Cahen** – the **Tempio**

Belvedere, the only above-ground remains of an Etruscan temple.

Just beside this temple is an unusual gem of baroque well architecture – the Pozzo di San Patrizio (St Patrick's Well – so called because of its supposed resemblance to a cave in which St Patrick dwelled in Ireland). Pope Clemens VI, after the sacking of Rome in 1527, was searching for a safe refuge. The **Rocca** in Orvieto suited his taste precisely, but it was lacking a well for use in the event of a siege. Sangallo, the fortress architect of Perugia, had a 197 ft (60 metre) shaft drilled into the rock and built a two-storey house over the shaft. Light shone through 72 large windows so that even the lowest steps were lit. In case of emergency, a mule train could transport the water to the top in buckets. The problem of two-way traffic was solved by means of a parallel stair construction; packhorses could descend by one set of steps to collect water and ascend by another, thus avoiding collisions. The idea, by the way, came from Leonardo da Vinci, who invented this

The lost soul in hell – a detail of the relief by Lorenzo Maitani on the cathedral facade.

type of double spiral stairway for a brothel. Orvieto was never under siege after that time. However, the city still profits from its well: queues of tourists pay dearly to make the difficult descent to the bottom of the well; worth it, though for the strange subterranean lighting effect.

Admission to the cathedral of **Santa Maria** is, on the other hand, free. It is one of the world's most beautiful cathedrals. For three centuries, countless artists and architects as well as many generations of Orvieto citizens strove to perfect the building. You can best appreciate its magnificent facade at noon, when the sun streams into all its pediments and portals.

The cathedral owes its existence to the miracle that ocurred at Bolsena, the small town on the shores of Lake Bolsena in Tuscany, 13 miles (21 km) west of Orvieto. The miracle occurred in 1263 when a Bohemian priest, travelling to Rome to resolve his doubts over the doctrine of transubstantiation, celebrated mass in the town: the communion host turned to literal flesh at the consecration and drops of human blood spilled on to the altar cloth. Pope Urban IV instituted the feast of Corpus Christi as a result, and Orvieto was chosen to house the blood-stained relic.

The first Corpus Christi Day Procession in honour of this miracle was held in Orvieto in 1337. This procession, still held today in period costumes, is Orvieto's largest festival. Another festival, second best to the Corpus Christi one, is that of Palombella. Its main attraction is a white dove, representing the holy ghost, which slides along a thin wire stretching from the roof of the church of St Francis to the main portal of the cathedral. This spectacle lasts no longer than a minute, and those who miss it must wait until next Pentecost to see it again.

The foundation stone of Orvieto's cathedral was laid in 1290 at a critical point in architectural history. Gothic was just becoming fashionable and work on the cathedral, planned in Romanesque style, ground to a halt until the

*he Fall of
*e Damned –
*esco in
*rvieto
*athedral by
*uca
ignorelli.

Sienese architect Lorenzo Maitani was brought in to graft a new design on to the partly built structure. He did a brilliant job and was responsible for the distinctive Sienese flavour of the building, built in narrow alternating bands of white travertine and dove-grey tufa.

The extraordinarily rich carving of the facade cleverly disguises four huge masonry pillars from the original Romanesque design. The bas reliefs (partly covered by perspex sheets because of repeated vandalism) are a *tour de force*, illustrating (from left to right) Genesis, the stories of Abraham and David, the Life of Christ and the Last Judgement. More than 150 masons contributed to the work, including Maitani himself, and Andrea Pisano. You could spend an hour or more absorbing these intricate scenes; note the humour of God delving into the side of Adam to get a rib from which to fashion Eve, and Eve hiding from her Creator in the bushes; the charm of the Nativity scene where Mary lifts the blanket to gaze at her sleeping son while Joseph nods, and the real human

misery in the faces of the wretched souls damned to eternal torment in the Judgement scenes.

Inside, nothing interrupts the view to tall east window filled with 14th-century stained glass, seen across a sun-dappled floor of ox-blood coloured marble. Signorelli's outstanding frescoes of the AntiChrist and the end of the world are under restoration and under covers. A small exhibition, with photographs of the cleaning work, serves to remind us of the terrifying force of these apocalyptic scenes in which metal-winged monsters, reminiscent of modern sci-fi and fantasy art, carry the damned to Hell and twisted bodies fly everywhere as if the laws of gravity have been suspended as the world ends in chaos and dissolution.

The **Archaeological Museum** of Orvieto is located in the **Palazzo Faina**, across from the cathedral. The collection is impressive but unfortunately provides the visitor with no explanatory information. The head of Medusa, probably of Etruscan origin, belongs to the collection. Two vampire teeth protrude out of her contorted mouth, proof that the idea of supernatural blood-suckers with a human face dates back to ancient times. There are also some delicate painted clay heads and a life-size rendering of a man.

Orvieto is a city of concentrated urbanism. Almost every square foot of the cliffs are inhabited. It is easy to see that the town enjoyed the patronage of a number of popes. The architecture is more varied than that of the other Tiber cities. It also enjoys a rich culinary heritage. Take the opportunity to sample the truffles, wine and wild boar ham in the shops under the arches of the **Corso Cavour** or at the weekly market. The latter is found at the foot of the impressive **Palazzo del Popolo**, a building which is being turned into a congress centre. If you visit the monastery of San Francesco, stop for an *espresso* at the popular **Piazza della Repubblica**, with a view of the octagonal campanile of the 11th-century church of **Sant'-Andrea**. In the evening, one should return to the animated Corso.

Left, medieval defensive tower. Right, the market in Orvieto in front of the Palazzo del Popolo. Following pages: statuesque cypresses near Via Flaminia; in the vineyards.

THE VIA FLAMINIA

On many maps, the road from Otricoli to the Scheggia Pass (a distance of about 103 miles/165 km) is simply called "No.3". But in travel guides, on road signs and in towns it bears its original name, the **Via Flaminia**. It is an extremely ancient road – its estimated date of construction is 220 BC – and was named after Gaius Flaminius, an ill-starred general under whose rule it was built. In 217 BC, Flaminius lost the Battle of Lake Trasimeno, along with his life, to the invading army of Hannibal.

Artery of Empire: The Via Flaminia linked Rome with the fortress at *Ariminum* on the Adriatic Sea (now the resort of Rimini) and was originally built as a military road, enabling the army to move men and supplies quickly between Rome and the northern frontiers of the empire. Starting in about AD 30, the Via Aemilia, which led to *Placentia* (Piacenza), joined the Via Flaminia. From Placentia, roads to the north and west fanned out. In short, one could journey as far as *Arelate* (Arles) in Provence by means of the Via Flaminia, continuing on to the Iberian peninsula.

Rome's network of roads provided it with the necessary means for expansion. As soon as the weapons of the conqueror were laid down, the picks and shovels were taken up. The streets ran as straight as a die and many were paved; in the mountains they usually narrowed to one lane. Sometimes columns of marching soldiers and the wagon trains transporting goods stretched as far as they eye could see, especially when Nero travelled with 1,000 wagons. Soldiers carrying baggage could march about 20 miles (30 km) per day, sometimes more. Caesar's forced marches were notorious. A post coach with changes of horses could travel 46 miles (75 km) a day. There were also trained messengers who ran at a speed of 62 miles (100 km) per day.

The military wayfarers were soon joined by civilian ones. The Roman Empire, as it grew, also became a world trading power, and the network of roads connected Rome to its many ports. From these, ships sailed across the Mediterranean and even as far as the Atlantic.

Settlements also flourished along the road. Some were deliberately planned new towns, called *coloniae*, retirement settlements for army veterans. Others were trading posts which grew into market towns in the plains, beneath the hilltop towns of the Etruscans and Umbrians.

Caesar Augustus, who was revered as a god for his vigorous expansion of the Roman Empire, was personally responsible for ensuring that Rome was attainable from all directions. He concentrated on the Via Flaminia, building several new bridges along this route, one of which is the superb specimen at *Narnia* (Narni), the Pons Augusti. With the completion of other roads – the Via Appia, Via Aurelia, etc – the Roman Empire had an extremely efficient transportation network at its disposal.

The roads were diverted when a dif-

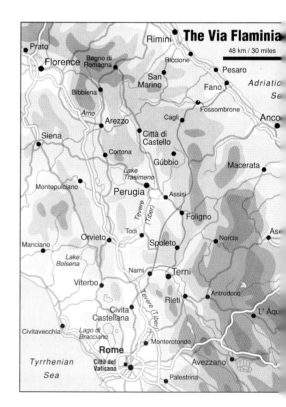

ferent route with new stations seemed more useful. Thus the old route from Narni to Bevagna to Forum Flaminii was abandoned and a new road leading through Narni, Terni, Spoleto and Foligno was constructed.

At Carsulae, the field of ruins near San Gemini Fonte north of Terni, one can glean an impression of the sad fate of a developing settlement when the road leading to it was abandoned. The people left the city in order to find a subsistence elsewhere and Carsulae was deserted. During the Middle Ages, two cloister orders settled into the ruins here, but by 1317 they, too, had abandoned the infertile region.

The great migrations: The Via Flaminia not only brought prosperity to Umbria; it was also the route by which the new religion of Christianity was introduced to the region by Syrian merchants who, landing at the Adriatic port of Ancona, or at Rome's own port of Ostia, travelled up and down this artery, buying and selling and spreading the Gospel message as early as the 3rd century AD.

Several of the region's saints (such as Assisi's San Rufino) became martyrs.

When the Roman empire started to crumble invading armies also found the Via Flaminia useful, conquering populations from Ravenna down to Rome. The Goths paralysed the empire, turning the transportation routes into arteries of blood. The Lombards settled into Spoleto and ruled as dukes until the 12th century, assimilating with the population by means of intermarriage. Later, the groaning carts of the merchants rolled over the route. Ancona grew into the Papal States' busiest port of trade.

But the road was not only a route for war and trouble. It was also a vital avenue of communication. Intellectual impulses followed along these lines, philosophies, scientific discoveries, religion, reforms and counter-reforms. St Francis of Assisi hastened down the Via Flaminia towards Rome in order to shore up the church of the Lord. And Michelangelo came from Florence to see the intensely coloured frescos of Fra Filippo Lippi in the cathedral in Spoleto.

NARNI

The bridge of Emperor Augustus was one of antiquity's most amazing feats of engineering. Stretching across the Nera Valley with four mighty arches, it was 525 ft (160 metres) long. The road over the bridge, a section of the Via Flaminia, was 98 ft (30 metres) above the river.

The middle part of the bridge suddenly collapsed around 1250. The exact date of this catastrophe is unknown, but history does note that about that time General Parcival Doria, astride his horse and in full battle array, drowned in the raging river as he tried to cross. In other words, the bridge was apparently no longer there at that date.

It is not clear why it was never rebuilt; perhaps the cost was prohibitive, perhaps the times were too uncertain or maybe the architects of the day were not skilled enough. Former travellers to Italy, particularly the Romantics, raved about the grand view at this spot, which combined so many elements so close to their hearts: the mighty ruins of the **Ponte d'Augusto**, the wild waters of the Nera, the monastery of **San Cassiano** perched atop a mountain and the buildings of Narni on a high mountain terrace, crowned by the **Rocca** of Cardinal Albornoz.

It still is magnificent spot today, though marred by a few ugly additions, including an electrical power plant. Further upstream, there is a heavily travelled viaduct. In the early 19th century a donkey path snaking its way to the old mountain monastery provided an ideal opportunity for hiking.

Narni, standing proud and high above the valley floor, is reached over a long and winding road. It is best to leave the car outside the city gate at the busy **Piazza Garibaldi**. The gate itself is part of the portico of the **cathedral of San Giovenale** (begun in 1043, consecrated in 1145). Although the facade is plain, the numerous annexes of the church are known for their beauty: chapels, towers, the lion stairs in front of the side portal, a fourth aisle and the flat arches of the

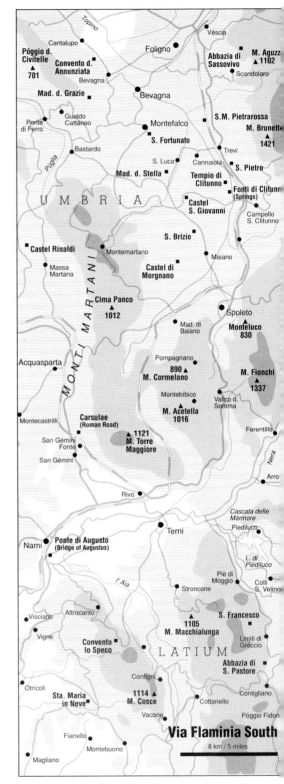

portico (a popular gathering place for the town's younger crowd).

Inside, Jacob Burckhardt's *Cicerone* highlights Sebastiano Pellegrini's **Cappella del SS Sacramento** (1499), designed in the form of a triumphal arch, in the aisle. The facade of the **Burial and Memorial Chapel** of the city's patron saints **San Giovenale** (6th century) and **San Cassio** (15th-century) is noteworthy. The strict proportions of the square spaces between the finely fluted pilasters and the ascetically concise decorations represent the dignity of early Christianity, the period in which both saints lived. The Romanesque pillars in the nave of the basilica, both pulpits by Tuscan masons (15th-century), the altar with baldachino (17th-century), the apse with frescoes and the beautifully inlaid choir stalls as well as the paintings, attributed to Lorenzo Vecchietto of Siena, are worth finding.

Also worth seeing is the **Torre Campanaria** (bell tower), reached through the characteristic old town alleyway of **Via Campanile**. This tower was built in the elegant brick architectural style of the 15th century on top of an intermediate layer of yellowish natural stones which is, in turn, on top of the original square base of rough light grey natural stones in the Romanesque style. The traces of time are evident in the walled-up windows and louvres, the crumbling embellishments, cracks, iron braces and the off-white statue of the patron saint perched high in a niche.

The *Nequinum* of the Umbrians was destroyed by the Romans and rebuilt as *Narnia* (named after the Nera) in 299 BC. Located on the Via Flaminia, the town developed into an important colony. The Narni of today has retained much of its medieval character. When the historical procession of the *Corsa dell'Anello* parades down the Corso between Piazza Garibaldi (with its Roman arch) and the **Piazzo Marzio**, it is following the Crodo Maximus of the Roman town. This particular festival, held on the feast day of the town's patron saint, Juvenalis, in May recalls the fact that the town was once famous for its

e Ponte
Augusto
low Narni.

brave soldiers; during the festival, horsemen in brightly coloured costume compete to thrust a lance through a small suspended metal ring.

The Roman forum today serves as the **Piazza dei Priori**, one of Umbria's characteristic squares. The chequerboard pattern of the Roman complex in the centre of Narni is especially appealing to the eye compared to the seemingly arbitrarily laid-out jumble of alleyways in the medieval sector between the cathedral and the rocca. The impressive structures around the square, including the **Palazzo del Podestà** (with reliefs from the 13th century), the 14th-century **Loggia dei Priori** with the outside pulpit for proclamations and the noble polygonal fountain (1303) are all expressions of a self-assured citizenry.

The greatest pleasure of this historical city centre lies in exploring its smaller churches and buildings. Some things remain a puzzle, for example the small sculptures (desecrated Penates perhaps?) on a door lintel across from **San Domenico**. The latter church, now an art gallery, contains Benozzo Gozzoli's excellent *Annunciation*. **San Francesco** has frescoes on its pillars depicting scenes from the lives of St Francis and St Benedict. The churches of **Santa Maria delle Pensole** (1175) and **Sant'Agostino** (15th-century) are as different from one another as a simple penitence shirt is from baroque vestments: and yet both are in their own way religiously pleasing. Santa Maria della Pensole is the more charming. An inscription above the figure of Christ in Majesty on the facade dates the church to 1175, and the central portal is flanked by carvings of lions devouring sacrificial lambs.

The **Sala del Consiglio** in the Palazzo Podestà contains pictures by Ghirlandaio (*The Crowning of Maria Accompanied by Saints and Angels*, 1486) and Benozzo Gozzoli's *Proclamation*, in tribute to his teacher Fra Angelico.

Two of Narni's most famous sons are the Emperor Nerva (AD 30–98) and the victorious Venetian mercenary commander Gattamelata (literally "Honey cat") who lived from 1370 to 1443 and whose equestrian statue by Donatello is now in Padua. There were no local heroes, however, to stop the soldiers of Emperor Charles V who, on returning from sacking Rome in 1527, robbed Narnia of its prosperity.

The town, with a population of about 21,000, is today enjoying a period of economic growth which is spreading throughout the valley. The annual craftsmen's trade fair and the antique fair, both held in September, have added to Narni's reputation. In the area of music, the concerts of the *Amici di Mozart* (Friends of Mozart) are recommended.

Excursions from Narni: Amelia, about 7 miles (11 km) distant, can be recommended for its wall of cyclopean stone between the Nera and Tiber valleys.

San Gemini, about 8 miles (13 km) away, has a lovely old town as well as the Palazzo Pretorio with its outer stairway under a pointed arch (12th century). To the south of the town is the former abbey church in Romanesque style. The richly decorated frame around the portal is a copy; the original has been in the Metropolitan Museum of Art in New York since 1934. A bit further (about 2 miles/3 km) is **San Gemini Fonte**, a mineral spa set in a park.

On the route from Fonte to **Carsulae** (about 1 mile/2 km), the ruins of a Roman city are located along an abandoned branch of the old Via Flaminia. Founded around 220 BC, Carsulae flourished briefly, declined when the Via Flaminia was rerouted further to the east, and was probably abandoned after an earthquake towards the end of the 1st century AD. Never rebuilt, the town was rediscovered in the 16th century and excavations have uncovered the extensive remains of the forum and law courts, bath houses and amphitheatre, and two temples whose delicate pink marble cladding hints at the lost splendour of this city described as very beautiful by Tacitus and Pliny.

In **Lo Speco di San Francesco** near **Vasciano**, 9 miles (14 km) to the southeast of Narni, is a Franciscan monastery enjoying an idyllic setting between holm-oaks and chestnut trees. St Francis himself visited here in 1213.

TERNI AND CASCATA DELLE MARMARO

As the Umbrian centre for heavy industry since the 19th century and centre for the electrical and chemical industries during recent decades, **Terni** isn't one of Umbria's tourist attractions. With a population of 106,000, Terni is Umbria's second largest city after Perugia; explosive suburban growth has changed the complexion of the city in recent years and much of the infrastructure, badly damaged in the war, has been rebuilt with little aesthetic consideration.

But travellers are able to make discoveries here which make the city worth exploring. Behind the **Giardini Pubblici** are the walls of the amphitheatre of *Interamnia*, as the Romans called their city located between the Nera and Serra rivers. And the **Via XI Febbraio** on the other side of the monument is also exceptionally picturesque. The cathedral of **Santa Maria Assunta**, an edifice rebuilt in baroque style in 1653, is located beside the heathen stadium. The main portal under the portico is a remnant of the original 12th-century Romanesque structure, as are certain architectural elements inside the cathedral. Across from the church, a fountain of the river god and goddess splashes beside a 17th-century palace facade.

An evening stroll from here along the **Via d'Arringe** to the lively **Via Roma**, provides the best opportunity to absorb the old city culture. Eventually the route reaches the **Palazzo Spada** (mid-16th century) on the **Piazza del Popolo**. This square is a good place to enjoy an aperitif. The works of Gozzoli, Alunno and the mysterious Umbrian master "della Annunciazione Gardner" can be seen in the **Palazzo Manassei's Pinacotheca** (behind the post office) along with the work of modern artists such as Miro and Chagall.

Across the huge main square, the Piazza delle Repubblica, the tiny church of San Salvatore alone makes a visit to this busy city worthwhile. The tiny circular sanctuary is shaped like a beehive. A porthole in the apex admits sunlight which shines down on the altar at noon. It was probably built by the ancient Umbrians as a temple to the sun around the 3rd century BC, incorporated into a Roman house which served as a meeting place for Christians in the 5th century AD and enlarged to form a church in the 12th century.

San Francesco (at Piazza San Francesco), with its elegant campanile, has beautiful frescos in its Cappella Paradisi. These were painted in about 1450 by Bartolomeo di Tommaso based on Dante's *Divine Comedy*.

The opportunity to visit the waterfalls, located about 5 miles (9 km) away in the direction of Ferentillo, should not be passed by. These famous falls are known as the Cascata delle Marmore, where, in the words of Charles Dickens, "the Velino plunges from the high cliffs in a rainbow-covered foam" The thundering waters can now only be seen in full flow on weekday evenings and at weekends. The rest of the time the hydro-electric power is used by the region's industry.

Practical for the narrow streets.

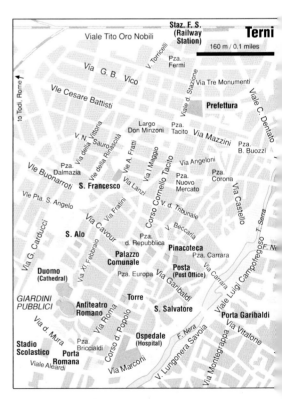

SPOLETO

Many roads lead to Rome. One of the most important, the Via Flaminia, used to be controlled by **Spoleto**. This town could open or close the road, just like a sluice. The valley of the Tessino narrows at this point between Monteluco (2,700 ft/830 metres) Colle Sant'Elia (1,486 ft/453 metres) and Colle Risana (1,040 ft/317 metres/). The city, perched on a hillside, is guarded by a castle, the **Rocca Albornoz**. This mighty fortress, spreading out over the rounded hilltop of Sant'Elia, and the fine-as-filigree **Ponte delle Torri** – aqueduct and road to Monteluco – are the classic landmarks of Spoleto. Today, this is where the tunnel of the Via Flaminia breaks through the fortress hill.

Archaeological finds have proved that the origins of this defiant settlement date back to the Villanovan culture, in the 9th century BC, the pre-Etruscan era. Piece by piece, the Umbrians erected the first city wall of Cyclopean stone. It was comparable in size to the surviving walls of Amelia near Narni. After *Spoletium* became a colony in 241 BC, the Romans expanded the city wall first with rough, and later with finished, stone blocks.

Roman influence is evident throughout this city. If you come off the Via Flaminia and enter the town on Via Nursina you will find parking space around the Piazza della Vittoria, a scruffy and unpromising introduction to the city, but surrounded by Roman remains. Under the adjacent Piazza Garibaldi you can see the so-called Ponte Sanguinario, built to carry the Via Flaminia over the river Tessino, now restored and open to the public.

Ponte Sanguinario means Bridge of Blood, and the name commemorates the legend that St Abbondanza, along with 10,000 Christian martyrs, were slaughtered in the town's amphitheatre (the ruins of which survive nearby, behind the barracks in Via dell'Anfiteatro) causing the river Tessino to run red with their blood. The church of San Gregorio Maggiore, on the west side of Piazza di Vittorio, commemorates the event and has been beautifully restored; its 12th-century crypt is a forest of reused Roman columns and contains the large sarcophagus of St Abbondanza.

Early Christian influence: While you are here, make a visit to the town cemetery, where the church of San Salvatore is an astonishing survival, an untouched 4th-century church facade, looking more like a domestic house than anything ecclesiastical, and a Carolingian nave, its dusty floor littered with fragments of fallen columns. This church was probably built as a *martyrium* for funeral banquets, a place to celebrate the passage of a member of Spoleto's early Christian community into the afterlife of eternal happiness. The ancient Etruscans held similar rites, so Spoleto's early Christians were, as it were, simply going back to their roots.

Now we enter the town proper, climbing up Corso Garibaldi, through medieval alleys to the Piazza del Mercato, site of the Roman forum and just as colourful and bustling today as in former times. Continuing the Roman theme, one side of the square is closed off by the 1st-century AD Arco di Druso, built to commemorate the Germanic victories of Drusus, son of the Emperor Tiberius. Remains of a Roman temple stand alongside and more of the temple foundations are contained in the crypt of San Ansano church, with its 12th-century frescoes. Further south is the Roman theatre, largely rebuilt after the war and used for summer festival events.

Returning to the north side of Piazza del Mercato, you will find the city's picture gallery tucked away to the right in the quiet Piazza del Municipio. The gallery is located in the upper floor of the Palazzo Comunale and the basement of the the palace contains the remains of a 1st-century AD Roman house with mosaics, once thought to be the home of Vespasia Pollo, mother of the Emperor Vespasian.

Out of the square, turn right into Via Aurelio Saffi and look for a gate in the wall on the left which takes you into the quiet courtyard of the Palazzo Arciv-

e cathedral
Santa
aria
ssunta.

escovile, the Archbishop's Palace. To its left is a real jewel of a church, Sant'Eufemia. Its pure Romanesque style dates from the 10th century and it is assumed that this was the royal church of the Lombardic Dukes of Spoleto. Inside, a *colonna santa* (second column on the right) has been integrated into the row of pillars, a richly decorated architectural element from the 9th century.

We have saved the best of Spoleto until now. By turning left from Sant'Eufemia into Via Aurelio Saffi you will soon reach the steps on the left that lead down to the stone-paved square in front of the cathedral of Santa Maria Assunta – the favourite place for young boys who want to practice a bit of football before supper. Two pilasters of Santa Maria della Manna d'Oro serve as the goalposts.

The stunning cathedral was built and destroyed several times. The campanile and parts of the facade date to the late 12th century and the colourful Byzantine style mosaic of *Christ in Majesty with the Virgin and St John* is signed and dated "Solsternus, 1207".

The lower central window, with its sculptural decoration, is one of the most suggestive works of the Umbrian Romanesque style. The spandrels of its square frame contain the symbols of the four Evangelists, and below this is a pillared gallery held up by two caryatids. The magnificent portico has five arches resting on slender pillars as well as a pulpit to the right and one to the left, both crowned by a balustrade. This portico was once attributed to Bramante, but it is now known that it was designed by Barocci from Milan (1491–1504). A brisk but subtle harmony exists between these different elements from such varying epochs, bringing the serene facade of the cathedral to life. The monolithic campanile beside the church seems to shoot up like the opening chord played on the organ. Construction of the cathedral, which had at least two predecessors, was begun in 1175 after Frederick Barbarossa laid waste the town, and was completed in about 1230. The inside was pretty comprehensively ruined, however, when it was remodelled in

baroque style by Luigi Arrigi in 1638 at the request of Cardinal Barberini.

Fortunately the remodelling spared Fra Filippo Lippi's sanctuary frescoes. It is very likely that Michelangelo visited this cathedral on his way to Rome and, impressed by Fra Filippo Lippi's work, gathered ideas for the colouring used in his work on the ceiling of the Sistine Chapel.

Sensuous Virgins: Filippo Lippi's frescoes were the last he ever painted. Lippi was a colourful character – a wayward orphan whose aunt abandoned him to the care of Carmelite friars, at the age of eight, because she found him impossible to control. His artistic talent was stimulated by his love of women. As Vasari recounts: "Fra Filippo Lippi was so lustful that he would give anything to enjoy a woman he wanted if he thought he could have his way; and if he couldn't buy what he wanted, then he would cool his passion by painting her picture". Thus Lippi is best known for his sensuous Virgins, many of them portraits of his mistress, the beautiful Lucrezia Buti.

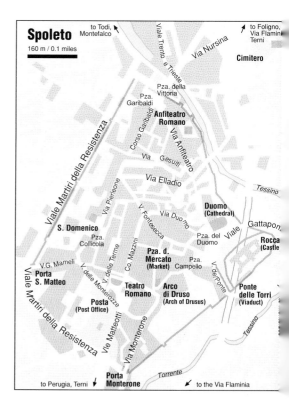

232

Lippi was invited to Spoleto in 1468 with a commission to paint a complete cycle on the Life of the Virgin, from the Annunciation to the Nativity to her Coronation in Heaven. Lippi died before he could complete the work, aged fifty-seven. Vasari, who loved gossip, reports: "they say that, in one of those sublime love affairs he was always having, the relations of the woman concerned had him poisoned".

Whether this is true or not, the artist died at the full height of his powers and these frescoes display the lyrical and tender figures and the vibrant colours that were his trademark. As the art historian, David Sante, has written, "The painter transformed the typical heavenly queen-like figure of the Virgin into one of a charming girl".

When Lippi died Spoleto was allowed to keep his remains and the Medici bank even donated one hundred gold ducats for a tomb; this was designed by Lippi's illegitimate son, Filippino, himself by now an accomplished artist. The tomb is found in the right-hand transept, carved with an epigram written by the humanist orator, Politian. Two other treasures are the 12th-century icon of the Virgin, in the chapel below the organ loft, said to have been looted from Constantinople by Frederick Barbarossa and given to Spoleto as a peace token in 1185, after the emperor had destroyed the town. Further up the nave, on the right as you leave, is a Crucifixion painted on wood, dating to 1187, and a beautiful set of mid 16th-century stalls.

The Museo Civico is on the right-hand side of the Piazza del Duomo, housed in the Palazzo della Signoria, next to an elegant octagonal chamber theatre, the Caio Melisso, built in 1880. The museum contains an enjoyable miscellany of architectural fragments and 12th to 15th-century sarcophagi. Two stone tablets, dating to the 3rd century BC, record the *Lex Spoletina*, a law forbidding the cutting of timber in the sacred groves around the city. Climbing back up the steps from the cathedral piazza, turn left to reach the imposing Rocca Albornoz and its partner, the

stroll
through the
streets of
Spoleto.

graceful Ponte delle Torri acqueduct. Rest awhile in the shade of the pavement cafes along the Via della Rocca and consider the history of this monumental fortress.

Totila the Goth first built a castle here in the 6th century, using masonry quarried from the town's Roman amphitheatre. It probably served the Lombardic Dukes who ruled Spoleto from the Thoedoric Palace, a structure that no longer exists today. Frederick Barbarossa destroyed the Spoleto of 100 towers, including those of the castle one assumes, because the citizens refused to pay him tribute.

"There were times in which Spoleto was the stake in a poker game being played for sovereignty over all of Italy," notes the historian Casimir Edschmid. In 1240 the pope held the better cards in his game against Frederick II and Spoleto fell to the Papal States. Men like the cardinal and papal legate, Gil d'Albornoz, one of the best of his trade, ensured that Spoleto remained under papal rule for the next 600 years. He built today's rocca as the base from which papal representatives subjugated the whole region. It was constructed from 1355 under the direction of Matteo Gattapone of Gubbio. In more peaceful times it was converted to a luxurious palace, a favourite papal retreat and home, for a time, of the Borgias.

It was still being defended in the name of the pope, by Major O'Reilly and his Irish comrades, when the national guard stormed the fortress bearing the Italian tricolour in 1860. The fortress was then turned into a prison – the would-be assassin of Pope John Paul II and members of the Red Brigades spent time here. Now it is facing a happier future; once restored it will house the city's art collection and serve as a cultural centre, the focal point of the city's Festival dei Due Mondi, the Festival of Two Worlds, founded by the Italian-American opera composer, Giancarlo Menotti, which takes place here every summer and brings world-class artists together from Europe and the Americas.

From the Rocca walls you can walk

Spoleto's Ponte delle Torri.

down and across the Ponte delle Torri aqueduct, incorporated into the rocca, though predating it, so as to supply water to the fortress and provide an escape route to Monteluco, the hill on the opposite side of the gorge. Statistics impress: the aqueduct is 750 feet/230 metres long and as you walk along the now dry water channel you are 260 feet/80 metres above the bottom of the Tessino gorge. Even more impressive, if you have a head for heights, are the extensive views.

Monteluco, the queen of Umbria's mountains, beckons the visitor to a spell of relaxation in its airy heights. In antiquity, it was considered one of the sacred mountains of the Mediterranean cultural region. When Christianity arrived, several hermits settled here, including the Syrian monk Isaac. In the 6th century, the St Julian monastery was built, and in the course of time, several other chapels were constructed in the woods. The landscape has inspired many visitors to wax lyrical, including Ferdinand Gregorovius: "the sweet aroma of the balsam greens streams out of the ground, the breezes swish through the tree-top leaves of the thousand-year-old oaks, and otherwise there is no sound to be heard. Looking up, one sees picturesque Spoleto; down below one sees the white road of Via Flaminia or gazes off into the stretches of the fragrant Tiber Valley." This wandering bard was mistaken in his last remark – this is actually the Tessino Valley.

The route down from Monteluco passes the church of **San Pietro Fuori le Mura**. According to legend, the chains of St Peter were kept here in the 5th century, having been stolen from Rome by Bishop Achillus. The church is built on a necropolis formerly used by the heathens and later by the Christians.

The nave of the church was destroyed by fire in 1893 and rebuilt in depressing baroque style in 1699. The 13th-century facade survived, however, and the portal is surrounded by a delicate floral frieze. Ten stone panels of 12th/13th century date have been set into the facade; their origin remains a mystery and the precise meaning of some of the scenes still eludes commentators. The two upper panels on the left show demons battling with angels for the soul of a dying man, and the dismembered body of an unrepentant sinner being fed into a cauldron. The next three are less easy to understand: each features a lion, first caught by the paw in a tree cleft, then being revered by a kneeling man and finally attacking a knight in armour; they may illustrate some lost allegory.

The first two scenes on the right show Christ washing the feet of St Peter and calming the waters of Lake Tiberias. The next two illustrate scenes from the popular medieval beast epic, the satirical *Roman de Renard*. In one, Reynard the Fox feigns death to ensnare two crows and in the other he is disguised as a monk reading the Bible while eyeing his next victim, a ram. Finally the lion appears again, chasing a dragon. These panels are carved with great skill and naturalism but perhaps the best is the charming rural vignette by the portal in which a ploughman plods timelessly behind his team of oxen.

Modern sculpture in Spoleto, a legacy of the Festival dei Due Mondi.

ART RESTORATION IN SPOLETO

There is no other country in the world which has such a rich tradition of art as Italy. From the Alps down to Sicily, it is brimming with prehistoric graffiti, necropolises, frescoes, temples, towers and churches. Some voices are calling for an international agency to protect this heritage because they fear that Italy does not have the ability to preserve it on its own. Nobody actually knows the dimensions of this art treasure. Registering the entire holding, however, is a prerequisite for preserving it.

There are 66 regional offices with seven supervisory bureaux which are responsible for Italy's archaeological treasures, the municipal complexes and the art works from the Middle Ages up through the present. For years they have demanded more freedom of decision and the dismantling of the ineffective centralised administrative structure.

The Ministry for "Beni Culturali ed Ambientali", which is responsible for art, museums, architecture, archaeology and urban heritage, was first established in 1975, as an off-shoot of the Ministry of Education. Even so, it would take an act of enormous political power to ensure the proper supervision, restoration and accessibility of all Italy's art treasures.

It seems that only the spirit of private enterprise will be able to save Italy's national heritage, but the scientific direction and control must remain in the hands of the political bodies responsible for historic preservation.

A good example of successful cooperation is found in Umbria. In 1987, the Ministry of Culture commissioned the private finance company ITALSTAT, a subsidiary of the state holding company IRI, to restore the papal fortress of Spoleto (built in 1359–70). This has been partially completed and a sector of the 12,000 sq. yard (10,000 sq. metre) construction site is already open to the public. A cooperative of art historians has laid bare

an unexpectedly high number of murals dating from various epochs. Some of these have turned out to be Gothic frescoes depicting courtly life.

Italian restorers have a good reputation. London's *Financial Times* once wrote that, next to Italian fashion, the "Istituto Centrale de Restauro" in Rome is Italy's most astounding phenomenon. Its employees receive requests for assistance in restoring art treasure from all over the world - from the bronze doors of the Hagia Sophia to the paintings hanging in Dublin's National Art Gallery.

One only wishes that institutes for restoration could be found throughout the entire country. Because there is no financial support from the government, the institutes must rely on private support. In Spoleto, highly qualified restoration workshops have been established. Architects, engineers, art historians and restorers work together with the state agencies for historic preservation in order to conserve the immense amounts of art treasures in Umbria.

Pinturicchio and Perugino, in whose school the young Raphael developed his talent, are Umbria's greatest contribution to art. All that came before and after was not even recognised for a long time. The rejection of the art of the 17th century lasted well into the 20th century. In the 1950s, the baroque interiors of numerous churches were destroyed, and many altar-pieces found their way from Perugia to South Carolina. Scientific research on baroque painting first began with the Caravaggio exhibit organised by Roberto Longhi in 1951. That was followed by the rediscovery of the Bolognese painters, the Caracci brothers, Guido Reni, Il Guercino. It was not until quite recently that the academic world even began studying the art of local schools.

A group of art historians from the Roman University searched through the entire eastern sector of Umbria, including the most remote mountain villages, looking for traces of baroque painting. About 2,000 pictures were found; of these, 600 were documented and restored. The whole project was crowned by a large exhibition in 1989 in the rocca of Spoleto.

In a large factory hall in the valley, the headquarters of a cooperative of restorers and art historians, pictures are removed from their worm-ridden frames and cleaned. All canvases are stretched on flexible metal frames. The technical difficulty of trying to extract the pictures from the altar constructions was not the only problem in their removal; the scepticism of the nuns and priests, reluctant to part with their devotional pictures even for the time necessary for their restoration, also had to be overcome. The priests of the tiny mountain village of Cancellara travelled to Spoleto every fortnight to reassure themselves that their treasures were being properly cared for by the restorers.

Almost all of the pictures were still hanging in the rooms and chapels for which they were painted more than 300 years ago; and they were all returned to these rooms after their restoration.

The churches in the mountainous region around Norcia have an extraordinarily large number of baroque altarpieces, executed by Florentine artists. Shepherds and lumberjacks working in Tuscany originally brought them home to Umbria when their seasonal jobs ended.

In Rome and Naples, early 17th-century painting diverged between two extremes – the profane naturalism of Michelangelo da Caravaggio and the idealistic realism of

the three Caracci brothers. The countryside remained aloof from this influence. As early as the 16th century, Umbria was under the control of the papal legates and there were no free towns. Art serving the church was forced to follow a certain type. The paintings, in large format, were an important instrument of the *propaganda fide* and you will find no naturalistic works here.

In Umbria, the people have long been known for the temperamental demonstration of their beliefs. From Agostino di Duccio to Pietro Perugino and Raphael, art was always religious. Even portrait commissions were rare. Many of Raphael's paintings, such as the *Madonna* from Foligno (today in the Vatican) or the *Crucifixion* of Città di Castello (today in the National Gallery in London),

hung in Umbrian churches in the 17th century. The artists remained true to forms which had become popular. The counter-reformation demanded a return to forms and symbols of Franciscan philosophy. The huge Basilica Santa Maria degli Angeli was erected in 1569 on the grounds where St Francis died and commissions were given to local artists as well as to the renowned ones in Rome and Siena. Art was seen as a way to portray beliefs which were not based on words but on the experiences of spiritual rapture, ecstasy and visions. Rather than being straitjacketed by this requirement, several Umbrian artists like Perugino (who, as a man, had no time for religion) developed painting techniques that use wonderful lighting effects as a symbol of spirituality.

A spiritual intensity of a completely different kind is attributed to a picture which was discovered on a side altar in the small village of Serrone. It depicts the holy family in Joseph's workshop. All the tools are reproduced in detail, just as the commissioners – lumberers and carpenters – probably requested. Mary sits and sews, the smiling Christ binds two pieces of wood together to form a cross and Joseph pauses in his work to look pensively at the symbolic activity of his son. It is thought that the artist was of French-Flemish ancestry. He was probably one of the many artists from the north who was unable to get a foothold in Rome and thus took his trade elsewhere.

Federico Barocci also lived apart. His atelier in Urbino was probably visited by many Umbrian painters. One of them extracted the most beautiful details from various works of this master and combined them into a scene of prophesy. The picture is in the Basilica Santa Maria degli Angeli near Assisi. The viewer is immediately drawn into the heart of the picture, past everyday objects such as a sleeping cat and a straw hat on the wall, over the threshold and into the celestial realm, finally to the face of God directly above. The castle of Urbino, on the other hand, the worldly home, is far off in the distance. The juxtaposition of cold steel blue, bright red, sulphur yellow and violet pink, marks the zenith of counter-reformationary art.

TREVI

Trevi is one of those perfect Umbrian hilltop towns where the modern world is left behind as soon as you leave the industrialised lower town and enter the walls of the medieval core. Streets too narrow for motor cars have been turned into works of art, paved with cobbles set in frames of stone to create patterns of squares, diamonds or herringbone. No street is straight and every turning offers a new vista of ancient buildings or flower-filled courtyards.

Threading through a maze of alleys, climbing to the highest point in the town, you will eventually reach the **Piazza Mazzini**, where craftsmen have converted the **Palazzo Comunale**, the **Pinacotheca**, into a restoration workshop, thus making the precious Lo Spagna panels inaccessible to outsiders. Also on this square is the **cathedral** (12th–19th century), dedicated to the missionary and martyr Sant'Emiliano – his statue can be seen between two lions on the beautiful but tightly closed Renaissance portal. The exterior is the best feature of this church so it does not matter that the interior, ruined by dull sub-classical remodelling in the 18th and 19th centuries, is usually closed. If it happens to be open, however, call in to see the splendid altar in the north aisle shaped like a triumphal arch and covered in grotesque work, with a niche containing Mattia di Gaspare da Como's realistic *Virgin and Child* (1524).

The town gives a lesson in what medieval urbanism under the sword and shield was – a labyrinth. The walls of the inner palace complex are towering. This complex probably grew up in early times around a castle on the top of the hill. Walking through sloping alleys, visitors intermittently catch glimpses of the countryside beyond.

Exiting through the gate on to the spacious **Piazza Garibaldi**, one experiences a feeling of liberation, of entering into the age of enlightenment, though this is perhaps a bit too flattering for this "modern" square with its bus station. One will also take away from here the memory of the **Madonna della Lacrime** and its enchanting *Adoration of the Magi* by Perugino (1512). This tiny church of the early Renaissance is located along the smaller road to the south towards Bovara.

This road rejoins the Via Flaminia and a tiny side road, after 1km, will take you to the Tempio Clitunno, or "tempietto" (little temple) as it is known locally, a mini Acropolis built in the 4th century and dedicated to the martyr, San Salvatore. The 7th-century frescoes here, depicting Christ with St Peter and St Paul, are among the earliest to have survived in Italy. Another kilometre south you cannot miss the large car park on the left serving the Fonti di Clittuno, the source of the river Clitunno, home to a river god who issued oracles in the time of the Romans, where the spring waters remain crystal clear. Countless visitors, from Virgil to the artist Corot and the poet Byron have been charmed by this idyllic spot.

MONTEFALCO

In 1249 the mercenaries of the German emperor, Frederick II, cut their trail through Corrone, as Montefalco was then called, leaving no building standing in the rebellious city; they didn't rest until the town was totally levelled. They even robbed this 1,000-year-old city of its name.

Frederick II, a keen falconer, left his eternal mark on the ruins, rechristening the place "Falcon Mountain", **Montefalco**. Soon thereafter, in the year 1250, he died, as politically ruined as the town was physically.

The peacefulness of a morning in Montefalco is enhanced by the view from the walls and from the **Torre Comunale** out across the landscape. The grandiose panorama merits three Michelin stars and has earned the city another name: Ringhiera dell'Umbria – the Balcony of Umbria. The piazza should be worth at least one star. Santa Chiara, a daughter of Montefalco (not the Clare that followed St Francis of Asissi), is the patron saint of a church and convent here, in Via Verde. The nuns will show you a tree grown from a staff given to Santa Chiara by Christ in a vision. The nuns use the dried berries of the tree to make rosary beads. The convent also has the heart of Santa Chiara, a precious relic that was found, after the saint's death, to be marked with a cross.

A life in pictures: One of the loveliest museums of sacred art in Umbria has been established in the former church of San Francesco. Without doubt, the highlight of the museum is the *in situ* fresco cycle in the sanctuary, painted by the Florentine artist, Benozzo Gozzoli, between 1450 and 1452. The 12 scenes from the life of St Francis are not as well known as Giotto's work, but they are easier to enjoy. You do not, as with Giotto's work, have to make allowances for the lack of sophistication, for Gozzoli was an artist working with the whole range of new techniques that had been developed by Florentine Renais-

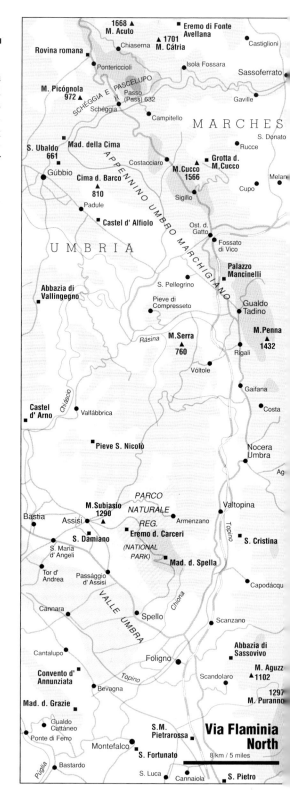

sance artists, including Gozzoli's own teacher, Fra Angelico.

What makes these works even more appealing is the realistic background detail, much of it corresponding to recognisable scenes and buildings that survive to this day. Thus anyone who knows Florence will recognise that the "church" in the vision of St Francis (below the central window) is in fact the Palazzo Vecchio, but given an extra campanile. St Peter's church in Rome features in the sixth scene, the meeting between St Francis and St Dominic, and Montefalco itself features in the best scene of all, to the right of the window, in which St Francis preaches to the birds.

The only works in the museum that compare in quality to those of Gozzoli are the two paintings at the rear of the north aisle. Here, two versions of the *Madonna and Child* are set side by side to invite comparisons. One is by Tiberio d'Assisi (1510), the other by Perugino (1515). Both are beautifully fresh and their colours – purples, oranges, reds and irridescent blues – are arresting.

In the opposite aisle, in the two easternmost chapels, are two *gonfalone* portraying the Madonna del Soccorso (the Madonna of Emergencies); one is anonymous (dated to around 1498) and the other is by Tiberio d'Assisi (1510). Both are highly comical and illustrate a popular local legend according to which a mother, exasperated by the bad behaviour of her child, wished him to the devil. The devil duly turned up to carry the child away so the distraught mother turned to the Virgin for help. In both paintings the Virgin is far from being the tender mother portrayed in most paintings; she is a club-wielding giantess from Umbrian folklore, ferocious enough to frighten any devil or any disobedient child.

Before you leave the town, be sure to sample its wine; Sangrantino, and the port-like Sangrantino Passito, are among the region's most distinctive reds, to be enjoyed with a meal at one of Montefalco's several good restaurants or bought from one of the wine dealers in the main street.

ontefalco,
Icony of
nbria.

BEVAGNA

Tiny, endearing Bevagna, is a quiet unspoiled gem of a town that was once a staging post on the Via Flaminia but went into decline when the route changed. Roman Mevania was famous for breeding Umbria's sacred white bulls, whose deer-like features made them highly prized as participants in religious ceremonies, usually to end up as sacrificial victims on an altar to Juno or Jupiter. Seutonius relates that this was the town in which Caligula developed his strategy for his Germanic wars. It was also the birthplace of the poet Propertius, who described his native town as "cloudy Mevania, standing among rain-soaked fields".

The town's best Roman relic also has a watery theme. To the right, off tree-lined Piazza Garibaldi, in the basement of Via Porta Guelfa 2, you will find a well-preserved bath-house mosaic, featuring the sea-god Triton and an entourage of dolphins, octopus, sea-horses and a delightfully realistic lobster.

The sleepy main street of today's town, the Corso Matteotti, leads (right) into the main square, the Piazza Silvestri, and the Palazzo dei Consoli. The wide steps of this palace provide the best seats for watching the street theatre. It seems that everyone – mothers on their way to shop, men and women on their way to work – must cross the Piazza Silvestri.

Across the square is **San Michele**, whose portal features the Archangel Michael in the form of a dragon slayer. Under the frieze is a tribute to the late 12th-century architects: "Rodolfo and Binelli built this structure, Christ and St Michael protect it".

Two lively angels guard the portal. One bears the scriptures and thrusts a spear into the mouth of a dragon; the other carries an orb and crucifix. The corbel table above is carved with grotesque beasts. Pairs of Romanesque triple lancets light the aisles. The rose window, too large in proportion to the

A local greengrocer

rest of the facade, is an unfortunate addition of the 18th century, but the 17th-century wooden tympanum, showing the Archangel Michael casting Lucifer from Heaven, is in sympathy with the original architects' work.

Inside, the nave is very tall, long and narrow, focusing attention on the altar, raised by some 10 ft (3 metres) above the floor. The nave is separated from the aisles by an eight-bay arcade of great elegance, supported on travertine pillars, sadly hacked about in the 18th century when the columns and walls were plastered over. Restoration in 1954 has given back to San Michele something of its original appearance, and the simplicity of this ancient church is just as pleasing as any more gorgeously frescoed one.

The **Piazza Silvestri** provides an impression of how a complete and unadulterated town centre of the Romanesque period looked. Besides San Michele, two other buildings complete an ensemble of total harmony: the **Palazzo dei Consoli** (built about 1270), high, wide and majestic, constructed at an angle to the square and with a regal stairway. The facade exhibits double-bay windows under pointed vaulted arches. The palazzo now houses the splendid Teatro Torti. Look inside, if you can, for the theatre, founded in 1886, has recently been restored to its 19th-century glory.

A flat archway links this building to the church of **San Silvestro**, a simple but symmetrical counterpart to San Michele. It is dated (1195) and signed by the same sculptor and architect, Binelli, who built San Michele. The church is almost windowless and dark, as if to heighten the mystery surrounding the rituals of the medieval Church. Binelli's columns in the nave have intrigued architectural historians; carved with a papyrus-like motif, they wonder if Binelli had seen some long-ruined Roman temple to an eastern deity – perhaps Isis – and copied its capitals.

Between these two monuments, a fountain – a smaller version of Perugia's Fontana Maggiore – dates from the neoromantic era of the 19th century.

nough to ard off any truder – this ngel guards e portal to evagna's urch of San ichele.

SPELLO

Driving towards the town of Spello, one notices that the town is only slightly elevated above the plains. The Roman city wall stretches to the south about as far as the country road, to the fields and gardens of the new part of the town where all the banks, petrol stations and larger shops are found.

The **Porta Consolare** (1st century AD) on the approach road leading from Rome boasts three statues. Contrary to impressions, it is not an emperor's triumphal arch, just a symbol of solid republican self-assurance.

Although the gate could theoretically still handle motorised traffic, it is only open to pedestrians. Spello, with its narrow streets and alleyways is actually a pedestrian town, although pedestrians don't have it particularly easy: the streets here are very steep.

Spello is full of historical sites. These include a complete town wall with impressive gates (**Porta Urbica** and **Porta Venere**) as well as several towers (Torri di Properzio) dating back to the time of the emperor Augustus.

A second wall leads into the the south of the town to form gorge-like alleys (just like the wall of **Arco Augusti**). In the north, this same wall clambers up the hillside above the plains. The view from up here makes the time and energy involved in the hike well worth while. Standing among the ruins of the **Rocca of Cardinal d'Albornoz**, one has a magnificent view across the plains of the Valle Umbra all the way north to Assisi and the dome of Santa Maria degli Angeli at the foot of the Franciscan city. To the south, the panorama extends past Foligno as far as Montefalco.

But apart from the Roman walls and the unadulterated medieval atmosphere, there is another reason to travel to Spello - its fine architectural and art work. About 100 metres past the Porta dei Consolari is a small chapel containing a fresco which has recently been restored, the *Crucifixion* by Niccolò Alunno

Preceding pages: Spello – like an island surrounded by a sea of colour. **Below,** happ▶ at last.

(1461). Outside, you will probably spot a builder's shovel stuck in a pile of sand. Not only here at the **Cappella Tega**, but throughout the entire town, restorers are hard at work trying to save the town's treasures from decay. It is not without reason that Spello's coat-of-arms contains a mason's hammer.

Just around the next turn is the **Piazza Matteotti** with its **church of Santa Maria Maggiore**. This church was completed in 1285; in 1644, it was lengthened in the front. In its **Cappella Baglioni** is one of the most wonderful treasures of murals which Pinturicchio bequeathed to his Umbrian home. On the left wall is the *Annunciation* (with a self-portrait of the artist in a golden frame). On the right wall is the young *Christ among the Scribes*, and the *Adoration of the Shepherds and the Arrival of the Magi* (1501) is found on the middle wall. The frescoes glow softly from behind their glass screen which reflects the flames of the votive candles.

The floor of the same chapel contributes to the rich effect. The 16th-century maiollica tiles, made in Deruta on the opposite side of the Vale of Spoleto, are decorated with dragons and griffins. They have the brilliance and intricacy of a Persian carpet.

A pietà fresco (1521) by the aged Pietro Perugino can also be found in the church. It is especially moving because of its naive iconography.

The only square on which Spello does not really live up to its image is the modern Piazza Repubblica with the simple **Palazzo Comunale** (1270). But there are more than enough alternatives.

Once a year, the grey cobblestone streets of Spello host a festival. Dozens of ingenious minds and hundreds of industrious hands prepare for the Corpus Christi Day procession, which is more magnificent and impressive each year. For weeks thereafter, the showcase windows are filled with photographs of this spectacle.

The realist, however, will be drawn to the Giardino all'Italiana of the **Villa Fedelia**, just beside the Via Flaminia, where you can rest your weary feet.

FOLIGNO

At first encounter Foligno seems rather an unappealing modern town with little to interest the visitor. Negligible evidence remains of the extensive Roman presence here. At the junction of the old and the new Via Flaminia, an encampment known as *Forum Flaminii* was maintained here (outside the town). Another road leads to *Asisium* (Assisi), and still another stretches through *Plestia* (near Colfiorito) all the way to the Adriatic coast.

War torn: Compared with most other Umbrian towns, Foligno is also short on medieval attractions. As a centre for the aeroplane industry in World War II, the town suffered heavy bombing. Likewise, during ground fighting for control of the road junction and bridgehead in the Topino Valley, the town was attacked by artillery shells. Consequently most of the roads one sees here today have been built since the war.

However, there are a few places where signs of former times are still evident. The **Piazza della Repubblica** in the centre of the medieval town, for example, is not one of Umbria's most triumphant squares, but is one of its most respectable. It is framed by the **cathedral of San Feliciano** (completed in 1113 by Attus), the **Palazzo Trinci** (basically constructed from 1389–1407) and the **Palazzo Comunale** (13th–17th century) as well as a number of other grand houses.

The main facade of the cathedral with its mosaic of *Christ in Majesty* from 1904 lost much of its earlier substance and beauty when it was restored. The magnificent facade, original and richly decorated, faces to the west where the cathedral is joined to the Trinci Palace by means of an archway. An inscription from 1201 credits Rodolfo and Binelli as the architects, the same ones who built the churches in Bevagna. As the site of a saint's tomb and as a bishop's church, the cathedral of San Feliciano occupies the superior position. A statue

Preceding pages: traditional costumes and broad smiles at the Quintana Festival. Below, a picture of Christ crucified dating from the Fascist era.

on the left portal pillar is in memory of Emperor Frederick Barbarossa who, in his time, added Montefalco and Bevagna to Foligno's territory. On the right pillar, the founder of the church, Bishop Anselmus, is depicted. Thus, as the congregation entered the church they filed past the personifications of both the temporal and the spiritual ruler.

Visitors are given an intimation of the magnificence awaiting them in St Peter's in Rome (or so Moritz thought) by the high altar under the church's dome, a replica of Bernini's baldachino, and the gold-plated columns. As a devotional figure for the pious, St Feliciano is presented in a life-size statue made of silver. It was crafted by Giovanni Battista Maini (1698–1752) and its silver pedestal was made by the German Johann Adolf Gaap. The statue is located in the right transept.

The crypt of the saint is much older than the cathedral. Feliciano was born in the year 159 in Forum Flaminii and was consecrated as a bishop by Pope Victor I. It seems appropriate that spoils from the time of the Romans have been put to use in his crypt – capitals, shafts of columns and building stones. These create a hallowed atmosphere reminiscent of that of early Christian catacombs.

Papal army: Take the time to enjoy a refreshing drink at one of the nearby cafes and gaze at the 14th-century facade of the Palazzo Trinci. The Trinci, supporters of the Guelphs in the 13th century, served as a military arm of the pope and thereby gained control over Foligno. They usurped the surrounding communities like fruits which had fallen from the tree of the Guelphs, from Montefalco and Bevagna all the way to Assisi and Nocera Umbra. At the beginning of the 15th century, they had established a kind of principality. The palace of this dynasty, extinguished by Cardinal John Vitelleschi in a family feud, is evidence of the family's wealth and appreciation of art. Wonderful fresco cycles, a collection of paintings mainly from the 15th century and one of the oldest antiquities collections in all of Italy are housed here. Normally the

display of orsemanship t the uintana estival.

Palazzo Trinci would be open to the public as a pinacotheca. However, in 1986, it was "temporarily" closed and remains so to this day. The damage caused by World War II bombings is finally being repaired.

A mini art gallery of sorts is the church of Santa Maria Infraportas, found by walking from the Piazza della Repubblica all the way down Via Mazzini. This ancient church, built on the foundations of a Roman temple to Diana, was, if you believe local legend, visited by St Peter himself, who celebrated mass here. The oldest parts probably date to the 8th century and many of the churches columns and side niches are painted with frescoes by local artists. Nerby San Nicolo has paintings by Nicolo Alunno; parts of his *Nativity* and *Resurrection* (you will have to go to the Louvre in Paris to see the rest) and his *Coronation of the Virgin* (1492).

Casimir Edschmid, a German author of many books about Italy, pointed out that Foligno is a kind of historical link between German printing and Italian

poetry. The students of Gutenberg spread out through all countries, like missionaries, carrying the message of "black art". They taught and practised their trade wherever they could find people who appreciated their knowledge and products and who were willing to pay accordingly. One day, a Gutenberg disciple named Neumeister arrived in Foligno and found in one of the citizens, a man named Orfini, a supporter and companion. In 1472, they created the first book to be printed in Italy and in the Italian language. It turned out to be the most distinguished book of Italian literature: Dante's *Divine Comedy*.

Further afield: Foligno stands on the eastern shore of an extinct lake. Like Lake Trasimeno today, it was never very deep and, helped by deliberate drainage by the Romans, it had dried up completely by the 17th century. It now forms a shallow bowl, called the Vale of Spoleto, which has been conquered by agriculture, and increasingly by industrial estates. If the view of that plain is depressing, head out of Foligno up the steep mountain road to the peaceful, timeless Abbazia di Sassovivo, just 4 miles (6 km) east of the town. The chances are there will be few other visitors as you explore this small Benedictine monastery, founded in 1070, with its gracious Romanesque cloister, set in a woodland clearing.

If remote, wild landscapes appeal to you, you could continue from the monastery along the little-used and highly scenic N77, which climbs to the high plains of Piano di Colfiorito, right on the border between Umbria and the Marches. Fortifications and sweeping views are the reward. Pale, with its castle and Grotta di Pale cave, is the first stop. Scopoli has another well-preserved 15th-century castle, and if your vehicle suspension is up to the strain you can follow the umetalled "white" road from this hamlet around the summit of Mount Aguzzo and back to Foligno. Or you can divert along the N319, through the delightful Menotre valley and, vehicle allowing, to the summit of Mount Tito (3,421 ft/1,043 metres) – true wilderness all the way.

Left, the Palazzo Trinci. Right, a parade before Foligno's cathedral.

NOCERA UMBRA

At the point where the Superstrada forks into the N3 and N75, the Via Flaminia continues from Foligno to the north in a fairly straight line. The hills range closer to the road and, as you head north, the light and wide-open panoramas of the Valle Umbra shrink into the distance behind you. North signifies shadows, dark tones: ombra, umbra, Umbria. This play on words may seem a bit far-fetched, but it is not so far from the truth. The colours of the narrow Topino valley are more muted than the bright fields of the Poverello valley.

Passing the signpost saying **Ponte-centesimo** – indicating the bridge's former status as a toll-bridge charging one centesimo for passage – head up to Nocero Umbra (22 miles/34 km).

Church steeples and a watchtower rise up over this little town situated on the crest of a hill. It's a town famed for its mineral springs, and to reach the spa – **Bagni di Nocera** – you must travel about 7 km (4 miles) further into the mountains. There, the **Sorgente Angelica** and **delle Caciatori** (the Angelica and Hunters springs) can be found. The waters from both these springs can be purchased in bottles, which are exported worldwide from the bottling plant by the railway station in the newer part of town

The old town is the real attraction, however. Behind a fountain, war memorial, ice cream parlour and gate a long climb up a steep slope, so typical for Umbrian towns, passes a series of medieval facades with a wealth of interesting details: inscriptions, portals, door knockers. At the top is a spacious square and some welcome stone benches in the shadow of **San Francesco**, the pinacotheca.

San Francesco houses a lovely and famed polyptych of the *Virgin* by Niccolò di Liberatore, known as Alunno (signed 1483), and a *Crucifixion* attributed to Cimabue.

A street with tastefully-restored **Nocera Umbra**.

houses (note that most of the cars in front have Roman licence plates) leads up to the cathedral of **Santa Maria Assunta**. The original Romanesque building was replaced by one in the baroque style; the only remnant from the former church is the side portal leading to the tower of the former castle.

The town's history is imbued with a touch of scandal. On 10 June, 1421, something happened in this castle which would have made headlines in today's tabloids. The castellan, Pasquale di Vagnolo, invited the powerful Trinci brothers from Foligno to a hunting party here. During the night, Vagnolo murdered the head of the Trinci family – along with his own wife.

Standing at the foot of the tower, looking out across the rolling green hills and the Topino Valley, it is easy to imagine how strategically advantageous the location of Nocera Umbra, the *Noukria* of the Umbrians, was. The Romans had a base here and, in AD 76, they built a shortcut branching off from the Via Flaminia and the valley, leading

directly over the mountains to Ancona on the Adriatic. After changing hands several times in the Middle Ages and following the fall of the Trinci dynasty the community came under the Papal States in 1439. Today, this town of 6,000 residents has spread beyond the ring wall on the hill and down into the valley.

The sign of *Specialità tartufo* (truffle specialities) tempts one to linger a bit longer here. After all, as Cicero said, lust makes the spirit blind. Who would travel on in such a dangerous condition? Perhaps the best place to sample the truffle is not in Nocera Umbra itself, but at the Albergo Ristorante Pennino in the mountain hamlet of Bagnara, 5 miles/ 8km east, named after the nearby Mount Pennino, a winter skiing resort. The restaurant's peaceful rustic setting makes the flavour of truffles and other homemade dishes all the more special. Afterwards you will probably be in no condition to make the three-hour walk to the summit, but you can drive up on the road from Colle Croce, to the south.

eramics and uriosities.

FROM GUALDO TADINO TO THE SCHEGGIA PASS

One often reads and hears tales about the destruction of Umbrian cities, and yet they still survived the ravages of history. They were repeatedly destroyed and rebuilt, and yet some Umbrian towns count among the most beautiful and precious architectural ensembles in Europe. **Gualdo Tadino** is one of them.

The town's compound placename combines its Roman and medieval names. After the legionnaires vanished, *Tadium*, the Roman centre of administration in the Tadino Valley, was drenched in the blood of the Byzantine Narses and the Ostrogoth Totila who battled here. The town was conquered by Emperor Otto III, destroyed by Frederick II and then rebuilt.

The new town was built at the top of a 1,640 ft (500-metre) hill in the year 1180 and became known as Gualdo (from the Lombardic *wald*, wooded). In 1237 it became a free town. The castle **Rocca Flea**, primitive and angular, dates from those times and has retained its original form. When the construction work inside the walls is finally finished, the castle can assume its function as a cultural centre.

One of the most attractive sites is the Romanesque facade of the cathedral of **San Benedetto** with its lovely rose window and richly-decorated main portal. Inside the church, the main altar has a 14th-century Renaissance baptismal font. The **pinacotheca** in the former church of **San Francesco** houses noteworthy paintings by Matteo da Gualdo and Alunno as well as an interesting altar-piece made of majolica by Florence's Bodega della Robbia. The town (population of 14,000) is renowned as a centre of ceramic manufacturing and a free tour of a factory is easy to arrange. Many workshops have grown up along the well-travelled Via Flaminia.

The backdrop of mountains, among them Monte Penna 4,700 ft (1432 me- **The Scheggia Pass.**

tres), lends this friendly town something of the character of an alpine village. As a matter of fact, there is great interest here in mountain hiking on the Monte Cucco range and mountain-climbing expeditions in the higher elevations are popular. White-water enthusiasts like to practise their rafting skills on the ice-cold waters of the Rio "Freddo" (*freddo* meaning cold). Five miles (8km) to the north, a road branches off near **Fossato di Vico** where the 11th-century **church of S. Pietro** is situated. This road leads over a mountain pass to Ancona, a port on the Adriatic Sea. Those with time to spare might like to continue along this road to the renowned baroque and paper-making town of **Fabriano** in the Marches.

The final stretch of the route to the Scheggia Pass leads through a valley basin dominated by a long mountain chain directly to the east. One of these mountains is Monte Cucco itself, Umbria's highest peak, which has an elevation of 5,138 ft (1,566 metres). No great effort is required to get to the summit, however, and it is a popular summer picnic spot. You can drive up from Sigillo, a distance of 6 miles/9km. If you are lucky it might be one of those occasional days when the caves at Ranco di Sigillo, the Grotta di Monte Cucco, are open to the public.

To the west the fields and meadows stretch down to Chiascio; on the other side of the river they back up the hillsides. The ruins of the Roman bridges near **Sigillo** and **Costacciaro** remind travellers that they are journeying along the Via Flaminia.

The tower in the centre of Scheggia, is a relic of the Roman city of *Shisa*. Just as in former times, here the old east-west road (from Gubbio to Arcevia and then on to the Adriatic Sea) joins the north-south axis, the Via Flaminia.

From the top of the pass, at an elevation of 2,073 ft (632 metres), one has a wonderful view into the valley to the north into which the road makes its descent. This idyllic Burano valley was once the main artery between Rome and Byzantium.

GUBBIO

In Umbria it is said that Gubbio was one of the first five towns which was founded after the great Flood. It is a known fact that Gubbio grew out of one of Italy's oldest settlements and was founded long before Rome. *Eugubium*, a flowering Roman town, developed out of *Ikuvium*, an Umbrian settlement. There are only a few relics of this era remaining; one of the most important is the well-preserved Roman amphitheatre in the plain below the medieval town, still used for summer theatrical performances.

Gubbio is a bewitching, mysterious medieval town, with a truly unique character. Whether viewing Gubbio from afar or strolling through the narrow alleys, visitors are constantly struck by the majestic turretted tower of the **Palazzo dei Consoli** ranging above the town. It is the symbol of Gubbio. The palace, built between 1332 and 1337, was commissioned by the citizens rather than a single sovereign. It was the era of free towns and democratic government, an era which lasted from the 12th to the 14th century. The consuls were elected by the population. And this in the midst of the so-called dark Middle Ages.

Ancient tablets: Today, a museum is found inside the Palazzo dei Consoli. Its most important exhibits are the famous Eugubine Tablets. These are written in the Umbrian language. Two different types of lettering, stemming from the Etruscan and the Latin, were used. The texts describe the ceremonies of an ancient college of priests, the Atiedii. They deal with the business of sacrifice, describing how sacrifices should be offered, specifying how the flight of birds should be interpreted and which formula should be used to cast a spell over an enemy city.

Significant as they are in archaeological terms, the Eugubine bronzes are nothing much to look at, but you will enjoy the view from the small loggia off the picture gallery (the door is in the main hall) from which there are dizzying views across the tumbling rooftops

of Gubbio. Note too the number of early stone toilet seats and basins in the main hall of the palazzo downstairs; Gubbio was one of the first cities in Umbria to organise a public water supply, piped to individual palazzi.

A stairway leads from the Palazzo dei Consoli to the **Piazza della Signoria**, also known as **Piazza Grande**. Because of Gubbio's location on the side of a steep hill, huge amounts of earth had to be heaped here before many of the buildings, and especially this square, could be built. Colossal pillared arches were constructed to support the square on the side facing the valley.

Two other palaces frame the square. One is the **Palazzo Pretorio**, today's town hall, and the other is the **Palazzo Ranghiasci**, the only classical element in the otherwise purely medieval scenery of Gubbio, which a young nobleman built for his English wife. The Palazzo dei Consoli was surrounded by the fashionable houses of the well-to-do. The height of the building signified how influential the inhabitants were.

Preceding pages: Gubbio's old town by night.

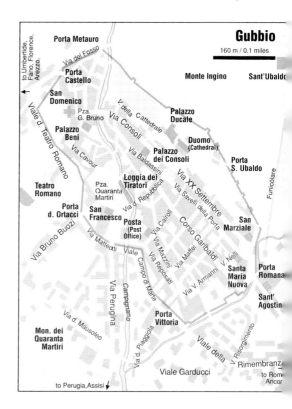

Gubbio
160 m / 0.1 miles

to Umberide, Fano, Florence, Arezzo

Porta Metauro
Via del Fosso
Porta Castello
San Domenico
Viale d. Teatro Romano
Pza. G. Bruno
V. della Cattedrale
Via Consoli
Palazzo Beni
Via Cavour
Via Baldassini
Monte Ingino
Sant'Ubaldo
Palazzo Ducale
Duomo (Cathedral)
Palazzo dei Consoli
Porta S. Ubaldo
Loggia dei Tiratori
Teatro Romano
Pza. Quaranta Martiri
Via XX Settembre
Via Savelli della Porta
Funicolare
Porta d. Ortacci
San Francesco
Via d. Repubblica
Posta (Post Office)
Via Cairoli
Via Mazzini
Corso Garibaldi
Via Maffei
San Marziale
Via Bruno Buozi
Via Matteotti
Viale
Campo di Marte
Via Reposati
V. Nelli
Via V. Armanni
Santa Maria Nuova
Porta Romana
Sant' Agostin
Via Perugina
Porta Vittoria
Via d. Mausoleo
Mon. dei Quaranta Martiri
Via d. Piaggiola
Viale della
Risorgimento
Rimembranz
to Rom Ancor
Viale Garducci
to Perugia, Assisi

By strolling along the Via dei Consoli, you arrive at the **Palazzo del Bargello**, an elegant Gothic palace which was built around the beginning of the 14th century. It was the headquarters for the communal police. The outside wall has a small hole which was used as an official post box. Thus, citizens could anonymously pass on requests to their rulers or file reports about annoying neighbours and other residents.

According to legend, anyone who circles around the fountain in front of the Palazzo del Bargello three times automatically becomes a citizen of Gubbio with all the accompanying rights. It might be as well to bear in mind that the name of this fountain is **Fontana dei Matti** – Fountain of Fools.

Heathen rite: With a wink of the eye, the residents of Gubbio are quite happy to acknowledge themselves to be crazy. Maybe they are referring to their tendency toward mysticism, their religious zeal, or just their enthusiasm during the annual **candle race**, held on on 15 May. This festival, the *Corsa dei Ceri*, is dedicated to St Ubaldo, the town's patron saint. This celebration probably originated from ancient heathen rites which were designed to please the gods of nature in the springtime.

The occasion is an animated and colourful affair centreing on the Palazzo dei Consoli. Three wooden poles, each 23 ft (7 metres) long, symbolise the candles; their phallic shape clearly hints at pre-Christian fertility rites. The Church has, however, rendered them safe by perching tiny figures of saints, dressed in costumes matching those of the candle-bearers, to the tops of the candles. Three teams of candle–bearers, known as *ceraiolo*, compete against each other: the fans and competitors representing St Ubaldo wear shirts of yellow; those who are competing in the name of St George (patron of the merchants) wear blue shirts; and all those with black shirts are associated with St Antonio Abate (patron of farm workers). Membership of a team is considered a great honour.

The candle-bearers raise the wooden

during the Corsa dei Ceri the streets are packed.

poles upright to the chanting encouragement of the crowds and carry them (each candle weighs about a hundredweight) through the streets of the town and up the 2,600-ft (800-metre) high Monte Ingino to the **church of Sant' Ubaldo**, where the body of this great saint lies in a glass casket. The candles are delivered to him as a sacrificial offering. Most people need about one hour to walk this route, but the *ceraioli* race up to the top in just 13 minutes, despite their heavy load.

The route up to Sant'Ubaldo is so narrow that the racing teams cannot overtake each other. Instead, they set off at intervals, and although the race is soon over, the rest of the day is spent in animated discussion about which team won – the one that demonstrated the most skill and prowess, the one that either closed or increased the gap between themselves and their pursuers.

Even when it is not festival time, the rich history of Gubbio is apparent at every turn in the town. Medieval gates, towers, idyllic squares, churches and

palaces abound. Only the clothing, the automobiles and the occasionally heavy traffic serve to jolt one back into the reality of the present day.

You will notice that many of Gubbio's houses have a narrow door next to their main, wide entrance. These were called death doors and were used purely for when there was a death in the house. The deceased left the house through them; afterwards, they were walled shut so that the dead could not re-enter.

Among the many noteworthy palaces and churches here, two which merit special attention are the **Palazzo Ducale**, with a lovely inner courtyard decorated with pillars, and the **cathedral**, directly across from this palace. The Ducal Palace is so named because it was built in 1476 by Frederico di Montefeltro, Duke of Urbino, the famed humanist and soldier, who was invited by the citizens of Gubbio to protect the town following their rebellion against papal rule.

The palazzo was built on the site of an older Lombardic palace where Charlemagne stayed on his way to be crowned Holy Roman Emperor in Rome in the early 9th century. The single-nave Gothic interior of Gubbio's cathedral is dark due to the absence of windows on one side.

This is compensated for by the 13th-century stained glass of the east window, and the serenity of the great stone arches rising to the apex of the nave like the ribs of a whale. The greatest treasure of the church is in the adjacent Museo Capitolare, a 16th-century Flemish cope embroidered with scenes from the Passion, given to Gubbio by Pope Marcellus, a native of the town.

At the lowest point in the town, on one side of the oval-shaped Piazza Quarant Martiri (Square of Forty Martyrs, shot by Nazi's in 1944 in reprisal for attacks by the Italian Resistance) is the church of San Francesco, a lovely 13th-century building adorned with Ottaviano Nelli's gorgeous frescoes on the *Life of the Virgin* (1408–13). The quiet shady cloister nearby has a shop where you can see and buy some of the fine ceramics for which Gubbio has been famous since the Middle Ages.

Young flautist.

IN THE POTTER'S STUDIO

Gubbio was a ceramic production centre even in ancient times, producing the elegant black-burnished bucchera wares that are found in Etruscan graves. The industry was revived in the Middle Ages and reached its zenith in the 16th century when Giorgio Andreoli da Intra, Gubbio's most famous potter, discovered the secret of making a ruby-red glaze. He refused to pass the formula on to anyone, and so the secret went with him to the grave until rediscovered earlier this century. His pottery works in Via della Fornace di Mastro Giorgio is now one of Gubbio's best restaurants.

Now Gubbio's pottery tradition is alive again, and though many local potters are content to produce reproductions of Etruscan and Renaissance wares, some are creating their own new designs. Such a craftsman is Leo Grillin, one of the town's most renowned artists, who operates from his studio at No. 78 in the ancient and steeply sloping Via dei Consoli. As well as being a potter he is a sculptor and painter. He hand crafts vases, plates, various containers and a wide variety of decorative items which he sells in his three shops. His wife and daughter are also employed in these shops.

Now 54 years old, Grillin has run the 200-year-old family business since 1960. By the age of eight Grilli had already discovered his artistic talents, and soon thereafter his love for both modern and traditional art. He has more respect for the latter because it is, as he says, "the basis for creative work, the basis for finding new ways and forms." Modern as well as traditional forms, colours and patterns are evidenced in his ceramics.

Many other establishments try to imitate the creations of this master and to produce them more cheaply by machine, but Grilli remains true to traditional working methods, the same ones which have been used for generations in the town. The creation of fine ceramic wares demands detailed technical knowledge as well as enormous precision. He uses different types of clay for the various products. These clays vary basically in their fat content, and the exact ratio and the consistency of

the individual raw ingredientss remain Grilli's well-guarded secret.

Grillo himself forms each article on an old potter's wheel. With simple "tools", such as a piece of wire or a favourite stick, an unassuming lump of clay is transformed into a true work of art. The pieces are then fired in an indirectly-heated oven, usually heated to a temperature exceeding 1,472°F (800°C). The slip, up to 1.5 mm thick, serves to make the still-porous clay watertight and to protect the decor from harmful effects from elements such as lactic acid. The next step is the painting of the still grey-brown clay artifacts with a special underglaze. Here the maestro has two female assistants. One is Sara, an 18-year-old American who came to Europe specifically to serve an apprenticeship under Leo Grilli. The other is Cinzia, a 26-year-old Gubbian woman who has been assisting Grilli for the past 10 years. Sara and Cinzia both describe the master as a spontaneous and strong personality with a wonderful love of life.

Pottery is one of the most ancient of man's inventions. Archaeological finds near Jericho in Palestine prove that ceramic products were being produced as early as 7000 BC. It has been proved that the use of the potter's wheel in the ancient Orient dates back four millennia. In Italian territory, the potter's craft had special significance especially among the Etruscans. Terracotta panels and clay statues of the gods were used in the decoration of the temples. Under Roman rule, *terra sigillata* found wide-spread usage. This technique, dominated by the colours of red and black, was first employed about 150 BC. It was not until the time of the Renaissance that Italy once again gained fame through the production of the Medici porcelain in Florence and with the development of important ceramic centres in Umbria such as Deruta, Orvieto and Gubbio.

What hopes for the future does an artist like Leo Grilli have, a man who lives solely for his art and who loves his craft as one would love his own children? His answer is simple:"That more young Italian men and women will become interested in this profession so that the potter's craft will live on in Gubbio.".

THE NERA VALLEY

The Valnerina, or Nera Valley, lies a bit off the beaten tourist track (it is impossible to explore the area without a car), and anyone who wants to become more intimately acquainted with this enchanting region should plan to spend more than just one day here. Find accommodation in the old ducal city of Spoleto, which makes the best base for exploring the area.

A choice of routes: If for no other reason, Spoleto is recommended for the stunning aproaches it offers to the valley via Monti Spoletini. Despite the lofty elevation, several roads cross the mountain range. One is the N395 which leads over the Forca di Cerro and joins the N209 above Grotti near the Castel San Felice or Piedipaterno. An alternative route is the one that starts at Valdarena (branching off from the Via Flaminia, the N3, in the direction of Valico, about 6 miles/9 km south of Spoleto) and leading thereafter to Ancaiano. This route is undoubtedly very picturesque, but the ride along unmetalled roads can be bumpy. There are two roads which lead into the Valnerina. Drivers can take either the southern route in the direction of Ferentillo or the northern one through Case and Ceselli. Both of these roads merge into the N209. Those who are a bit anxious about driving over the pass, or who have limited time, can travel via Montefranco and Arrone or through Terni in order to reach the N209.

Travellers arriving from Florence can even use the A1 which leads to Rome. In this case, exit from the autostrada at Orte – not far from where the Nera flows into the Tiber River – and follow the N204 directly to Terni.

There are various theories explaining the origins of the name Nera. The one propounded by Antonio, a barber and unoffical historian in Terni, is that in about 300 BC, before the Roman legions marched this far north, the valley of the Nahar was inhabited by a tribe of the Sabines who named themselves af-ter the Naharci River. In those days, and still today in the region of Triponzo, at the northern end of the valley, the river was fed by sulphur springs. And, in the language of the Sabines, the word for sulphur was "nahr".

The Virgilian commentator Maurus Servius Honoratus was probably the first proponent of this theory. Other explanations include the theory that the name Nera comes from the Greek word *nar*, meaning strong, vehement, fierce. This could refer to the ferocity of the valley's inhabitants, or to the strength of the rushing river Nera itself, which has cut several deep gorges in the layers of limestone rock.

There are further fanciful explanations. The source of this river, located in the region around Monte Cornaccione, is found in a cliff with two openings. People of former times thought they saw here the snout of a calf with two nostrils, two *narici*, and thus named the river Nar.

In ancient times the Nera formed the border between the Umbrians to the **Preceding pages:** a welcome break – the Nera Valley is a paradise for cycling and walking excursions. **Below,** ruling the roost.

west, and the Sabines to the east until the Romans arrived. After conquering the Umbrians, between 310 and 295 BC, the Romans marched through the valley, defeating the Sabines in the year 290 and the Picenti in the year 268. Connecting roads were built, including one leading to Triponzo. Because of the location of thermal springs here, this town acquired a certain amount of renown during the time of the republic.

After the Romans came the Ostrogoths, then the Byzantines and finally the Lombards. The Lombard king, Authari, reorganised his kingdom in the 6th century, and replaced all of the former administrative districts with duchies. And in each he installed a *dux militum* as sovereign. One of these duchies stretched from Assisi to Norcia, and its duke, a certain Faroaldo I, chose Spoleto as the site of his residence. In making this choice, he laid the foundations for the important cultural and political role which Spoleto would play throughout the turbulent history of the Nera Valley.

To the Abbey of San Pietro: San Pietro in Valle, also called **Abbazia di Ferentillo**, Umbria's oldest monastery, thus became the burial place for the dukes of Spoleto. The rebellious son Trasmondo was also buried there in 739 as was his successor, Hilderic Dagileopa, in the year 740 and, the last of the line, a certain Vinigisius in 822.

Two small roads wind up to the monastery from the N209. One is an attractive cypress-lined drive leading up a steep incline. This road, which branches off to the left where the main road curves to the right, 3 miles (4 km) past Ferentillo, is recommended for travellers who are arriving from the direction of Terni. The other possibility, a metalled road, branches off to the left about 1,000 ft (300 metres) after passing through Macenano. The car park for the monastery can be found in a clearing behind the church.

The monastery's location is idyllic. It nestles between olive groves and dense woods. But it is not just because of the enchanting landscape that a visit to this

lot to be uffled.

monastery can be recommended. Its other attractions include a collection of Roman sarcophagi and the abbey's unique high altar.

It appears that, outside the main season, so few tourists come to this out-of-the-way place that local entrepreneurs have not thought it worthwhile to establish any souvenir shops. Usually there isn't a single parked car to be seen outside the abbey, apart from a small *cinquecento* belonging to the custodian of the church, a smiling old man who wears a knitted cap. He is always delighted to have reason to fish the church keys out of his pocket.

The five important Roman sarcophagi are not difficult to find. The first one is located just before the transept, on the left side. It is decorated by a mythological scene – the journey across the river Styx to Hades. The second sarcophagus serves as an altar in the left-hand apse. The custodian tells us that John and Lazarus used this. There are reliefs of the dead as well as scenes from a banquet and a hunt.

The main altar is of special significance. It is a rare example of Lombardic sculpture, a masterpiece completed in 742 by a mason named Ursus. This was two years after the death of the man who commissioned it, Hilderic Dagaileopa, the former duke of Spoleto who had been deposed and sought refuge in the abbey just as Faroaldo II had before him. The inscription on the sarcophagus reads: *Hildericvs Dagileopa in honorem sancti Petri et amore sancti Leonis et sancti Grigori pro remedio animae. Ursus magister fecit.* Two men, clad only in loincloths and surrounded by trees of life and other symbols of Christian mysticism, confront the viewer with outstretched arms. The man on the left is Ursus. He is holding in his left hand the sign of his art. Above the head of the man on the right, who is probably meant to depict Christ, the cup of life floats between two doves signifying love and freedom.

In the top of the tree, which resembles a sun, the architect Ursus placed isosceles crosses, symbols of an all-embrac- **San Pietro in Valle.**

ing unity, for the harmony between God and man. Note the unusual headgear of the two men, their hair, their facial expressions as well as the symbolic circular ornamentation of the back of the altar. Instinctively, one thinks of the covenant of the rainbow (Genesis 9:11) and the story of the Creation

The third sarcophagus is just in front of the east pillar of the right-hand aisle and is said to contain the remains of Faroaldo II. It is particularly unusual, with a remote resemblance to the columned sarcophagi of Asia Minor. It dates from the first half of the third century – it was common for Roman sarcophagi to be reused by the early Christians.

Under the middle arch is the Greek god of fertility, Dionysos, with a satyr. To the left, a maenad dances with a satyr and to the right a silenus with Pan. On both of the long sides, a griffin-like figure lurks, a kind of cross between the Siren and Pegasus. The lid is not as old as the sarcophagus itself; it dates from the Middle Ages.

The fourth sarcophagus is on the side wall of the right-hand transept. This, too, dates from the third century and its reliefs depict the story of *Cupid and Psyche*. Finally, the last of the stone sarcophagi, dating from the latter part of the third century, is on the right-hand wall of the nave and depicts sumptuous scenes from a hunt for wild boar and antelopes.

Returning to the car park, be sure to glance across to the other side of the valley. There the next destination beckons – a former *castello*, today a quaint village bearing the charming name of **Umbriano**.

Land of castles: The journey continues in the direction of Sambucheto. Customarily, when one speaks of the Valnerina, one means the entire region which includes Monti di Spoleto and Monti Sibillini. In reality, however, due to various local characteristics, history and the type of settlements, two differing zones can be recognised here.

The first, which is made up of the area along the Nera and its tributaries, is

he high altar
n the abbey
hurch.

SAN PIETRO IN VALLE

During the time of Theodoric, the Ostrogoth king, the Nera Valley experienced perhaps the most important wave of immigration in its history: Syrian hermits who were fleeing from the persecution of the Aryan emperor of Ostrom, Anastasios Dikoros, came to this region to settle. In the year 514, about 300 of these hermits arrived in Umbria.

Two of them, named John and Lazarus, settled at the foot of Monte Solenne on a small hill on the right side of the river Nera, between today's Sambucheto and Ferentillo. They lived there as ascetics for 40 years.

When John died, Lazarus prayed to the Lord to comfort him in his loneliness. It thus came to pass that St Peter appeared to the seventh Lombardic duke of Spoleto, Faroaldo II, in a dream and advised him to build a church at the solitary place where a hermit lived. Interpreting the dream as a revelation, Faroaldo promptly ordered the construction of a church and monastery during that same year, 703. It was built in honour of St Peter on the site where the hermitage of Lazarus was located.

Faroaldo II himself moved to the monastery and became a monk after his son, Trasmondo II, removed him from power around 720. He lived strictly according to the tenets of St Benedict and died there in the year 728. Towards the end of the 9th century (perhaps 881), the abbey was badly damaged by the Saracens. To protect it, the fortresses of Matarella, Precetto and Umbriano were built. In the year 996, Germany's King Otto III, on his way to Rome to be crowned as emperor, ordered the restoration of the abbey. Thus, some art historians have justly termed San Pietro in Valle a "unicum", or "an island of Ottonian culture in Umbria".

Under the express wishes of Emperor Henry II ("the saint"), the restoration work, carried out under Abbot Luitprand, was completed in 1016. Towards the end of the 11th century, the frescoes of the church's nave were commissioned. In the year 1190, Spoleto took over control of the region's protective fortresses. This slowly led to a decay of monastical power. The cloister and today's monks' building were added in the 12th–13th century.

In 1226, the treaty of San Germano granted the pope sovereignty over the abbey and its possessions. In the year 1234, the pope placed these under the control of the Cistercian Abbey of Fiastra in the Marches. Quarrels among the monks led Pope Boniface VIII to issue the Bull of 1300 (or perhaps 1303), placing the abbey directly under the control of the Lateran Chapter. One decision they made was to reduce the number of monks in San Pietro in Valle, a move which led to the practical disintegration of the institution.

Fortunes changed for the better in 1346, when the abbey was freed from all interest payments. In the mid-15th century, the abbey was able to commission the frescoes in the apse. In the 1470s, the Lateran Chapter transferred the spiritual and administrative responsibilities for the abbey to Pope Sixtus IV. He, in turn, granted them as a benefice to Bartolomeo della Rovere. Under Sixtus' successor, Pope Innocent VIII, the abbey was placed under the control of the family of the Cybo-Malaspina, the lords of Ferentillo.

At the beginning of the 16th century, under Abbot Attone II, the cloister and the monks' building were restored and the facade was rebuilt. In 1730, the last descendant of the Cybo, Alderano Malaspina, sold his property to the prince of Umbriano and Precetto – a Frenchman named "Luigi Desiderato di Montholon". In 1848, the spiritual sovereignty for the monastery was transferred, with the consent of Pope Pius IX, to the archbishop of Spoleto.

"Di Montholon" sold his property in 1860 to the town of Ferentillo, from whom the Costanzi family purchased it. This family still owns the property, which now incorpoates a restaurant, except for the abbey church which was bought by the state as part of the national cultural heritage. The church's most recent restoration was completed in 1931.

Because of the large number of sculptural fragments dating from the 8th century and set into the walls of the belfry and the nave, as well as other architectural elements – such as the horseshoe arches of two of the windows – many art historians date the construction to the time of Faroaldo II. They point to models such as San Salvatore in Spoleto. Other art experts reject this theory, resting their case on the ground plan which they say is an example of the so-called T form. This is typified by a nave, in front of which is the choir with three apses. According to Adriano Prandi, this clearly follows the Benedictine pattern of the augmented church of the monastery at Cluny.

Cluny, however, was first consecrated in the year 981; the date of construction of San Pietro in Valle must be about 100 years later. This assumption is based on the fact that this pattern did not spread throughout Italy until the mid-11th century. The local historian Fabbi offers a third hypothesis. For him, the form of the present church is the result of two different construction phases. The first structure was an early Christian one, modelled on the crypts of the Galla Placidia in Ravenna. This structure is now the transept. In the 8th century, Fabbi argues, it was expanded; the design being modelled on San Salvatore.

Perhaps the following compromise is the answer to the puzzle: an original church, modelled on Spoleto's structure from the time of Faroaldo II, was destroyed by the Saracens. Enough material remained to rebuild it, incorporating the former nave as a transept. This reconstruction, ordered by Otto III, was based on the Cluniac floor plan.

On the northern arm of the transept is the campanile, or bell tower, dating from the first half of the 11th century. Its architecture is in no way Umbrian, but rather in the so-called Lombardic style which prevails throughout all of Latium. However, it has its own special features – it is not a true square. It is composed of five storeys each with two round-arched windows, has brick cornices, is divided by marble corbels and has decorations of brick.

Set into the walls are the surviving relics of earlier structures or sculptures. For example, a statue of St Peter from the 11th century on the fourth storey greets visitors. A portal dating from

Guardians of San Pietro: <u>left</u>, the abbey's custodian; <u>above</u>, a sculpture flanking the door.

the same era leads through the right-hand wall of the church's nave into the 12th-century cloister. Sculptured scenes on the outside of the portal, probably from the 11th century, depict St Peter and St Paul.

So much for the outside. The inside of the church houses the legendary high-altar and the five Roman sarcophagi. The walls of the nave provide evidence of early Umbrian painting of unequalled quality. This is a three-tiered cycle depicting scenes from the Old and New Testaments. Although it has not been preserved in its entirety, that which still remains is definitely worth the journey here.

The scenes depicted on the frescoes are as follows, beginning with the rear wall of the facade. Left wall, uppermost level: God separates light from darkness, the creation of Adam and of Eve, Adam gives names to the animals, the origin of Original Sin and the banishment of Adam and Eve from Paradise.

Right wall, uppermost level: the prophets Samuel and Daniel as well as two angels, again two angels. Left wall, middle level: Cain and Abel offer sacrifices, Cain kills his brother Abel, God appears to Noah, construction of the ark, life aboard the ark, Abraham and three angels, Abraham sacrifices Isaac, Isaac blesses Jacob.

Right wall, middle level: the birth of Christ is proclaimed to the shepherds, the Three Kings, adoration of Christ by the Three Kings, Herod's murder of the children of Bethlehem, the baptism of Christ and finally the marriage at Cana.

Left wall, lower level: the paintings on the bottom level are no longer visible except for a few discernible traces of a scene showing Benjamin standing in front of Joseph.

Right wall, lower level: the entrance of Jesus into Jerusalem, the Last Supper, the Apostles washing Christ's feet, the way up to Calvary.

These 12th-century frescoes are among the oldest examples of how local artists attempted to replace the predominant Byzantine style of the time with a naturalistic style. Their careful observation of man and nature is clearly seen – a path which would, centuries later, lead to the Renaissance. These pictures represent the beginnings of an independent Umbrian school of painting.

marked by steep wooded hills and is bordered by numerous *castelli*. These castles were constructed for strategic reasons, in order to guard the connecting roads. The second zone is made up of the regions around Norcia, Cascia and, to a certain extent, Sellano. This region is characterised by its wide and almost flat mountain plains . The highest points of these slopes are usually crowned, also for strategic reasons, by small settlements.

Aside from the *castelli*, innumerable *torri* (towers) are also found here. In former times, these towers functioned as beacons to spread the word that plunderers were approaching. This network grew up as a protective measure after the attacks by the Saracens in the 9th and 10th centuries. The conflict between the emperor and the papacy, as well as the resulting battles by aspiring communities for more independence, made structures of this sort even more necessary.

Papigno and the **Rocca** on the other side of Monte San Angelo are the first of this network of more than 20 *torri* lying along the N209.

Travellers journeying along the Corno in the direction of Cascia will pass by the picturesque *castelli* of Nortosce, of Argentigli and Biselli. The tower of Serravalle passed the signals on to the tower of Collegiacone and so forth. A similar chain is found in Valle Castorina from Torre del Nera through Preci, Todiano and Campi and then on to Forca d'Ancarno.

The plan of the *castelli* were almost all identical – a walled triangle or trapezium with square corner towers at the acute angles and semi-cylindrical or polygonal towers at the obtuse angles. The four-cornered towers were constructed of ashlar blocks between which peepholes were left open. Tower-like front structures served to protect the pointed arch entrance gate. In the gateway of Geppa Castle, the recess for the drop-gate can still be seen. The tallest structure was invariably the castle tower with its small doorway high above the ground, attainable only by means of a

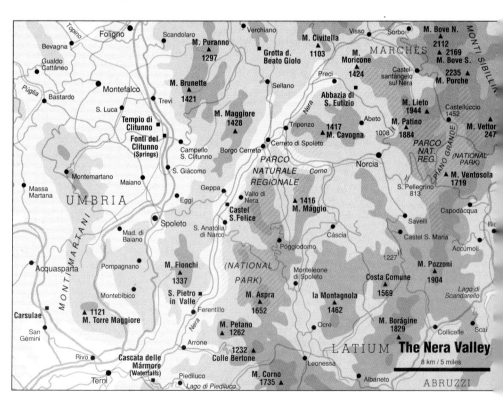

ladder. It had several upper storeys made of wood and often had a secret subterranean passageway. **Montefranco** and **Triponzo** are just two lovely examples of this type of hilltop fortress.

The final consolidation of papal supremacy at the end of the 14th century led to the demilitarisation of this region. Many *castelli* and *torri* were abandoned and only ruins or memories of their names still remain. Others were converted into villages with an open structural form, typical of the peasant settlements of this region. However, with the advent of the 19th century, when migration to the towns was already underway, many of these settlements were deserted; today the ruins are the preserve of grazing sheep and cattle. Umbriano is a good example of just such a village.

To Umbriano: Just at the end of Macenano, a small road turns off to the right, across the Nera. This is the Via di Colleponte. Crossing over the river along this road, one travels further in the direction of Colleponte. After about 1,000 ft (300 metres), there is a gravel road to the right which is wide enough for cars to park.

Invariably you will see groups of women women washing their laundry in a large stone trough, one of several hereabouts (they lead up the hillside in step formation towards the village). The function of these troughs is to collect the rain and spring water which is filtered by the numerous and dense reeds growing there. This is an extremely effective and ecologically sound purification plant – a system seen relatively frequently in this region.

Two paths lead up to the village and both are fairly easy to follow (it takes, at the most, one hour to walk to the top). The one leads up the hillside along the paved road to Colleponte. Beyond the village there is a wood where a *sentiero* (path) forks off to the right (it might be hidden by the dense undergrowth). The other route follows the river.

Few people, however, visit Umbriano by foot. Nobody lives in the village any more, most of its former residents having moved away after World War II and

he unspoilt
andscape of
 e
 alnerina.

the rest about 20 years ago. Younger residents moved to Rome or Milan to earn a living and the older inhabitants eventually moved to Colleponte, leaving the village to the goatherds and their flocks. At one time several thousand goats were herded annually from their summer grazing areas in the mountains to the Etruscan Maremma or the Roman campagna for the winter months.

The most interesting of the two routes to Umbriano is probably the one that follows the the river. To tackle it in comfort, you will need sturdy footwear and a picnic lunch. It starts gently: a loose covering of gravel leads along the Nera out of the valley, passing several houses along the way. On the other side of the valley San Pietro in Valle can be seen. A wooded hillside lies to the left and to the right lie lush riverside meadows. After walking for about 25 minutes, you should leave the well-worn path, which continues in a southwesterly direction, and turn left on to a path leading up the hillside. Shortly after this point a chain blocks the path (these

barriers indicate that the region is still used for grazing), but it is quite easy to cross. The trail turns to the left, leads past the ruins of a house and turns into a 5-ft (1-metre) wide path. It is again crossed by a barbed wire fence and leads alongside a spring spurting out of a pipe on the right-hand side.

Shortly afterwards the *sentiero* forks. Those who follow the lower fork, leading slightly downhill, will reach a bend. The path, protected on the right by old retaining walls built into the hillside, leads again uphill and then along the top of a retaining wall. A few steps above the wall is a small clearing. It is Umbriano's old threshing floor, covered with flagstones. Again and again it comes into view, while San Pietro in Valle shines in the sunlight on the opposite hillside. It is said that the monastery and the village have approximately the same elevation – 1,200 ft (370 metres) above sea level.

Shortly before reaching the first houses of the village, you see on the right a small stone drinking trough for

Triponzo lies at the confluence o the Nera and Corno rivers.

cattle. To the left are the remains of the church of Umbriano and to the right is the castle. Despite its age, it is still at least 50 ft (15 metres) high, has a square foundation (15 x 15 ft/4.5 x 4.5 metres) and a massive wall. Inside, it is covered by a barrel vault.

Ghost village: The houses are practically ruins, and no furniture or domestic utensils are left inside. A few of the wooden doors are still hanging on their hinges. The wooden floors do not look particularly stable, but it is worthwhile taking a look behind the old walls. Wild blackberry and raspberry brambles clamber up the old house walls, and alleyways, sometimes built as steps, become more and more impassable. The path which leads up from the Nera Valley crosses over a hillside to the west of Umbriano. Centuries ago, this hillside was terraced.

Nowadays even the main street leading through Umbriano is becoming overgrown. Sloping gently upward, it leads in a northeasterly direction to a wooded hillside. In the shade of the trees, it

merges into a wide path approaching from the right. This leads back to the starting point.

Because of the poor soil of the area, the villagers could never rely only on the harvests they managed to extract from their own land. The necessary supplements were provided by means of collective ownership of the woods and pastures as well as the granting of rights to collect wood and to graze the herds on public or even private grounds. By combining the sparse yields from the jointly-farmed land with the crops from their own gardens, villagers managed to eke out a living. Such communal principles, once applied in the entire region, are still practised in the mountain region, especially around Norcia.

To reach Norcia, continue up the N209 to **Triponzo** (from *tre ponti* meaning three bridges), the *castello* at the junction of the Corno and Nera, where there is a beautiful castle and thermal springs. It is thought that the community was built around a former hermitage. One of the owners, Domenico Bucchi-Accica,

many llages only e old have mained ehind.

bishop of Norcia, erected a portico here in 1887 along the bath houses. The remains can still be seen.

From Triponzo, the N396 is a fast road that will take you straight to Norcia It would be quite possible to visit this town without realising that it was the birthplace of St Benedict, the founder of western monasticism and a man who has been described as one of the architects of modern Europe. Whereas Assisi honoured St Francis with one of the greatest medieval churches in Christendom, Norcia has no more than a second-rate statue of St Benedict standing in its main square.

The town is much more preoccupied with its reputation as a centre for the processing and curing of pork. The Piazza San Benedetto is ringed by *norcineria*, butchers' shops selling the excellent locally produced prosciutto and numerous varieties of salami, ranging from tiny sausages to great meat-filled balloons.

The appearance of Norcia owes much to the regular occurrence of earthquakes.

Houses were deliberately built low (after the destructive tremor of 1859 an edict was issued setting a maximum height of 40 ft/12.5 metres). Many buildings are still being reconstructed after the last violent earthquake which occurred in 1979.

The centre of Norcia has a certain rough charm. The church of San Benedetto has an elegant Gothic portal and the upper portion of the facade has a pretty geometric window, added when the church was rebuilt after the devastating 1859 earthquake. The interior is sombre and uninviting but the crypt is worth exploring. It is built up against the foundations of the main temple of the Roman forum, and on the spot where St Benedict is supposed to have been born in AD 480.

The town's most appealing building by far is the extraordinary Edicola (also known as the Tempietto, or little temple) on the corner of Via Umberto in the north of the town. This low tower, built in the mid 14th century, is covered in inscriptions and tiny but very detailed

Far from the madding crowd.

bas reliefs of masonic tools, the sun, Christ the Lamb and the instruments of the Passion, as well as very complex geometrical patterns and a corbel table of animal heads. Nobody knows for certain what purpose this building served, but it may have been associated with a trade guild.

To the north of this building you will find the narrow streets and low houses of the Quartiere Capolaterra, the shepherds' quarter. Though this is in the process of redevelopment, you can still see ancient and crumbling houses where as much space was given to the winter quarters of sheep as to human habitation. The area reverberates to the sound of concrete mixers as the interiors are gutted and rebuilt. The reason is Norcia's latest phase of development as a ski resort: in a good year, the snows on the surrounding mountains remain until June (Virgil called the town *frigida Nursia* – icy Norcia).

Due south of Norcia, a dead straight road passes through the town's industrial estate to the hamlet of Santa Scolastica and a left turn takes you to Castelluccio. When you reach the top of the pass, you drop over rim of Mount Ventisola and see the vast Piano Grande spread out before you. The Piano Grande (literally Great Plain) is the largest of three natural basins surrounding Castelluccio, the lone village just visible in the distance. The empty plain, 5 miles (8 km) in length, is as flat as a cricket pitch, and virtually empty except for the odd haystack and field hut. If you come here in winter the plain is bleak and dangerous to cross on foot – on the worst days bells are rung continuously in Castelluccio to guide inhabitants home. In early summer, by contrast, the grassland of the plain is one continuous flower meadow and later in summer, during the holiday season, the air is filled with hang-gliders who launch themselves from the rim of the surrounding mountains and coast down to the plain.

Rural idyll: Tiny Castelluccio is a working village that seems uncertain whether it wants the attention of tourists and greets them warily. If you stop for coffee, fierce sheep dogs will bark at you and chickens, scrabbling among the manure heaps piled in the streets, stop for a while to look quizzically in your direction. Castelluccians crop hay from the plain to feed their cows, and grow tiny sweet lentils for which the area is famous all over Italy. The village is, though, a perfect base for walking, surrounded as it is by a landscape of great natural beauty and interest. Immediately to the east, Monte Sibillini rises to over 8,000 ft (2,448 metres) but is not an especially difficult climb in good weather if you are fit and properly equipped. It is a walk that will reward anyone interested in alpine flora.

The return journey to Spoleto, via Norcia, could take in Cascia, a pilgrim town dedicated to Saint Rita, patron saint of infertility, parenthood and those in desperate situations. If you are fortunate not to be so afflicted, you can at least enjoy an invigorating walk in the alpine meadows around St Rita's birthplace, near Cascia, the scenic hamlet of Roccaporena.

ennine othills.

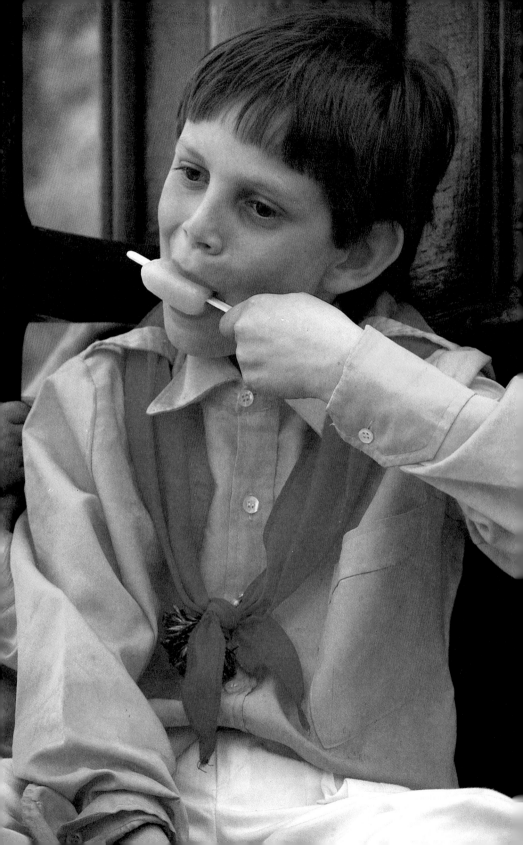

TRAVEL TIPS

GETTING THERE

BY AIR

Umbria is easily accessible from the international airports in Pisa, Rome, Bologna and Florence. Of the four, Pisa is the most convenient. There are frequent scheduled and charter flights into Pisa and the airport is less prone to industrial action than larger airports such as Rome. A number of travel agents specialising in Italian travel offer attractive fly-drive deals aimed at villa owners, but they are heavily booked in summer, so reservations need to be made well in advance.

From Pisa airport it is less than two hours' drive on the autostrada, by way of Florence, to Perugia, capital of Umbria.

The journey from Rome airport by car is about the same distance by autostrada – 176 km/110 miles – but the route passes through a heavily industrialised region of Italy. Rome's airport is a major international hub, served by trans-Atlantic and inter-European flights; for that reason it is a busy airport and cheap package deals are not so easy to find.

Bologna's airport is, by contrast, a good choice if you make a last-minute decision to visit Umbria and find that all other flights are booked. Several car rental firms have offices in the airport which is next to the A14 Adriatic autostrada; this takes you to Faro and then inland on the Ne to Gubbio and northern Umbria, a distance of 290 km (180 miles).

Florence Peretola airport now receives a limited number of international flights. These are primarily geared at business travellers and, at present, represent the most expensive option. The airport is located 6 km (4 miles) northwest of the city and you will have to negotiate busy suburbs to reach the A1 autostrada for Perugia.

BY RAIL

Connections can be made into two trans-European rail services that call at Florence, where you can change for onward services to Umbria: the Palatino from Paris to Rome via Turin and Genoa and the Italia Express from London to Rome via Lille, Strasbourg, Basel, Milan and Bologna. In both cases, the cost can exceed that of a scheduled flight. Advance reservation is obligatory and you have to book a couchette or sleeping compartment on the Palatino.

There is a motorail service from Boulogne to Milan operated by SNCF French railways during the summer. At Milan you can either drive on down to Umbria, or continue with Italian motorail services. Be warned: this is probably the most expensive way to get to Umbria.

BY ROAD

On a good day it is just possible to drive from northern Europe to Umbria in 24 hours using the main north-south motorways, but during the holiday seasons these roads are heavily congested and you may have to allow for two or even three overnight stops. The combined cost of tolls, petrol, insurance, accommodation (and cross-Channel ferries) makes this an expensive option unless you are travelling as a group of three or more (and sharing the stress of driving).

If you choose to drive, however, you can buy petrol coupons at the Italian border (or in advance through motoring organisations such as Britain's AA and RAC) which will give you a 15 percent discount on petrol in Italy, where prices are considerably higher than elsewhere in Europe.

There is also a long-distance coach service from London to Florence via Paris, Turin, Genoa, Milan, Venice and Bologna (details from National Express, Victoria Coach Station, London SW1. Tel: 071-730 0202).

TRAVEL ESSENTIALS

VISAS & PASSPORTS

US, EC and Commonwealth citizens can visit Italy for up to three months with a valid personal identification card or passport. Children under the age of 16 must have their own passport, or be entered in the passport of one of their parents. Citizens of other countries should apply for a visa from Italian embassies or consulates.

Anyone entering Italy by car must carry a valid driver's licence, car registration papers and an International Green Insurance Card (you may be requested to present all three at a random traffic check).

Cats and dogs must have an official health certificate, issued by a vet and dated no earlier than 30 days prior to arrival in Italy. They must also have been inoculated against rabies; the certificate of vaccination must have been issued at least 20 days and no more than 11 months before entering Italy. Officially, owners have to bring muzzles and leashes for their dogs.

CURRENCY

There is no limit to the amount of currency that can be imported into Italy. It is possible to take up to 1 million lire out of the country. Visitors planning to take the equivalent of more than 4 million lire (per person) in foreign currency out of Italy should declare the total amount they have in their possession upon their initial arrival in the country.

CUSTOMS

Arrival: Items intended for personal use may be brought into Italy free of duty. The usual European Community regulations apply to the import of coffee, alcohol, perfumes and cigarettes. All video equipment must be declared upon arrival. Neither big knives nor reserve canisters of petrol are allowed into the country, for safety reasons. Information regarding the import of hunting weapons is available at Italian embassies and consulates.

Departure: Goods acquired in Italy whose total value does not exceed the equivalent of US$500 may be exported duty-free. Art objects and antiques can only be exported under licence and an application must be made to the Italian Chamber of Art.

MONEY MATTERS

The unit of currency in Italy is the lire. There are 1,000, 2,000, 5,000, 10,000, 50,000 and 100,000 lire bills. Expertly forged 50,000 lire notes are also in circulation. Pay special attention to the watermark and don't be surprised if the cashier to whom you present a 50,000 lire bill examines it – literally – under a magnifying glass. Coins come in denominations of 50, 100, 200 and 500 lire.

There's been considerable discussion over recent years regarding currency reform in Italy. Some people believe change is imminent, but there has been no official announcement yet. The idea is to knock off three zeros, thereby considerably simplifying things for native Italians and foreigners alike (i.e. 1,000 lire under the present scheme would become 1 lira under the new). Until this reform actually becomes reality, there is one small comfort to ease the wait: on the basis of the current rate of exchange in Italy, it is relatively easy to become a lire-millionaire.

EUROCHEQUES

Eurocheques are very widely accepted as a means of paying for goods or obtaining hard cash. Currently, you can get up to a maximum of 30,000 lire per cheque. Don't forget that once the currency indication has been entered it cannot be changed; always fill out the name of the bank where you are cashing the cheque, the date, the appropriate form and last but not least, sign the cheque in the presence of a bank employee. The person helping you at the bank will want to see your passport or personal identification card, so come prepared. Cheques cashed for foreign currency incur no commission or additional charges.

EC CARDS

With a Eurocheque card and PIN number you can withdraw money at any time of the night or day from cash machines located at various Italian banks, recognisable by their blue and red EC sign. You have three chances to feed in the correct PIN number. If you fail by your third try, the machine will give you back your card with the message that from now on, this card will not be accepted at any other cash machine. However, you can still use the card in conjunction with Eurocheques to obtain money.

If your EC card should, for some reason, be swallowed by the cash machine, you can get it back by presenting your passport or personal identification card at the bank within three days.

EXCHANGE MACHINES

Airports, railway stations and many city centre banks in Italy now have 24 hour automatic currency exchange machines that give you lire in exchange for bank notes. The rate of exchange is excellent and there is only a small commission fee, usually around 1,500 lire. The machines accept bank notes in most European currencies, plus US dollars and Japanese yen. When you press the button to denote the currency you intend to feed in, instructions appear on the screen in your own language (i.e. if you press the sterling button, you will be given instructions in English).

Feed your notes into the slot indicated; the machine may reject notes with deep creases, so flatten the note and try again. The screen shows the amount you have fed in, and the number of lire you will receive in exchange. If you are happy, press the "enter" button to complete the transaction; if not, press the "reject" button to receive your money back.

CREDIT CARDS

Diners Club, American Express, Visa and Mastercard are accepted in most hotels and restaurants and in many up-market shops. Establishments that accept credit cards usually display a sign saying *Carta Si* (Card Yes) on their door or window.

Despite the high price of petrol in Italy, very few petrol stations currently accept credit cards. A few in city centres now accept American Express, but they are the exception rather than the rule.

TRAVELLER'S CHEQUES

You will not have any problem exchanging traveller's cheques for lire at any bank. The advantage of this particular form of currency is its security; lost or stolen cheques can be replaced quickly and without complications. Traveller's cheques can be purchased at all banks.

GETTING ACQUAINTED

GEOGRAPHY

Umbria is the only region of the Italian peninsula which has no coast. This emerald-green, hilly heart of Italy is surrounded by Tuscany to the west and north, the Marches to the east and Latium to the south, and it is composed of two provinces (Perugia and Terni). About 800,000 people living in 92 communities are spread out over an area of 8,500 sq. km (3,280 sq. miles). Fifty-three percent of Umbria's land area is mountainous, 41 percent is hilly and only 6 percent is relatively flat. The population is evenly distributed over the entire region; there are no densely populated areas and few completely uninhabited areas. Even Umbria's capital city, Perugia, has a population of just 150,000 people.

The many cities and towns of Umbria are connected by a well-developed network of roads. The two major arterials are the N3, still called the Via Flaminia after the ancient Roman road whose route it follows, and the N3 bis which follows the Tiber valley. The A1, Rome to Florence motorway (the Autostrada del Sole) just skirts the western borders of Umbria. The enchanting green of Umbrian meadows, forests and fields is intermittently interrupted by lakes and rivers.

The largest body of water in the region is Lake Trasimeno, Italy's largest freshwater lake, with a surface area of 128 sq. km.

RECOMMENDED MAP

The Touring Club Italiano's map of Umbria and the Marches in its *Grande Carta Stradale d'Italia* series, at 1:200,000 scale, is indispensible to anyone travelling in Umbria. It is clearer and more up to date than any other map of the region. If you read Italian, there is a rather expensive companion book to the map which, in small dense type, gives you the facts on literally every site of interest in Umbria.

CLIMATE

Despite the fact that Umbria is landlocked and mountainous, the region enjoys a Mediterranean climate – if in a somewhat weakened form. This means that Umbria is subject to warm, dry summers and relatively mild winters. Recent winters have been considerably drier than in the past, so that some rivers are well below their normal level, and the lack of rain has increasingly become a real problem for the entire area.

The Apennine Mountains protect Umbria from the climatic influences of the Adriatic Sea, and against cold air-masses coming in from the northeast. Because of the wide variety of topographical features found in the region, there are innumerable microclimates in Umbria: the area surrounding Lake Trasimeno is blessed with mild temperatures all year round and in the high Apennines it is refreshingly cool in summer; snow lies on the peaks from December through to April or May, and there are several ski resorts in the Norcia area. Apart from the Apennines, it rarely gets severely cold in Umbria, and the typical regional flora is Mediterranean. Irrefutable proof of this is the presence of healthy, thriving olive trees, which as a rule are notoriously sensitive to cold.

Average Temperatures in Umbria:

Month	Maximum		Minimum	
	°C	°F	°C	°F
January	9	48	5	41
February	9	48	3	37
March	12	54	4	39
April	16	61	9	48
May	20	68	12	54
June	22	70	14	57
July	30	86	19	66
August	29	84	19	66
September	24	74	14	57
October	20	68	13	55
November	10	50	5	41
December	8	48	3	37

BUSINESS HOURS

In Umbria getting to a shop or business when it's actually open is more or less a matter of luck. It's nearly impossible to say with 100 percent certainty when exactly anything will be open or closed. In particular, seasoned travellers in Italy know to keep an eye on the festive calendar; many businesses close down not just for bank holidays, but also for local feast days; moreover, a wise traveller will always be sure to have ample money and petrol for the weekend; you cannot be sure of finding a bank open after Friday lunchtime or a petrol station on Saturday or Sunday.

BANKS

Banks are generally open Monday–Friday 8.20 a.m.–1.30 p.m. Some banks in the cities also open in the afternoon, usually 2.30–3.45 p.m.

SHOPS

Shops are usually open Monday–Saturday 9a.m.–1 p.m., and again from 4–8 p.m., but bear in mind that these are only general guidelines. During the summer shops – especially those located in tourist areas – may remain open longer in the evenings and are sometimes open even on Sundays. To compensate for these later hours, they often do not open their doors for business much before 5 p.m. In many places during winter stores close at 7 p.m. In small towns you can expect that all stores – even those selling groceries – will be closed on Wednesday and Saturday afternoons.

CHURCHES

Churches are generally open in the morning from 7.30 a.m.–noon and in the afternoon 4–6.30 p.m. Churches and cathedrals which are especially popular with visiting tourists remain open until 1 p.m. Sightseeing is not permitted during services. Some churches, operate a very strict dress code; you will be rudely turned away if you try to enter the Basilica di San Francesco in shorts of T-shirt or with bare shoulders. It is no good protesting that God made man and is therefore not likely to be shocked by the sight of human legs and arms; the bully boys hired (or do they volunteer?) to exclude you will physically manhandle you and even your children out of the church if they don't like your appearance.

The solution for women is relatively simple; carry a large but lightweight wrap or two, one for the shoulders, and one to tie around the waist, like a skirt or sarong, when you enter the church. Men will either have to wear long trousers and suffer the heat, or do their church visiting (in long trousers) in the relative cool of the morning and then change into more comfortable attire for the rest of the day.

The dress code is strictly enforced in Assisi and Orvieto. For some reason, Spoleto and Perugia take a more enlightened attitude and in the countryside you should have no problems at all.

MUSEUMS

Museums usually open their doors from 9 a.m.–2 p.m. (on Sundays until 1 p.m.), and are generally closed all day Monday. Here again these given hours should be considered merely as guidelines. If you end up somewhere that really should by all accounts be open at that particular time, and find a sign proclaiming "Chiusu" hanging in the doorway for some totally inexplicable reason (though usually because the beligerant staff have decided to go on lightning strike), don't bother getting upset; just set out the following day again – unless, of course, the next day happens to be a Monday! Another tip when visiting museums; make sure you have plenty of small change for the entrance fees. Bored museum attendants get sadistic pleasure from refusing to give change for high-denomination notes.

POST OFFICES

Most post offices are open 8.10 a.m.–1.25 p.m. Monday–Saturday. In larger cities they frequently remain open until 8.25 p.m., and in smaller cities and towns, they are often closed on Saturday.

PETROL STATIONS

Petrol stations in Umbria warrant an entire chapter to themselves! You can just about count on them being open 7.30 a.m.–12.30 p.m. and again from 3.30–7 p.m., Monday–Friday. Many are closed on Saturday and nearly all are closed on Sunday. If you are short of petrol at the weekend, all you can do is find several brand-new 10,000 lire bills pressed flat as a pancake and look for one of the relatively few filling stations that have automatic petrol machines (*Aperto 24 ore*). If the 10,000 lire bill really is not hot off the press, or at least as good as new, the machine will probably swallow it whole, but will not give you any petrol in exchange. This may present something of a problem if the station does not open until Monday morning; the cheated driver will be left standing minus a tank full of petrol, but also 10,000 lire short.

TIME ZONE

Italy is on Central European Time, which is one hour ahead of GMT in winter, and two hours ahead in summer when Daylight Saving Time comes into force at the end of March, lasting until the end of September.

ELECTRICITY

The electrical supply in Italy is AC 220 volts.

HOLIDAYS

1 January
6 January (Epiphany)
Good Friday
Easter Monday
25 April (Liberation Day)
1 May
15 August (Ferragosto)
1 November (All Saints' Day)
8 December
25 and 26 December

All banks, shops and businesses, except for a few bars, restaurants and cake shops, are closed on the days listed above. In August practically the whole of Italy goes on holiday! During this month numerous stores, petrol stations, bars, restaurants and other businesses are *chiuso* for two weeks at a time, though you should rarely be stuck for an alternative that is open.

MARKETS

Weekly markets (mostly selling food and clothing) are generally held in the mornings between 8 a.m. and noon. The following is a list of market days in certain cities:

Tuesday: Deruta, Foligno, Gubbio, Perugia
Wednesday: Nocera Umbra, Spello, Umbertide
Thursday: Orvieto, Perugia
Friday: Spoleto
Saturday: Assisi, Orvieto, Perugia, Todi.

Antique markets take place in Gubbio on the second weekend, and in Città di Castello and Narni on the third weekend of every month.

FESTIVALS

In Umbria festivals abound throughout the year. Celebrations are the means by which the people of the region give expression to two different aspects of their cultural identity: the folkloric and the modern.

Remnants of early pagan traditions mixed with Christian and political elements all play a part in the folkloric events. Medieval traditions and customs, such as *Palio dei Terzieri* and *Calendimaggio* in Assisi, or *Cantamaggio* in Terni are just as enthusiastically celebrated as any of the theatre festivals, concert events and art exhibits, many of which extend beyond regional or even national boundaries, for example the *Festival of Two Worlds* in Spoleto, or *Umbria Jazz* in Perugia.

Following is a list of the most important festivals and events arranged in chronological order so you can see at a glance exactly what is going on during your holiday.

Visitors interested in knowing more about folk festivals, exhibits and smaller theatre performances should enquire at local tourist information centres. The staff will be glad to supply you with detailed information.

Last week in March – mid-April
Italian Antiques in Todi.

This antique market takes place on the Palazzo Comunale, located in the heart of the city. Leading antique dealers from all over Italy gather to sell furniture, paintings, rugs, bronze figures and antique porcelain.

First or second Sunday in April
Tulip Festival in Castiglione del Lago.

A parade of vehicles decorated to the gills with tulips and accompanied by groups of people dressed in ethnic costumes.

Last week in April – first week in May
National Antiques Fair in Assisi.

This is an antiques fair of very high quality. In the last few years it has taken place in conjunction with the Philatelic Show and the Numismatic Exhibition.

30 April
Cantamaggio in Terni.

A traditional folk festival dating back to the 19th century, celebrating the advent of spring Inhabitants of the city's various districts, and those from outlying areas, get together to decorate festive vehicles, which later form a parade. Many theatrical performances, art exhibitions and so on, also take place on and around 1 May.

25 April – 1 May
Coloriamo i cieli (Heavenly Painting) in Castiglione del Lago.

Every even-numbered year a Kite Festival is held on the banks of Lake Trasimeno. In addition to kites, there are hot-air balloons and fireworks to marvel at.

Second Sunday in May
Corso all'Anello (Ring Race) in Narni.

This festival is held in honour of the patron saint of Narni, San Giovenale and dates back to the 14th century. Young men dressed in medieval costume attempt to thrust the tip of a lance through a ring which is suspended on a string between the houses along the Via Maggiore. On the evening before the festival a lively and colourful procession, complete with flags and flaming torches, winds its way through the festively decorated city.

First Tuesday in May
Calendimaggio in Assisi.

A three-day celebration in commemoration of St Francis, who one day while still in his youth went through the city singing serenades and was suddenly struck by a vision of the Madonna of Poverty. There is a competition between two groups, the members of which are attired in antique garments. Each group tries to assert its superiority in singing, theatre performances, dance, processions, archery, banner-waving, etc. Knights and maidens in full regalia wend their way through the festively decorated city singing love songs.

15 May
Corsa dei Ceri (Candle Race), in Gubbio.

Three gigantic wooden candles, each weighing about a hundredweight and mounted with statues of saints, are carried by young candle-bearers to the Basilica di Sant'Ubaldo, situated on top of Monte Ingino.

21 and 22 May
Celebrazioni Ritiane in Cascia.

On the feast day of St Rita literally thousands of tiny oil lamps are lit at sundown in the Corno Valley. On the following day a procession makes its way from her birth place in Roccaporena to her shrine at Cascia.

Last Sunday in May
Palio della Balestra in Gubbio.

During this festival you'll see crossbow tournaments, target shooting contests with medieval bows and arrows, two groups attired in medieval costumes competing against each other and people waving banners. The celebration's grand finale is marked by a procession threading its way through the city.

Sunday following the Feast of Corpus Christi
Infiorata del Corpus Domini in Spello.

Religious and liturgical scenes are created out of flower blossoms and laid out in the city streets.

Sunday following the Feast of Corpus Christi
Corpus Domini in Orvieto.

This procession is held to commemorate the Miracle of Bolsena which is said to have happened in the year 1246 when, during a mass, blood flowed on to the altar cloth. During the procession this holy relic is carried through the city while 400 actors dressed in historical costumes do their best to remind everyone of the time when Orvieto was the city in which the pope resided.

June
Concorso Internazionale Pianistico in Terni.

Every even-numbered year, an international piano competition is held here. Accomplished pianists can register up until the end of March. Competitors have to perform four times in all; three times as soloists and once with the accompaniment of the entire orchestra. The jury consists of internationally renowned musicians. This contest is one of the most important piano competitions in Europe.

Last 10 days in June
Rockin' Umbria in Perugia.

This rock festival has taken place each year since 1986 not just in Perugia, but also in Umbertide and Città di Castello. Although you won't find the rock world's big stars here, you will find promising up-and-coming musical performers.

Last 10 days in June
Festivale di Teatro Citta di Narni in Narni.

Young Italian avant-garde groups perform different kinds of experimental theatre. Since 1989 foreign performing artists have also been permitted to participate in the festival.

Last 10 days in June – first 10 days in July
Mostra Mercato Nazionale dell' Artigianato in Todi.

A national exhibition of handicrafts, held on the Palazzo Comunale. Emphasis is on Umbrian arts and crafts, fine carpentry, furniture, jewellery, lace, woven goods, etc.

Last week in June – second week in July
Festival dei Due Mondi in Spoleto.

International prose, theatre, dance and musical performances by leading artists from Europe and the Americas. This is one of the high points of the Italian social and artistic calendar, and you will have to book well in advance if you want to attend any events, or even find a hotel room in the city. If you leave it too late, you can always stay in a nearby town and come in for the numerous free fringe events and street performances that take place in the city.

Mid-July
Umbria Jazz in Perugia.

One of the most important jazz festivals in Europe. From early in the morning until late at night you'll find over 100 concerts taking place in Perugia as well as in other Umbrian cities. Young people come from all over the world to get a chance to listen to some of the biggest names in jazz.

Last two weeks in July – first week in August
Festa Musica Pro Mundo Uno in Assisi.

Concert performances held under open skies, in churches, etc.

Mid-July – mid-August
Spettacoli Classici in Gubbio.

Classical drama performed in the ruins of the Roman theatre.

August/September
Concorso Mostral Internazionale della Tadini Ceramica in Gualdo Tadino.

An international ceramics exhibition and competition. Potters from all over the world gather together here to display their work.

Second Sunday in August
Palio dei Terzieri in Città della Pieve.

Over 700 citizens attired in historical costumes parade through the city streets accompanied by jugglers, fire-eaters, etc. on their way to the *Campo dei Giochi*, where a crossbow shooting competition is held.

Last week in August – first week in September
Festival delle Nazioni di Musica da Camera in Città di Castello.

A national and international chamber music festival of the highest order.

September
Segni Barocchi in Foligno.

This festival is devoted to everything baroque; art, music, theatre, cinema – anything and everything that bears the influence of this period and not just works dating from the 17th century.

First 10 days in September
Todi Festival in Todi.

A wide variety of works in the fields of music, ballet and film produced by young, up-and-coming artists hailing from Italy and abroad.

First two weeks in September
Sagra Musicale Umbra in Perugia.

This is a highly-regarded event in the European music world at which sacred 20th-century religious music is performed.

End of September
Teatro Lirico Sperimenta in Spoleto.

Award-winning singers and songwriters from around the world finish up their studies in Rome with performances in Spoleto.

Last week in September – first week in November
Rassegna Antiquaria in Perugia.

An exhibition of antiques.

November
Mostra Mercato del Tartufo in Città di Castello.

The entire city is transformed into a (very expensive) heaven for truffle fans.

24 December - 6 January
Celebrazioni di Santo Natale in Assisi.

During this time Christmas concerts are held in all the churches of Amelia and Assisi. In many other towns the Nativity scene is portrayed by live actors.

For **further information** regarding events in Umbria contact:
Audac – Associazione Umbria Decentramento Artistico Culturale
Via del Verzaro, 20, 06100 Perugia
Tel: 075-63 645

General information is also available at all local tourist information centres.

WHAT TO WEAR

It will take you probably no more than three seconds to realise just how elegantly most Italians are dressed. The sensitive visitor will want to do likewise rather than be seen parading around town in shorts, T-shirts or other items of clothing that immediately call attention to his or her tourist status.

Bear in mind that towns located at higher elevations maybe cool in the evenings, even at the height of summer. If you intend to buy clothing in Italy, remember that the sizes run a bit differently. The rule of thumb is to increase your usual size by 2: size 36 = 40, size 38 = 42, size 40 = 44, size 44 = 48.

COMMUNICATIONS

NEWSPAPERS

The daily newspaper printed in Florence, *La Nazione*, is one of the most popular middle-of-the-road newspapers in all of Italy and is found on all newsstands in Umbria.

National Newspapers:
Corriere della Sera (centrist)
Il Giorno (left of centre)
Il Messaggero (right-wing)
La Repubblica ((left-wing)
La Stampa (centrist)
L'Unità (communist)

TELEPHONE

You'll find public telephones everywhere, in bars, restaurants, at street corners and in many shops; look for the symbol of the yellow dial posted somewhere outside. As a rule post offices do not have public telephones, although there may be the rare exception. If you want to make a call, you'll need to track down telephone tokens (*gettoni*) which can be bought for 200 lire apiece in bars and tobacco shops (*Tabacchi*).

Some of the more modern public telephones will also accept 100, 200 and 500 lire coins. The cost of local calls depends upon how long you talk, but the minimum is 200 lire.

EMERGENCIES

MEDICAL AID

Hospital and medical care in Umbria is first class though you will be expected to pay the cost in full. In theory, EC nationals can reclaim the cost if they have had the foresight to obtain an E111 form in advance of their visit. Even if you are so well-organised, there is a lot of form-filling involved both to receive treatment under the scheme and gain reimbursement. In practice, it is simpler to take out a travel insurance policy that will cover emergency medical expenses, as well as cancellation fees, loss of valuables, etc.

CHEMISTS

Chemist shops (*Farmacia*) display a sign consisting of a green cross on a white background and are open 9 a.m.–1 p.m. and 4–8 p.m. except on Saturday, Sunday and holidays. You'll find a list of chemists in the vicinity on duty for emergencies posted in the shop's window. If you find yourself in an emergency in a small town, it is acceptable to ring the chemist's doorbell. If there is no answer, enquire at the local bar as to his/her whereabouts. It is generally easier in Italy than in many other EC countries to obtain medicines – including antibiotics – without a prescription. Therefore there's no need to panic – even if you've forgotten your birth control pills you should be able to get at least something similar without major problems.

FIRST AID

Every public hospital has an emergency clinic, a *Pronto Soccorso*, where medical treatment is free.

THEFT

By comparison to the rest of Italy, Umbria is relatively crime-free, but even this region is not entirely without its crooks. Consequently, it always pays to be careful and take a few precautions. Keep an eye on your possessions and your money clamped tightly to your person. Don't leave any valuables, or, better still, don't leave anything at all in your car. Italians themselves often remove their car radios after parking; they tuck them under their arms and walk off with them like other people carry handbags!

It makes good sense to have all your important papers and documents copied so that in case of theft or loss, their replacement may be as expedient as possible. Don't be tempted to exchange money on the streets for an exceptionally good rate, or purchase a gold watch or video recorder still enclosed in its original packaging, all for special discount prices. In such cases, you'll always turn out to be the loser. The designer purses, belts, etc that are sold for such hot prices at various markets are, without exception, counterfeit.

If you have something stolen, report the theft immediately to the police; the key word is *denuncia*, meaning statement – without making a signed and dated statement to the police you will not be able to make an insurance claim.

If you find yourself in the terrible position of not having a penny in your pocket, the quickest way to have money sent from home is by international money order which can be sent from your bank via fax or telex to the post office or a correspondent bank in the town where you are staying. Usually, the entire process only takes a few hours, assuming it is not a holiday or weekend.

If your passport has been lost or stolen you must contact your embassy promptly, as well as the police, and the loss of credit cards should be reported to your bank without delay.

EMERGENCY NUMBERS

Carabinieri (general police): tel: 21 21 21
Vigili police (traffic and accident rescue): tel: 113
ACI Breakdown Service (Italian Automobile Association): tel: 116

GETTING AROUND

BY RAIL

The fares on Italian trains are remarkably low and are cheaper still if you hold a student card that entitles you to discount fares. The main disadvantage of train travel in Umbria is related to the region's geography. The railways follow the valleys, and most of Umbria's towns are situated on high hilltops; the station is often as much as 2 to 3 miles (3 to 5 km) from the historic centre of the town, and it is a long, hot uphill climb in summer, especially if you are carrying luggage. Neither do the railways go to the more remote rural areas of Umbria, though bus and coach services, tied into railway timetables, will take you to just about anywhere in the region.

Information about **National Italian Railways** (Ferrovie dello Stato) is available in:
Perugia
Piazza Vittorio Veneto
Tel: 075-70 980

Terni
Piazza Dante Alighieri
Tel: 0744-401 2873

The main rail routes to Umbria are as follows:
From the north:
Florence – Terontola – Chiusi – Orvieto – Attigliano – Orte – Rome.

From the south:
Rome – Orte – Terni – Spoleto – Foligno – Assisi – Perugia – Terontola – Florence.
Rome – Orte – Attigliano – Orvieto – Chiusi – Terontola – Florence.

From the Adriatic:
Ancona – Foligno – Spoleto – Terni.
Ancona – Foligno – Assisi – Perugia.

Information regarding the **Italian Local Railways** (Ferrovia Centrale Umbria) is available in:

Perugia
Via Sant'Anna
Tel: 075-29121

Terni
Piazza Dante Alighieri
Tel: 0744-15297

Tickets for Italian trains can be purchased at railway stations and in nearly all travel agencies in the region. Travel agents can also supply details of (approximate!) departure times.

BY BUS

It is possible to take a regular bus to just about every town in Umbria. Buses run daily, except for Sundays and holidays. Schedules are available at the following bus company offices:

Perugia
Autoservizio Perugia, Loc. Pian del Massiano, Perugia
Tel: 075-751 145

Spoleto
Soc. Spoletina di Imprese e Trasporti
Via Flaminia KM 127,700
Tel: 0743-59541

Terni
Azienda Trasporti Consortili (A.T.C.)
Piazza Europa 19
Tel: 0744-59541

Information on bus services is also available at tourist information centres and travel agencies (ask about the "Autobus" or "Pullman"). Don't forget to ask where exactly the bus departs from, as there may not be a central bus station in every town. Travelling by regular bus is a relatively inexpensive mode of transport and frequently, special combination train and bus connections are offered.

Buses and trains departing from Perugia, the capital of Umbria, travel in the following directions:
Bevagna (via Foligno).
Montefalco (via Foligno).
Norcia–Cascia (via Spoleto).

Chiusi–Chianciano–Montepulciano.
Cortona (via Terontola).
Ipogeo dei Volumni.
Magion–Torricella–Passignano–Tuoro–
    Terontola–Arezzo–Florence.
Orvieto (via Terontola).
Bastia–Assisi–Spello–Foligno–Trevi–
    Spoleto–Terni–Narni–Amelia–Orte–
    Rome.
Nocera Umbra–Gualdo Tadino–Fossato di
    Vico–Gubbio–Fabbriciano–Genga S.
    Vittore–Falconara–Ancona.
Terontola–Chiusi–Siena.
Umbertide–Città di Castello–Sansepolcro.
Todi–Acquasparta–Sangemini–Terni.

BY ROAD

CAR RENTALS

Cars can be rented at the airports in Pisa, Rome or Bologna on arrival. Otherwise, look in the Yellow Pages of the local telephone book under *Noleggio* for the addresses of car rental agencies in the area. In order to rent a car, you'll need a national driver's licence (an international driver's licence is not required) and a valid passport.

TRAFFIC REGULATIONS

Lights should be turned on before entering a road tunnel, no matter how short it is.
Outside of built-up areas you are required to honk the horn before overtaking another car; the same method should be employed at blind curves and intersections!
During the night and in built-up areas, flash your headlights rather than using the horn.
The speed-limit in built-up areas is 50 kph (30 mph); outside of built-up areas the speed-limit depends on the size of the car's engine and is different on trunk roads and motorways. The maximum speed-limit for cars on trunk roads is between 80 and 100 kph (50–63 mph); on the motorways between 80 and 140 kph (50–90 mph).

Breakdown Assistance: The following emergency numbers can be used throughout Italy:
Accident Rescue: tel: 116
Road Patrol: tel: 113

FINES

Parking and other traffic regulation offenders in Italy – even if they're foreign tourists – pay juicy fines if they're caught; the *Polizia Stradale* show no mercy in this respect. at all. There have been cases where tourists have received, via registered mail, notification of payment due on a parking ticket or some other such misdemeanour, incurred weeks before while on holiday.

WHERE TO STAY

Accommodation is plentiful in Umbria; there is something for every taste and wallet. You will find hotels of every category, private rooms, campsites, chalets, youth hostels, holiday houses and apartments, as well as Agriturismo ("vacation on the farm") opportunities.

The local tourist information centres can help with the search for accommodation if you arrive without a booking. It is, however, advisable to book ahead, especially in the month of August and during the Easter holidays when rooms are at a premium.

HOTELS

Umbria has 420 hotels and a total of about 18,000 beds. You'll find a range of hotels to choose from at every important centre. Hotels are categorised by the Umbrian Tourist Information Office by stars: a ☆☆☆☆☆ indicates the ultimate in luxury, while hotels with ☆ ratings cater for tourists with fairly modest demands. Prices are set in relation to the quality and different services offered at each hotel. Depending upon the place and season, the cost of a single night in a double room at a ☆☆☆☆ or ☆☆☆☆☆ hotel will run you between 80,000 (minimum) and 200,000 lire. In a ☆ hotel rates fall between 30,000 and 50,000 lire (with bathroom), at ☆☆ hotels between 50,000 and 60,000 lire,

and at ☆☆☆ hotels between 70,000 and 80,000 per night.

The Umbrian regional Tourist Information Office will send you a free hotel listing on request (ask for the *lista degli alberghi*).

CAMPSITES

You'll find campsites in just about every town in Umbria. Drop the Umbria Tourist Information Office a line and they'll send you a complete listing (*lista degli campeggi*).

Keep in mind that camping in Italy in general is comparatively expensive and in Umbria this is no exception; you can easily pay 20,000 lire a night for two people, just for a little tent and your car. In spite of this, it is not a good idea – for reasons of law and security – just to pitch your tent anywhere.

In addition to published camping guides, further information is available from the Federazione Internazionale di Campeggio e del Caravaning, Casella Postale 23, V. Vittorio Emanuele, 500041 Calenzano (Firenze). Tel: 055-882 391.

There are about 35 campsites and several "camping villages" situated around Lake Trasimeno where you can rent caravans, two or four-bed chalets or bungalows with kitchen facilities, a bathroom, patio, parking place, electricity and bed linen all included in the rental price.

One of the best is Cerquestra (Villagio Turistico), Monte del Lago, 06060 Lagione, Perugia. Tel: 075-840 0100.

Weekly Rates During the Peak Season:
Chalets: 553,000 lire
Bungalows: 502,000 lire
Caravans: 360,000 lire

MONASTERIES

Overnight guests are put up in dormitories, usually in monastic cells each containing five or six beds. There are a number of "guest" monasteries in Assisi; for further information, contact the tourist information centre. The only drawback is that early each morning – at the crack of dawn in fact – churchbells calling the pious to early mass are rung with a vengeance! The monastery doors are locked at the stroke of 1 a.m. and if you arrive five minutes too late, plan on spending the night somewhere in the garden.

The compensation for these disadvantages is that spending the night at a monastery is relatively inexpensive and is sure to be an experience of some kind or other.

YOUTH HOSTELS

There are five youth hostels in Umbria:
Assisi
Albergo per Giovani – Fontemaggio
Strada per l'Eremo delle Carceri
Tel: 075-812 317

Foligno
Ostello – Fulginium
Piazza S. Giacomo
Tel: 0742-52882

San Venanzio
Casa per Ferie – Centro Turistico Giovanile
Località Monte Peglia
Tel: 075-870 9124

Sigillo
Ostello – Villa Scirca
Loc. Villa Scirca
Tel: 075-917 0307

Trevi
Casa per ferie – Casa S. Martino
Viale Ciuffelli 4
Tel: 0742-78297

It is no longer absolutely necessary to have an International Youth Hostel Card in order to stay at a youth hostel. You can also join the YHA on the spot at any hostel, but it is cheaper to join in your own country before you leave for Italy.

The Italian Youth Hostel symbol consists of a house with a leaning pine tree beside it.

If you want to be sure of getting a bed upon arrival, it is a good idea to fill out and send the Youth Hostel Association's reservation form to the *ostello* of your choice; during the peak season this should be done at least two weeks prior to your intended arrival. Make sure you include the international reply form, or at least the request for a written confirmation. The price for one night is 11,000 lire.

Staying at a youth hostel in Italy requires nerves of steel and pretty modest demands – at least during the peak season times. On the positive side however, the people here are usually quite friendly and helpful.

ON THE FARM

Agriturismo – holidays on the farm – is a concept that originated in Sardinia and has become increasingly popular on the Italian mainland too. Guests are accommodated in comfortable apartments converted from farm buildings and are served traditional meals made from ingredients straight from the smokehouse and vegetable garden. Guests are treated as part of the family and various activities, including horse riding, are often available. A basic working knowledge of Italian is helpful if you want to take full advantage of the experience. For visitors desiring something out of the ordinary, this is often a most delightful way of getting to know the rural Umbrian lifestyle.

Prices are stipulated by the region and fall between a minimum of 14,000 and a maximum of 28,000 lire a night per person. Included in the price is bed linen, a bathroom (though not always a private one) and use of the kitchen. There are additional charges for other services or goods, for example food from the fields or garden, wine, oil, etc. Recreational activities are also paid for separately, according to prearranged agreement.

Farmers interested in participating in the *Agriturismo* project are first required to apply for permission from their local authority which will inspect and register the accommodation to ensure that it meets minimum standards. However, like just about everything else in Italy, these are only official regulations and may or may not be adhered to in practice.

Further information regarding Agriturismo is available from the following:
Agriturist Umbria
c/o Federumbria Agricoltori
Via Savonarola 38
06100 Perugia.
Tel: 075-32028 or 33674
Fax: 075-32028

Terranostra Umbria
Via Campo di Marte 10
06100 Perugia.
Tel: 075-74559 or 72196
Fax: 075-62255

These offices will supply a brochure in Italian or English listing all Agriturismo opportunities in Umbria, including information about the farm and its activities, as well as the number of beds reserved for guests and details about meal arrangements. Facilities for shopping, swimming, tennis, horse riding, etc., are also described. At present the list has information about approximately 60 farms located throughout Umbria.

HOLIDAY APARTMENTS

As part of their room-finding service, tourist information offices will let you know about furnished flats available for rent (usually for a minimum of one week) in the area. You can also write to the tourist office for details and make bookings in advance. Prices fluctuate considerably from season to season. And, of course, the more people that share an apartment, the cheaper it is per person.

PRIVATE ROOMS

In nearly all Umbrian cities and towns you'll find quite a large selection of private rooms to choose from. Information is available at local tourist information centres. The price for a comfortable double room, excluding breakfast, is about 40,000 lire a night.

FOOD DIGEST

WHAT TO EAT

It is almost impossible not to eat well in Umbria. However, it is quite possible to commit a *faux pas* while dining out if you're not aware of certain Italian customs. The following are a few you should bear in mind. A restaurant meal always consists of three courses. The first of these is the *primo*, and consists of pasta, *risotto* or *minestra* (soup). This is followed by the *secondo* (main course) – a meat or fish dish with *contorni* (side-dishes). Next on the culinary agenda is *frutta* (fruit), *dolce* (dessert), *gelato* (ice-cream), *formaggio* (cheese), or, at the very least, a

caffè (espresso). *Antipasti* (appetisers) are more or less "voluntary". Italian restaurateurs will not take kindly to foreign guests who only order a glass of wine and a plate of spaghetti, and then have the audacity to spend a leisurely hour or two blocking the table for more lucrative business. Children are the only segment of the population excused from this unwritten code of ethics.

You will almost always find a separate charge on your bill for *pane e coperto* (bread and tableware). The flat fee runs about 2,000 lire, even if the only items on the table were a paper napkin, knife and fork, and you only ate a single piece of bread.

If you're looking for good value for money and do not want a typical, multi-course Italian meal, your best bet is to find a *pizzeria* or *spaghetteria*. In these establishments it is perfectly acceptable to order just one course – a pizza or serving of pasta – though there is a charge for *pane e coperto*.

Upon entering a restaurant do not immediately fly to the first empty table you see; the customary – and polite – thing to do is wait until the waiter assigns one to you.

The tip is either included in the price (*servizio compreso*), or is added separately to your bill. However in both cases it is customary to leave a little something on your table for the waiter.

In Italy – contrary to popular belief – it is not customary to eat spaghetti with the help of a spoon. Italians are actually quite surprised to discover how other Europeans think they eat. Native Italians eat their spaghetti by simply rolling it around their forks.

If you order a cup of coffee in Italy, you will automatically get an espresso. Cappuccino is generally only drunk at breakfast as an alternative to *caffelatte* (coffee with a generous dose of hot milk in it). Chances are that anyone spied sipping cappuccino after breakfast is more than likely a tourist.

In Italy you don't buy ice-cream cones – *cono* or *cornetto* – by the scoop. For a fixed price of about 1,500 lire you can have the person waiting on you pack as many different kinds into the cone as will more or less stay there.

UMBRIAN CUISINE

Although the cuisine of Umbria chiefly consists of simple, country fare, it is nevertheless delicious. This is due, at least in part, to the fact that nearly all the ingredients are locally produced and fresh; fruit and vegetables will have been harvested that morning and the region is famed for the high quality of its olive oil. (Climatic conditions are decisive for the ultimate quality of an oil; a long period of gradual ripening and the precise moment of harvest are essential ingredients to success. About 80 percent of all Umbrian olive oil is produced by using simple presses.) Excellent, tender meat is produced by local cattle farmers, and the fish caught in local rivers and lakes is both fresh and tasty. A special delicacy are the black and white truffles harvested from the Valnerina.

Appetisers, *antipasti*
Antipasti include a mouth-watering array of different kinds of sausage, lean, dried ham, air-dried neck of pig spiced with garlic (*coppa*), or air-dried pork sausage. Other favourite starters are a type of quiche *alla Perugina*, garnished with ham or minced pork, pizza-bread with sage and onions, *crostini* accompanied by chicken liver, crêpes served warm and sprinkled either with salt or sugar, and black olives.

First Course, *primo*
Typical first course dishes include *ciriole* – hearty noodles tossed with oil and roasted garlic, *strascinati* – pasta prepared with fried minced pork, eggs and Parmesan cheese, *umbrici* – a home-made, rather crude looking spaghetti, and risotto served with a sprinkling of grated black or white truffles.

Second Course, *secondo*
Traditional Umbrian main courses include roast suckling pig (the Umbrian national dish), snipe roasted on a spit and pork intestines which are smoked and grilled. Wild hare braised in white wine with olives and herbs is another regional speciality. And last but certainly not least are the myriad fish dishes, such as *tegamaccio*, consisting of bite-sized pieces of several varieties of deep-fried fish.

Dessert, *dolce*
Two especially sweet specialities of the region, *torciglione* (a kind of almond cake) and *bustengolo* (polenta with apples and a variety of nuts including pine kernels) will be sure to get your mouth watering again no matter how full you are.

During the Easter holidays special treats such as *ciaramicola* (pastry garnished with egg white and sugar), *pinoccate* (pastry with pine kernels), and *panpepato* (goodies made with sultanas, candied fruit and almonds) are available for sweet indulgence.

Wine
Of all the different wines produced in Umbria, Orvieto is probably the best known. This particular wine has quite a distinctive yellow colour and a very pleasant bouquet. In the last few decades the area used for wine cultivation has increased from 1,500 to 23,000 hectares (from about 3,700 to 56,830 acres) and production currently exceeds over 1 million hectolitres.

RESTAURANTS

In bars and *pasticcerie* (singular *pasticceria*) you can get both alcoholic and non-alcoholic beverages of every description. As far as eating goes, snacks are about it. *Pasticcerie* usually have the larger assortment of cakes, baked goods and *dolci*.

Ristorante are often quite charming establishments intended for guests who want to enjoy their food in tastefully decorated surroundings. Most are more up-market and more expensive than *trattorie*.

A *trattoria* is generally more casual (although these days the differences are becoming less distinct), and often has a relatively limited menu. Often, *la Mamma* herself is standing at the stove.

Tavola calda refers to a snack-bar where you can get a warm appetiser in a hurry; food is generally consumed here while standing.

You'll only find *rosticcerias* in larger cities. These establishments offer warm dishes (mostly food you can eat with your fingers) either to eat on the premises or to takeaway.

In addition to pizza, *pizzerias* often serve a variety of other snacks.

As everywhere else in Italy, bars in Umbria are important institutions. A rule of thumb is that the smaller the town is, the more important the role of the bar is. Bars are great sources of all kinds of information and meeting places for the local population. This is the place to hear and discuss the latest soccer results and political news, or to find out where someone is and how to reach them. In short, this is where the action is. And of course, they are also the right spot for a reviving shot of excellent espresso (*caffè*). Sometimes you can get a bite to eat here and tobacco, cigarettes and sweets are always available. You can make a telephone call if there is a sign depicting a yellow dial hanging somewhere in the bar; and in many cases tickets for public transport are also sold here – provided there's a square sign with the letter "T" on it posted somewhere outside. Most bars are open continuously from early in the morning until late at night.

CULTURE PLUS

CULTURAL INSTITUTIONS

It is possible to attend courses at the:
University of Perugia
Piazza dell' Università
6100 Perugia
Tel: 075-4691
This is one of the oldest universities in the entire country. It boasts a large number of both Italian and foreign students who fill the city with life.

University for Foreign Students
Università per Stranieri
Palazzo Gallenga, Piazza Fortebraccio 4
6100 Perugia
Tel: 075-64344
This interesting university was established just for foreign students in the year 1926. Students can take courses in Italian language, history and culture. It is a popular university for those wanting to learn Italian. Language courses lasting one to three months are offered for beginners and advanced students throughout the year. In addition to these regular courses there are also intensive language programmes. Courses cost between 230,000 lire (per month) and 450,000 lire

(for an intensive course). The university will do its best to help students find living quarters for the duration of their stay. More detailed information is found in the brochure *Corsi di Lingua e Cultura Italiana* (published in Italian), available upon request from the above address.

The Pietro Vannucci Academy of Art
Piazza San Francesco 5
6100 Perugia
Tel: 075-29106
Courses are offered here in painting, sculpture, set design and nude painting. In July there are a series of international summer classes, as well as courses in ceramics and graphics.

The Giulio Briccialdi Institute of Music
Via Massani
05100 Terni
Tel: 0744-549 602
This is an old music school dedicated to the flautist and conductor Giulio Briccialdi.

The University of Jazz
Via Muratori 2
05100 Terni
Tel: 0744-58926
A university for jazz students; courses are offered from January to June.
For further information contact:
Arci Nova-Terni
Tel: 0744-57888 or 57743

Multinational Chamber Music Festival Courses
These courses have taken place every year during August and September in Città di Castello since 1973. Further information is available at:
Azienda di Promozione Turistica dell' Alta Valle del Tevere
Via Raffaele di Cesare 2/B
06012 Città di Castello
Tel: 075-8554 817

"Festa Musica Pro" Courses
Accademia Musicale Ottorino Respighi
Via Villa Maggiorana 20
00100 Rome
Tel: 06-336 261
Classes offered by the Ottorino Respighi Academy of Music, organised in Rome. Courses take place in July, in Assisi.

"Pro Civitate Cristiana" Courses

Pro Civitate Cristiana – Sezione Musica
Via Ancaiani 3
06081 Assisi
Tel: 075-812 308.

Courses in musical education offered throughout the entire year in Assisi.

NIGHTLIFE

As you'll find everywhere else in Italy, nightlife during the summer months means taking to the streets for the evening stroll, the *passegiatta*, followed by a good meal.

For those whose concept of nightlife revolves around dancing, bars and discos, the following list of addresses may give you a few ideas:

ASSISI

Hermitage
Via del Pozzo 1
Tel: 075-816 671

CITTÀ DI CASTELLO

Dankar 26
Via Parini, Trestina
Tel: 075-854 0125

Discoteca
Via Bologni (N. 2 Linee)
Tel: 075-855 0300

Nemesys
Via Liviero 2
Tel: 075-855 6505

CORCIANO

Dejavu
Via Luigi Pasteur – Ellera
Tel: 075-799 162

Discoteca Conca del Sole
Str. Prov. Corcianese
Tel: 075-79249

DERUTA

Billo Dancing Discoteca
S. Niccolò di Celle
Tel: 075-974 398

Norman e il Presidente
S. Fortunato Bonveggio
Tel: 075-38584

Discoteca Gizia
S. Niccolò di Celle
Tel: 075-974 226

GUBBIO

Capocont Music S.R.L
Via Contessa 6
Tel: 075-927 7679

MASSA MARTANA

Riccardi P.
Via Tiberina 117
Massa Martana Stazione
Tel: 075-885 6106

MONTECCHIO

Straccia R
Via Cavour 46
Tel: 0744-951 611

NARNI

Dancing K 2
Via San Faustino 12
Tel: 0744-744 278

NORCIA

Strike Discoteca
Via della Stazione
Tel: 0743-816 171

ORVIETO

Break di Rosetti
Iolanda 7, Via I. Maggio
Orvieto Scalo
Tel: 0763-90216

PERUGIA

Angelucci Dino
S.a.S. 3 Via Naspo
Tel: 075-22646

Black Box
10c, Fontana
Colle della Trinità
Tel: 075-799 319

Brooklyn Superdancing
Via Fabrianese 2
Ponte Vallecippi
Tel: 075-692 9745

Casanova Club
Via Panoramica
Città della Domenica
Tel: 075-690 520

Etoile 54
Loc. Mad. Piano 109
Tel: 075-38710

Giles Keith
A.D. 1 Via F.lli Cervi
Tel: 075-694 869

New Odeon Spa
Via Montalcino 2/c
Ponte Valleceppi
Tel 075-692 9091

Privilege
S. Martino in Colle
Tel: 075-607 177

SPOLETO

Torricella Club
10c Torricella 170
Tel: 0743-44591

TODI

New York, New York
Ig. Faichi
Tel: 0744-59338

Globus Tenda
Via Trieste
Tel: 0744-285 061

Sabatini M.
108 voc. Gabelletta
Tel: 0744-241 626

Tiseo M
Via Noceta 6
Piediluco
Tel: 0744-69114

TERNI

Discoteque Joys
Via Angelo Cortesi
Tel: 075-882 608

TUORO SUL TRASIMENTO

Ciao Ciao Discoteca
Via Sette Martiri
Tel: 075-826 461

SHOPPING

The nicest gifts to bring home with you from Umbria are edible and include fresh or marinated truffles, olive oil (extra-virgin and bought where you discovered the "*olio*" sign at the side of the road), and the dark-brown, fragrant vinegar known as "Aceto Balsamico" (while the vinegar may not have been produced in Umbria itself, it's readily available in supermarkets, such as the Co-op, and considerably less expensive than what you'd pay for it back home. Wine is, of course, another gift sure to be appreciated, as is pasta in all its delicious varieties, air-dried ham and sausage, sheep's milk cheese, olives, a slab of crumbly Parmesan, Formaggio di Norcia, or salami made from wild boar meat.

CERAMICS & TERRA COTTA

An especially popular souvenir is hand-painted ceramic ware from Deruta. Pottery is one of the oldest crafts practiced in Umbria. The production of ceramics according to traditional techniques and patterns is mainly carried out in the cities of Gubbio, Gualdo Tadino, Deruta, Todi, Orvieto, Città di Castello, Perugia and Umbertide; Ficulle is the centre for the art of terra cotta.

LACE & WOOD-CARVING

A simple crochet hook is used in the making of the exquisite "Irish lace" mainly produced on Isola Maggiore (an island in Lake Trasimeno). Ars Wetana, a very special kind of Irish lace which is known and treasured throughout the world, is currently produced in Orvieto. In Umbria you'll also find a variety of both skilfully made and restored furniture (Assisi and Perugia are veritable strongholds of antiques). Workshops in Orvieto turn out wonderful, modern-style furniture and in Gubbio look for reproductions of antique weapons.

On a stroll through Orvieto it is common to see wooden objects by the artist Gualtiero Michelangeli proudly displayed in many shop windows.

WINE

Wine produced in Torgiano, the wine capital of Umbria located between Perugia, Assisi and Todi, can be highly recommended. Torgiano Rubesco, a blended wine pressed in accordance to traditional methods from a mixture of both red and white grapes, is also delicious. Check to make sure the word "Riserva" is printed somewhere on the label; this indicates that the wine's alcoholic content is 12 percent and that it has been aged for at least three years. Vino Santo is also quite good. This dessert wine tastes especially good when served with *ghiottini* (hard almond biscuits). Its name (Holy Wine) derives from the fact that priests are said to be fond of it.

SPORTS

WINDSURFING, WATER-SKIING & SAILING

In terms of total area, Lake Trasimeno is the biggest lake in Italy (128 sq. km/50 sq. miles). However, the lake is only a few metres deep and its banks are relatively flat. Windsurfing and sailing schools are to be found all round the shores of the lake, especially around Passignano and Castiglione del Lago. For further information contact: **Azienda di Promozione Turistica per Lago Trasimeno**
Piazza Mazzini 10
06061 Castiglione del Lago
Tel: 075-952 184 or 953 583

There are a few areas in Lake Trasimeno, marked with red and white buoys, where water-skiing is allowed. Since 1988 prior permission has had to be obtained from the Province of Perugia. Requests should be addressed to:
Lake Trasimeno Department of Environmental Protection
Via Europa 4
06065 Passignano
Tel: 075-827 125

Lake Piediluco is the second largest lake in Umbria. It is situated at an elevation of 365 metres (1,220 ft) above sea level, is 19 metres (63 ft) deep and has a circumference of 17 km (11 miles). The lake is suitable for sailing, water-skiing (with certain limitations) and fishing. Lake Piediluco is also the official training lake for the Italian Rowing Association.

CANOEING

Canoeists will find a variety of different routes – some easy, some more challenging – along the Tiber and Nera rivers, as well as on Lake Piediluco. Superb conditions await white water fans in Forra di Rio Freddo (M. Cucco), Forra di Pago del Fosse (M. San Vito, Scheggibo), in Forra die Parano and in Forra di Prodo (Orvieto).

FISHING

It is possible to fish anywhere in Umbria with a licence. Your best course of action is to enquire at the fishing association responsible for the area you're interested in; they will be happy to give you details regarding regional regulations (a list of fishing association addresses is available at the Trasimeno Tourist Information Centre). You can fish in Lakes Trasimeno, Piediluco and Corbara (sturgeon, carp, tench, eel, perch and whitefish), as well as in the following rivers: Chiascio, Assino, Nera, Corno, Clitunno (trout), and in sections of the Tiber around Città di Castello, Umbertide, Ponte San Giovanni, Ponte Pattoli, Ponte Valle Ceppi, Fanciullata and Monte Molini (near Todi).

GOLF

There is an 18-hole golf-course (plus 9 training holes) situated in the midst of exquisite countryside in Sodi di Santa Sabina Ellera di Perugia. Further information, tel: 075-79704.

HANG-GLIDING

Aficionados can spread their wings from the summits of Monte Cucco, the Monti Sibillini range, or Monte Subasio.

MOUNTAINEERING

The most important faces for rock-climbing are located in Pale (Foligno), Monte Tezio (Perugia), in Monte Vettore (Norcia) and Ferentillo.

HIKING

At present there are marked hiking trails in the Lake Trasimeno Nature Reserve, in the area around Monte Cucco (Gualdo Tadino), in the Sibillini Mountains (Norcia), near Stroncone, and in the upper Tiber region. Further information is available from:
CAI in Foligno, Via Piermarini
CAI in Perugia, Via della Gabbiaia 9

CAI in Spoleto, Via Pianciani 4
CAI in Terni, Via Roma 96
You will find additional suggestions and hiking options in *Camminia Umbria* (Arcadia Edizioni), a guide published in cooperation with the region of Umbria by the Worldwide Fund for Nature. Information in this guide includes the description of 26 hiking trails, optimal hiking times, how to get there, where to eat and spend the night, what kind of equipment is necessary, interesting things along the trail to look out for, detailed maps and a description of 80 of the most common plants and animals of the region. This is a wonderfully informative book with only one drawback: it is published only in Italian.

SKIING

The area around Norcia is developing as a ski resort, though a series of snowless winters has left hoteliers desperate for trade. Few people as yet think of Umbria as a place to ski, but there are plenty of opportunities, snowfall permitting, for downhill and cross-country skiing, as well as ski-touring in the Sibillini Mountains. Cross-country skiing and ski-touring are also possible on Monte Cucco and Monte Serra Santa (Gualdo Tadini).

CYCLING

If you're interested in cycling through Umbria it's best to bring your own bike, and preferably a mountain bike. At the present time the one and only place in all of Umbria where you can rent a bicycle is in Passignano, near the Esso Petrol Station Ragnoni, Via II Gingno 30, tel: 82 72 12. Rates are quite expensive at 25,000 lire a day.

THERMAL BATHS

Fontecchio Thermal Baths: These baths are located not too far from Città di Castello. The waters here are described as semi-mineral and contain chiefly bicarbonate and sulphur. They are considered beneficial in the treatment of respiratory and joint ailments, gynaecological complaints, digestive tract difficulties, vascular problems and burns. They are also used for beauty treatments, rehabilitation from orthopaedic afflictions and pulmonary diseases. Healing waters for internal consumption, baths and mud-packs are offered here.

Sangemini Thermal Baths: The mineral waters at Sangemini have a slight carbon content and contain calcium salts, a touch of chlorine and sodium. In addition to being deemed healthy for children (taken internally), the waters are suitable for digestive and urinary tract ailments, and metabolic disorders. At this health resort you can also participate in water therapy using Fabia Water, a semi-carbon water containing a variety of minerals and said to be especially beneficial in the treatment of hepatitis and digestive tract disorders.

Amerino Thermal Baths: The Fonte Amerino is situated in Acquasparta. The waters here are semi-mineral, composed of carbon and lime and said to be good for treating predominantly digestive tract disorders, gout, kidney stones and arthritis.

San Faustino Thermal Baths: These baths are located in Massa Martana. The waters here contain alkaline bicarbonate rich in earth particles. They are said to be of benefit in the treatment of indigestion, enteritis, cystitis, liver and kidney cholic, as well as in digestive tract disorders.

Thermen del Cacciatore di Nocera Umbra: These waters have a relatively low mineral content and are especially recommended for internal consumption to alleviate gastro-intestinal complaints and metabolic and urinary tract disorders.

Santo Raggio Assisi Thermal Baths: The thermal waters here have a low mineral content which includes bicarbonate and minerals. They are used primarily in the treatment of uric-acid disorders, gout, dyspepsia and gallstones.

SPECIAL INFORMATION

PUBLIC TOILETS

Ladies' toilets: *donne* or *signore*; men's toilets: *uomini* or *signori*. It's a good idea to commit these terms to memory in case you find yourself standing in front of two doors marked with words rather than some kind of graphic gender symbol. Finding a public convenience in Umbria is pretty much a matter of luck. In an emergency don't hesitate to ask in a bar or café for the *bagno*. If you've forgotten this word, don't worry: chances are good that "toilet" will also be understood. If the lavatory door is locked, ask for the key (*chiave*) at the counter.

WATER

Unless there is a sign saying *non potabile* (not drinkable), it is usually safe to drink water from taps and stand pipes dotted around the streets of Umbrian towns. Usually these supply deliciously cool water, straight from an underground spring. The water tastes good and is free, which explains why you will see Italians drive up and fill a box load of plastic bottles from time to time.

PHOTOGRAPHY

CAMERAS

It's best to bring any film you think you'll need during your holiday with you from home, as it is considerably more expensive to buy in Italy than elsewhere. If you have a camera that requires a battery, it's also a good idea to bring along an extra one, just in case. In Italy the search for the right battery could take days.

LANGUAGE

PRONUNCIATION

The following pronunciation hints are designed to help broken, guide-book Italian be a bit more comprehensible:

In Italian, a *c* appearing before either *e* or *i* is pronounced *ch* as in church. Example: *Cesare* is pronounced *Chesareh*, *città* like *chittah*.

A *g* appearing before *e* or *i* is pronounced soft as in agent, or like a j in journey. Example: *gelato* becomes *jelato* and *Gina* becomes *Jina*.

Ch appearing before *e* and *i* is pronounced like the letter *k* : *marche* becomes *marke*.

Gh appearing before *e* and *i* is pronounced like the letter *g* : *Margherita* becomes *Margerita*.

Sc appearing before *e* and *i* is pronounced like *sh* : *scena* becomes *shena*.

FURTHER READING

The history, art and festivals of Umbria are lovingly described in Michael Adam's book *Umbria*, first published by Faber and Faber in 1964, reissued in 1988 as a Bellew Publishing paperback.

Giorgio Vasari's *Lives of the Artists* (sev-eral publishers, including Penguin) was written in the 16th century and remains a good read; his biographies are studded with gossip and scurrilous details and you have to make allowances for his personal prejudices – he adores Giotto's frescoes and hates Perugino. As for Gozzoli, he is dismissed by Vasari as a painter for people who do not like art – all superficial brilliance and no context. Carry Vasari with you and see whether you agree with his judgements.

Umbria has featured little in literature, unlike its neighbour, Tuscany. That may yet change with the number of artists, dropouts and would-be writers seeking a haven in what is still a relatively cheap place to live. Already William Trevor (not a dropout, one hastens to add, but an accomplished and award-winning novelist) has used the region as the background to his story *My House in Umbria*, published along with *Reading Tergener* under the collective title *Two Lives* (Viking, 1991).

USEFUL ADDRESSES

TOURIST INFORMATION

The following regional tourist information agencies (APTs) will be happy to supply you with both written and verbal information pertaining to Umbria:

Via Orvieto 1
05022 **Amelia**
Tel: 0744-981 453

Piazza del Comune 12
06081 **Assisi**
Tel: 075-812 450 or 812 923

Piazza Mazzini 10
06061 **Castiglione del Lago**
Tel: 075-952 184

Via R. De Cesare 2b
06012 **Città di Castello**
Tel: 075-855 4817

Porta Romana 126
06034 **Foligno**
Tel: 0742-60459

Piazza Oderisi 6
06024 **Gubbio**
Tel: 075-927 3693

Via Vespalia Polla
06043 **Norica**
Tel: 0743-71401

Piazza Duomo 24
05018 **Orvieto**
Tel: 0763-41772 or 42562

Corso Vannucci 94a
06100 **Perugia**
Tel: 075-23327

Piazza della Libertá 7
06049 **Spoleto**
Tel: 0743-220 311

Viale C. Battisti 5
05100 **Terni**
Tel: 0744-43047
Piazza Umberto 6
06059 **Todi**
Tel: 075-883 395 or 883 062

Comprehensive information about the whole of Italy is available from ENIT (Ente Nationale per il Turismo Italiano) – The National Italian Tourist Information Office. Their headquarters are located at:
Via Margherita 2
00185 Rome
Tel: 0039/6/49 711

In the UK, contact the:
Italian State Tourist Office
1 Princes Street
London W1R 8AY
Tel: 071-408 1254

ART/PHOTO CREDITS

Photography by

Page 70/71, 87, 108/109, 111, 112, 113, 142/143, 150/151, 157	Hans Jürgen Burkard/Bilderberg
40/41, 114/115, 160, 161	Christopher Catling
92/93, 94, 95, 96, 97, 98, 99	Heinrich Decker
107	European Community Photo Service
54	Patrizia Giancotti
20/21, 30/31, 64, 78, 131, 144/145, 146/147, 172, 208/209, 212, 214, 215, 217, 218/219, 237, 267	Thomas Höpker/ Anne Hamann Picture Agency
16/17, 37, 38L, 38R, 39, 68, 76, 79, 84/85, 88, 89, 90, 91, 102, 103, 105, 135, 165, 168, 174, 186, 225, 235, 239, 246, 247, 263	Hans Jörg Künzel
180/181, 187, 188, 189	Leo Linder
3, 24/25, 28, 29, 46, 52/53, 62/63, 65, 118, 123, 126, 127, 129, 140/141, 156, 158, 162/163, 169, 173, 178/179, 183, 184, 191, 194/195, 220/221, 250, 254, 257, 261, 269, 271, 273	Gisela Nicolaus
32, 137, 177, 256	Paul Otto Schulz
14/15, 35, 122, 132/133, 134, 138, 243, 268, 272, 276, 277	Wilfried Taschner
9, 100/101, 255	Cliff Vestner
18/19, 22, 26, 34, 57, 67, 72/73, 74/75, 77, 80, 81, 82, 83, 86, 104, 116/117, 120, 121, 139, 148, 152, 153, 155, 159, 167, 170, 171, 173, 175, 192, 196, 197, 199, 200, 201L, 201R, 202, 203, 204, 205, 206, 207, 210/211, 223, 227, 229, 230, 233, 234, 236, 238, 241, 242, 244/245, 248, 249, 251, 252, 253, 258/259, 260, 262, 264/265, 266, 270, 274, 1275, 278	Bill Wassman
27, 36, 69, 130, 136, 164, 185, 190, 216	Gerd Weiss
119	Karsten Welte
Maps	Berndtson & Berndtson
Illustrations	Klaus Geisler
Visual Consultant	V. Barl

INDEX

T

U

V – Z